English-Medium Instruction Practices in Higher Education

Also Available from Bloomsbury

English-Medium Instruction in Higher Education in the Middle East and North Africa, edited by Samantha Curle, Holi Ibrahim Holi Ali, Awad Alhassan and Sergio Saleem Scatolini
The Value of English in Global Mobility and Higher Education, Manuela Vida-Mannl
Teaching English-Medium Instruction Courses in Higher Education, Ruth Breeze and Carmen Sancho Guinda
Language and Decoloniality in Higher Education, edited by Zannie Bock and Christopher Stroud
Researching Language Learning Motivation, edited by Ali H. Al-Hoorie and Fruzsina Szabó
Rethinking TESOL in Diverse Global Settings, Tim Marr and Fiona English

English-Medium Instruction Practices in Higher Education

International Perspectives

Edited by
Jim McKinley and Nicola Galloway

BLOOMSBURY ACADEMIC
LONDON • NEW YORK • OXFORD • NEW DELHI • SYDNEY

BLOOMSBURY ACADEMIC
Bloomsbury Publishing Plc
50 Bedford Square, London, WC1B 3DP, UK
1385 Broadway, New York, NY 10018, USA
29 Earlsfort Terrace, Dublin 2, Ireland

BLOOMSBURY, BLOOMSBURY ACADEMIC and the Diana logo are
trademarks of Bloomsbury Publishing Plc

First published in Great Britain 2022
Paperback edition published 2024

Copyright © Jim McKinley and Nicola Galloway and Contributors, 2022

Jim McKinley and Nicola Galloway and Contributors have asserted their
right under the Copyright, Designs and Patents Act, 1988,
to be identified as Authors of this work.

Cover design: Charlotte James
Cover image © Klaus Vedfelt/ Getty Images

All rights reserved. No part of this publication may be reproduced or transmitted in
any form or by any means, electronic or mechanical, including photocopying,
recording, or any information storage or retrieval system, without prior
permission in writing from the publishers.

Bloomsbury Publishing Plc does not have any control over, or responsibility for, any
third-party websites referred to or in this book. All internet addresses given in this
book were correct at the time of going to press. The author and publisher regret any
inconvenience caused if addresses have changed or sites have ceased to exist, but
can accept no responsibility for any such changes.

A catalogue record for this book is available from the British Library.

A catalog record for this book is available from the Library of Congress.

ISBN: HB: 978-1-3501-6785-8
PB: 978-1-3501-8960-7
ePDF: 978-1-3501-6786-5
eBook: 978-1-3501-6787-2

Typeset by Newgen KnowledgeWorks Pvt. Ltd., Chennai, India

To find out more about our authors and books visit www.bloomsbury.com
and sign up for our newsletters.

To Jim's mother, Jane E. McKinley (1941–2021), teacher and writer, who passed away at Easter towards the final stages of preparing the manuscript

Contents

List of Figures	x
List of Tables	xi
Foreword *by Ernesto Macaro*	xii
Notes on Contributors	xiv

Introduction
  Nicola Galloway and Jim McKinley   1

Part I Macro-analysis

1 English-Medium Instruction in Bangladeshi Higher Education: A Policy Perspective
   Obaidul M. Hamid and Md Al Amin   13
2 Brazil Trying English-Medium Instruction On for Size: Emerging Trends and Policy
   Ron Martinez and Ane Cibele Palma   25
3 English-Medium Instruction in Mainland China: National Trends and Institutional Developments
   Sihan Zhou and Heath Rose   35
4 English-Medium Instruction in Danish Universities: An Unintended Policy?
   Anna Kristina Hultgren   47
5 Policy Analysis of English-Medium Instruction in Ethiopian Higher Education
   Tolera Simie   59
6 English-Medium Instruction as Neoliberal Endowment in Nepal's Higher Education: Policy-Shaping Practices
   Pramod K. Sah   71
7 Provision for Partial English-Medium Instruction Programmes in Turkish Higher Education: All or Nothing?
   Kari Sahan   85

Part II Meso-analysis

8 English-Medium Education in Austria: General Trends and Individual Initiatives in Institutional Policy
Ute Smit and Miya Komori-Glatz — 99

9 Profiling English-Medium Instruction in Colombian Universities: Policies and Practices
Norbella Miranda and Mario Molina-Naar — 111

10 A Longitudinal Perspective on Language Ideological Debates in Estonian Higher Education: Current Trends and Tensions
Josep Soler — 125

11 Perceived Needs of English-Medium Instruction Lecturers in an Italian University: Before and after Training
Francesca Costa and Roberta Grassi — 137

12 English-Medium Instruction in Polish Higher Education: Insights Provided by Classroom-Level Analysis
Agata Mikołajewska and Izabela Mikołajewska — 149

13 Finding Space for Languages of Instruction alongside English: Language Management in South African Higher Education
Christa van der Walt — 161

14 English-Medium Instruction in Vietnamese Higher Education: From Government Policies to Institutional Practices
Huong Thu Nguyen — 173

Part III Micro-analysis

15 English-Medium Instruction in the South Caucasus: Listening to the Positive Voice
Andrew Linn — 187

16 Translanguaging and Trans-semiotizing in English-Medium Instruction Tertiary Classrooms in Hong Kong: Creativity and Trans-semiotic Agency
Phoebe Siu and Angel M. Y. Lin — 199

17 It's Worth the Extra Effort: Behind Student Perceptions of Success in the Study of Content via English-Medium Instruction in Japan
Gene Thompson, Samantha Curle and Ikuya Aizawa — 213

18 Comprehension Issues in English-Medium Instruction Classrooms: Kuwait's Public Institutions
Abdullah Miteb Alazemi and Abdullah Ali Alenezi — 225

19 English-Language Proficiency Pre- and Post-immersion Courses in Mexico for Pre-sessional Students at a Bilingual International and Sustainable University
   Myrna Escalona Sibaja and Gabriela Zamarrón Pérez   239
20 The Englishization of Higher Education in a Dutch University Context: The Glocalization of English-Medium Instruction
   Robert Wilkinson and René Gabriëls   253
21 English-Medium Instruction in Tunisian Higher Education: A Desired Target but with Uncertain Consequences
   Khawla Badwan   265

Index   277

Figures

6.1	Neoliberal agendas shaping the EMI policy in Nepal	76
6.2	The model of EMI in Nepal's higher education	79
16.1	The multimodalities-entextualization cycle	200
16.2	YouTube screenshot from 'Trapped inside Hong Kong's cage houses'	204
16.3	Hong Kong cage housing student design board	205
16.4	A student's L1/L2 process-map	207
19.1	Map of the Mexican Republic	242
19.2	Pre-sessional course and training cycles implemented at technological BIS institutions	242
19.3	Pre-sessional course and training cycles implemented at polytechnic BIS institutions	243
19.4	Overview of pre-sessional course for EMI in Mexico	244

Tables

8.1	Overview of Austrian Higher Education Institutions	101
9.1	Colombian Universities and Documents Analysed	114
9.2	Participants	115
10.1	List of Items of the 2012 and the 2018–20 Language Ideological Debates at the University of Tartu	129
12.1	Number of EMI Students and Lecturers in Poland	155
14.1	Types of EMI Programmes in Vietnam	175
16.1	Summary of Hong Kong Students' Online Multimodal Resources	206
17.1	Interview Participants	216
18.1	Students' Perceptions of the Impact of EMI on Academic Development in Kuwait	230
18.2	Students' Perceptions of the Impact of EMI on the Classroom Environment in Kuwait	231
18.3	Students' Perceptions of the Impact of EMI on Language Skills	232
19.1	Participants' Proficiency Levels before and after the Pre-sessional Course	246
19.2	Respondents' Confidence Levels after Their Participation in the Immersion to English Language Course	247
21.1	Participant Details for EMI in Kuwait Study	270

Foreword

Ernesto Macaro

Having personally been caught up in the surge of interest in English-medium instruction (EMI), the kind invitation by the editors to write a foreword for this book very appropriately forced me to ask myself the following questions: Why is there currently such a burgeoning endeavour by researchers to describe the phenomenon of EMI? Are we just following a trend and jumping on a bandwagon? Or are there such important issues arising from EMI in higher education that it would be a manifest failure on the part of the research community to ignore them? Is there something particularly extraordinary and new about content subjects being taught through the medium of English in settings where one would 'normally' expect them to be taught in the first language of the majority population?

The answer to these questions is, in my view, that there are indeed many issues arising from the EMI phenomenon that are of major educational importance, and the reason for the surge in academic interest is that the research community has, to a large extent, been playing 'catch-up'. EMI existed well before the considerable volume of research and commentary output of the past fifteen years, in various parts of sub-Saharan Africa, Hong Kong and Singapore, to name only the most obvious. Moreover, the community has been playing catch-up because the drive to introduce EMI in higher education has largely been propelled by policymakers and institutional managers. Thus, the theoretical foundations for examining the EMI phenomenon have mostly had to come *after* the frantic attempts at gathering the empirical evidence. That empirical evidence will (one would hope) lead eventually to some overarching theories and a confluence of recommendations.

Of course, the surge in interest is not simply a reaction to an accelerating type of educational offer. It lies in the complexity of an international situation where EMI manifests itself in multiple ways. These divergences are driven not only by geography, language and politics but also by the multiple ways in which the practice of EMI can be introduced and then moderated. It is therefore of paramount importance that the phenomenon be considered, as in this volume, from its multilayered perspectives. Location, policy decisions, models adopted and the different disciplines/subjects offered through English, all impact on the multifaceted nature of EMI, and therefore all require careful 'situating' before we can understand what is actually going on in classrooms, lecture theatres and examination rooms.

Another aspect of EMI which has played a major role in kindling a research interest is, of course, that what is being taught in EMI classrooms is not the English language – at least not directly. It is merely the vehicular language (or one of the vehicular languages) for learning content. This fact immediately leads to researchers asking themselves whether EMI actually improves the students' level of English proficiency and, perhaps even more importantly, if it improves it more than would be the case were students to be studying English in classrooms where language learning was the predominant focus. Moreover, what kind of proficiency should we be expecting from a student who studied, say, engineering through English? How should we be measuring that progress and at what time points? The flip side of the coin, of course, leads us to the question as to whether the content subject knowledge is adversely affected by EMI, and if it is, by how much and for how long?

Academics focusing on EMI have also considered the impact on different social groups such as gender and those of different socio-economic levels. This is of enormous importance as higher education has already, in some countries and jurisdictions, been the prerogative of the wealthier strata of society and, in others, evidenced itself by larger intakes of male when compared with female students. The issue then for researchers is whether EMI intensifies those inequalities or acts as a catalyst for reducing them. This impact on different sections of society is at the heart of some of the ideological debates currently taking place in the EMI research and commentary, and they are addressed in this volume.

Once researchers and commentators have had their say, then what is to be done? As academics we do not have the direct power to bring about change – we may have some, but it is limited. An area that we can clearly contribute to is the professional development of EMI teachers. Research to date has shown that EMI teachers are dissatisfied with their pedagogy. Or, to put it differently, they do recognize that their pedagogy has to change with respect to how they used to teach using the first language. A great deal of research focus has centred on the interaction of the EMI classroom, and that, in my view, is how it should be. But for that focus on classroom interaction to be both informed and incisive, it, I am increasingly of the conviction, has to be a collaborative focus. Applied linguists need to work with content specialists to arrive at the right research questions, devise the most appropriate research designs and draw the most thoughtful conclusions from the research. I hope that the issues raised in this volume will help to incentivize such collaboration.

Contributors

Md Al Amin (PhD) is Assistant Professor in the Department of English and Humanities at the BRAC University, Dhaka, Bangladesh. He teaches applied linguistics and ELT-related courses and supervises thesis students. He has taught in several countries, including Bangladesh, the United Kingdom and New Zealand. He has a strong interest in researching English-medium instruction, teacher education and English teaching in Bangladesh. ORCiD: 0000-0002-6867-1594

Abdullah Miteb Alazemi (PhD, University of Exeter, UK) is Assistant Professor at the Language Centre at Public Authority for Applied Education and Training, Kuwait. He teaches various ESP courses for adult learners at the university level. His current research interests concern critical applied linguistics and language policy, which relate to English as a medium of instruction.

Abdullah Ali Alenezi (PhD, University of Newcastle, UK) is Assistant Professor at the Language Centre at Public Authority for Applied Education and Training, Kuwait. He teaches a variety of ESP courses for adult learners. In addition to his interest in investigating the role of communication in different social settings, his current research interests concern EFL classroom communication in Arabic contexts.

Khawla Badwan is Senior Lecturer in TESOL and Applied Linguistics at Manchester Metropolitan University, UK. She has interdisciplinary research interests in areas related to language and social justice, intercultural communication, sociolinguistics of globalization, migration research and education research. She has recently published a monograph entitled *Language in a Globalised World: Social Justice Perspectives on Mobility and Contact*.

Francesca Costa is Associate Professor in English Language and Linguistics at the Università Cattolica del Sacro Cuore of Milan, Italy. She taught scientific English at Università degli Studi di Pavia from 2006 to 2014 and English for primary education at Università degli Studi di Bergamo from 2017 to 2019. Her area of research focuses on CLIL (content and language integrated learning), ICLHE (integrating content and language in higher education) and EMI (English-medium instruction).

Samantha Curle is Assistant Professor at the Department of Education, University of Bath, UK. She teaches subjects related to applied linguistics and is currently the director of the MRes programme in Advanced Quantitative Research Methods. Her main research interest lies in factors affecting academic achievement in English-medium instruction. Her research has been published in journals such as *Language Teaching, Studies in Higher Education, Applied Linguistics Review, System* and *International Journal of Bilingual Education and Bilingualism*.

René Gabriëls is Lecturer at Maastricht University, the Netherlands. His main fields of research are in social philosophy, sociolinguistics, philosophy of language and sociology of stratification. His research focuses on democracy, inequality, human rights, linguistic justice, poverty and the relation between semantics and pragmatics. He has written books and articles on intellectuals, racism and local democracy. Currently he is researching EMI at universities and food banks in the Netherlands. ORCID: 0000-0002-2259-0983

Nicola Galloway is Publications Lead, Senior Lecturer and Programme Director in Education (TESOL) at the University of Glasgow, UK. She has extensive experience researching EMI and working as a consultant for the British Council and the University of Tokyo in the subject area. She is currently writing a textbook for use in EMI teacher training courses (forthcoming) and has published EMI research in British Council reports, the *Higher Education Journal*, the *EAP Journal* and the *ELT Journal*. She has worked with the University of Tokyo to develop two MOOCs on EMI and coordinates an international EMI network (https://globalenglishes-emi.network/).

Roberta Grassi is Associate Professor in Language Teaching Methodology at the Università degli Studi di Bergamo, Italy. She has been engaged in teacher training at all levels since 1998. Her main research areas encompass ISLA and educational linguistics, with a special interest in teacher training (in Italian as a second language and in early EFL) and in immersion education in plurilingual contexts (including EMI). She has been working on classroom interaction (teacher talk and interactional feedback) as well as on translanguaging.

Obaidul M. Hamid is Senior Lecturer in TESOL Education at the University of Queensland, Australia. Previously he worked at the University of Dhaka, Bangladesh. His research focuses on the policy and practice of TESOL education in Asia. He is a co-editor of *Language Planning for Medium of Instruction in Asia* (2014). He is on the editorial boards of *Current Issues in Language Planning, Discourse: Studies in the Cultural Politics of Education, English Teaching Practice & Critique, Journal of Asia TEFL* and *Asiatic: IIUM Journal of English Language and Literature*.

Anna Kristina Hultgren (DPhil Oxon, MA Copenhagen, Cert LSE, SFHEA) is Professor of Sociolinguistics and Applied Linguistics and UKRI Future Leaders Fellow at the Open University, UK. She is currently leading an interdisciplinary project funded by UK Research and Innovation on English as a Medium of Instruction. She serves on the editorial boards of the *Journal of English-Medium Instruction*, the *Journal of English for Research Publication Purposes*, the Routledge Studies in English-Medium Instruction and others.

Ikuya Aizawa holds a DPhil (PhD) in Education from the University of Oxford, Department of Education, UK, and is a researcher in the EMI Oxford research group. His EMI-related research focuses on Japan and has most recently appeared in the journals *Higher Education*, *Studies in Higher Education*, *System*, *Language Teaching and Research* and *International Journal of Bilingual Education and Bilingualism*.

Miya Komori-Glatz is Senior Lecturer at WU Vienna University of Economics and Business, Austria. Her research examines English in a range of business and educational contexts, particularly English-medium education and internationalization, teaching business communication and English as a business lingua franca. Her publications reflect this interdisciplinary focus, with papers in outlets ranging from *Applied Linguistics* and the *Journal of English as a Lingua Franca* to the *European Journal of International Management*.

Angel M. Y. Lin received her doctoral degree from the University of Toronto, Canada, in 1996. Her research and teaching have focused on classroom discourse analysis, bilingual and plurilingual education, academic literacies, language across the curriculum, content and language integrated learning (CLIL) and translanguaging and trans-semiotizing. She has published six research books and over one hundred research articles and book chapters. In 2018 Angel Lin moved from the University of Hong Kong, Hong Kong, to Simon Fraser University, Canada, to take up the position of Tier 1 Canada Research Chair in Plurilingual and Intercultural Education.

Andrew Linn is Pro Vice-chancellor for Research and Head of the College of Liberal Arts and Sciences at the University of Westminster, London, UK, and was previously professor of the history of linguistics at the University of Sheffield, UK. He has published books and articles on the history of linguistics, language policy and planning and EME, focusing on Scandinavia. He currently works on EME in Central Asia and the South Caucasus.

Ernesto Macaro is Emeritus Professor of Applied Linguistics and a Senior Research Fellow at Worcester College, University of Oxford. He is the founding

Director of the Centre for Research and Development in EMI. Before becoming a teacher educator and researcher, Ernesto was a language teacher in secondary schools in the UK for sixteen years. Ernesto's current research focuses on second language learning strategies and on the interaction between teachers and learners in second language classrooms and in those where English is the medium of instruction. He has published widely in these areas.

Ron Martinez holds a doctorate in English from the University of Nottingham, UK, in addition to a master of science in applied linguistics and second language acquisition from the University of Oxford. He is an English-language specialist for the US Department of State, and in that capacity he has been invited by numerous institutions around the world to advise on matters concerning internationalization and language policy. He currently directs the language centre at the University of Arkansas.

Jim McKinley (SFHEA) is Associate Professor at the UCL Institute of Education, University College London, UK, where he teaches on the MA TESOL and applied linguistics programmes and supervises PhDs and EdDs in higher education studies and applied linguistics. His interests focus on implications of globalization for L2 writing, language education and higher education studies, particularly concerning EMI (with funding from British Council) and the teaching-research nexus (with funding from British Academy). He is an editor-in-chief for the journal *System*.

Agata Mikołajewska is Doctoral Researcher at the Centre for Applied Linguistics at the UCL Institute of Education, University College London, UK. Her research concerns various issues in higher education, but currently her particular focus is on internationalization and EMI. Agata is a co-author of the British Council report *Global Mapping of English as a Medium of Instruction in Higher Education: 2020 and Beyond*. Other publications feature in *Higher Education*, *Studies in Higher Education* and *ELT Journal*.

Izabela Mikołajewska is a pedagogue and philologist by passion and education, as well as coach of aggression replacement training. Her areas of interest include human behaviour, media in education and teaching in higher education, especially regarding EMI. She is lecturer and researcher at the Maria Grzegorzewska University in Warsaw (APS), Institute of Education, Department of Didactics and Media Pedagogy, Poland.

Norbella Miranda is Professor in the School of Language Sciences at Universidad del Valle, Cali, Colombia. She holds a PhD in educational sciences from Universidad del Quindío, Armenia, Colombia. Her research focuses on educational language policies, multilingualism and language curriculum. Her most recent publications include: *Appropriation of Colombian ELT Policy in a Targeted School: The Creation of an 'Elite' yet Still Needy School in the Public Education System* and *Unsettling the 'Challenge': ELT Policy Ideology and the New Breach amongst State-Funded Schools in Colombia*.

Mario Molina-Naar is a full-time Professor at the Department of Languages and Culture at Universidad de los Andes in Bogota, Colombia. He holds a BA in foreign language teaching (Colombia) and an MA in TESOL (United States). He is currently conducting his doctoral studies in education at the Autonomous University of Barcelona, Spain. His research interests include language teaching and pedagogy, action research in teacher education, English for academic purposes and EMI policies and practices.

Huong Thu Nguyen is E-learning Advisor at the Institute for Teaching and Learning, University of Queensland, Australia. Her research interests are language policy and planning, English as the medium of instruction, and internationalization of higher education. Her current project 'Students' Cross-Cultural Well-Being through Story, Art, and Film' explores how the connection among students across cultures through digital platforms and how their shared experience contribute to enhancing the exploration of self-identity as well as mutual understanding.

Ane Cibele Palma has a PhD in Applied Linguistics focusing on EMI and the theory of emotions. She holds a master's degree in applied linguistics, which focuses on the subjectivity of writing evaluation. She is Professor in the Language Arts Department of the Federal University of Paraná (UFPR), Brazil, and her main area of work is English teacher education. She has also worked as an English teacher and coordinator at Inter Americano Binational Center for sixteen years and as professor and coordinator at the Catholic University of Paraná (PUCPR) for fifteen years.

Gabriela Zamarrón Pérez has been involved in the implementation of a new bilingual, international and sustainable (BIS) educational modality in Mexico since its creation in 2012. She has proposed new strategies for bilingual education and developed partnerships with American and Canadian universities. With more than twelve years of experience in education, she is currently in charge of the International Strategic Development office at Universidad Tecnológica Metropolitana de Aguascalientes, Mexico. She is a psychologist with a master's degree in systemic family therapy.

Heath Rose is Associate Professor of Applied Linguistics in the Department of Education at the University of Oxford, UK, where he is also coordinator of the EMI Oxford Research Group. His previous EMI research has included policy-related research in Japan and explorations of success indicators in EMI programmes. He has also worked on several British Council EMI projects, including one in China and an ELTRA project in Italy. Heath has authored several books about the impact of globalization on language teaching.

Pramod K. Sah is a PhD candidate and Killam Laureate in the Department of Language and Literacy Education at the University of British Columbia, Canada. His scholarship focuses on EMI, language planning and policy, language ideology, translanguaging and teacher education. His works have appeared in *Journal of Bilingual Education and Bilingualism, Journal of Multilingual and Multicultural Development, International Multilingual Research Journal, Asia Pacific Journal of Education, English Teaching & Learning* among others.

Kari Sahan (DPhil Oxon) is Lecturer in Second Language Education at the Institute of Education, University of Reading, UK. She is also a member of the EMI Oxford Research Group and an Honorary Norham Fellow in the Department of Education, University of Oxford, UK. Her research focuses on language policy, teacher–student interaction, and the use of the L1 in EMI classrooms. Her work has appeared in journals such as *ELT Journal, System, Language Teaching Research, Teaching in Higher Education*, and the *Journal of English for Academic Purposes*.

Myrna Escalona Sibaja has worked as a lecturer, English-language teacher, and teacher trainer in higher education for more than eighteen years in Mexico. She has also led the implementation of training for lecturers and English-language teachers at public and private universities and organizations. Additionally, she has had opportunities to develop English-language teaching skills in the United States, Cuba and the UK. She holds a master's in ELT and in education.

Tolera Simie is a PhD candidate at the UCL Institute of Education, University College London, UK, and ESOL lecturer at South Thames College, London, UK. He has previously worked as a teacher trainer in Ethiopia. His PhD project explores the impact of EMI on quality of education in Ethiopian universities. His research interests encompass EMI, ESOL/TESOL, language-in-education policy and teacher education.

Phoebe Siu is Lecturer at College of Professional and Continuing Education, the Hong Kong Polytechnic University, Hong Kong. She is a doctoral candidate

(English-language education) at the University of Hong Kong, Hong Kong. Her research projects focus on multimodalities, content and language integrated learning, social semiotic awareness and EMI higher education. Her conference papers were accepted at international academic conferences such as AERA, AAAL, AILA and ISFC. Siu is a postgraduate researcher in the Translanguaging-Trans-semiotizing Research Group developed by Angel M. Y. Lin.

Ute Smit is Professor of English Linguistics at the University of Vienna, Austria. Her applied linguistic research focuses mainly on English in, and around, education at the crossroads of classroom discourse, language policy, internationalization, English as a lingua franca and multilingualism. Her publications include *ROAD-MAPPING English-Medium Education in the Internationalised University* (2020), various edited volumes and numerous journal articles (in *Applied Linguistics, System, International Journal of Bilingual Education and Bilingualism, TESOL Quarterly*).

Josep Soler is Associate Professor of Applied Linguistics at the Department of English, Stockholm University, Sweden. He obtained his PhD in linguistics and communication from the University of Barcelona, Spain. His main research interests cover the areas of language policy and linguistic ideologies. Josep specializes in the study of the sociolinguistic impact of the internationalization of higher education; in addition, he has written about the role of English in research publication, multilingual families and the sociolinguistics of minority languages.

Gene Thompson is Associate Professor in the Department of Global Business at Rikkyo University in Tokyo, Japan. He is the director of the Bilingual Business Leader programme, and his research related to EMI has appeared in journals such as the *International Journal of Bilingual Education and Bilingualism, Studies in Higher Education* and the *Journal of Education for Business*.

Christa van der Walt is Professor in the Department of Curriculum Studies at Stellenbosch University, South Africa, where she is currently also vice-dean research. Her research focuses on teaching English in multilingual contexts. She has published widely, including *Multilingual Higher Education* (2013) and chapters in sixteen books; she has also co-edited three books. A forthcoming work is a book, co-edited with V. Pfeiffer, entitled *Multilingual Classroom Contexts: Transitions and Transactions*.

Robert Wilkinson, Visiting Research Fellow in the Department of Philosophy at Maastricht University, the Netherlands, conducts research on EMI and multilingualism. He worked at the Language Centre of the same university and previously in Scotland, Czechoslovakia and France. He has conducted training courses and consultancies in EMI and languages for specific purposes in many countries. He is currently chair of the ICLHE Association. ORCID: 0000-0002-8737-3357

Sihan Zhou is Lecturer in the English Language Teaching Unit at the Chinese University of Hong Kong, Hong Kong. Prior to this, she was a doctoral researcher in the EMI Oxford research group at the University of Oxford, UK, where she also taught on the MSc Applied Linguistics for Language Teaching. Her research focuses on self-regulation, listening and language support in EMI and transnational university programmes in China and has appeared in *System*, *ELT Journal*, *Applied Linguistics Review* and *RELC Journal*.

Introduction

Nicola Galloway and Jim McKinley

With the exponential growth of English-medium instruction (EMI) in higher education on a global scale, we have seen a similar growth in EMI research. EMI has become one of the most significant global phenomena in higher education in non-Anglophone contexts in this century. However, growing EMI research reveals that policy implementation, and the driving forces behind this, is certainly not uniform across the globe. Given the diversity of EMI contexts, complexities of educational contexts, sociolinguistic landscapes and the different disciplines of EMI, this is both unsurprising and a welcome endeavour. While some contexts have witnessed a backlash against EMI and a return to national languages, overall, EMI provision is growing globally. Provision continues to outpace research, but as a growing field of study, EMI research is providing increasing insights into EMI policy implementation, or EMI *practices*, and revealing how these vary at the national or regional (macro), institutional (meso) and classroom (micro) levels.

Our edited volume responds to the need for a global exploration of EMI practices. In a sense, it responds to the requirement for large-scale needs analysis of EMI in different contexts to showcase differences, and some commonalities of course, in policy implementation. In doing so, we provide insights into various driving forces, perceived benefits, approaches to policy implementation, challenges and responses to EMI in various contexts around the globe via different levels of analysis.

EMI has become commonplace in many educational policies around the world and subject to mass government funding. Dedicated research centres (http://www.emi.network/) and online communities of practice (https://globalenglishes-emi.network/), journals (*Journal of English Medium Instruction* publishing from 2022) and a quickly growing number of full-length books and edited volumes also demonstrate both the status of this phenomenon/interest and growing interest in this field. While EMI, by definition, might be expected to primarily involve educational policy researchers, the majority of research has fallen within the broad field of applied linguistics (and recent publications have also examined the impact of EMI on the field; see e.g. Galloway and Rose 2021). The use of English to teach university subjects across various disciplines means that there are implications for the entire university as the issues surrounding it (politics, pedagogy, etc.) are interdisciplinary.

The growth of EMI research and provision has seen the development of EMI as a research paradigm, both in its own right and as one that has implications for several paradigms. English, the global lingua franca of academia, the dominant language of the academy taking the lion's share of academic outputs and now a language increasingly replacing national languages as a medium of instruction, has very much become synonymous with internationalization, sometimes referred to as Englishization, in higher education. As evidenced by the range of chapters in this volume, EMI practices have educational, political, societal, economic and cultural consequences, impacts and implications.

Approaches to EMI policy implementation (or EMI in practice)

Given the differences in definitions, conceptualizations and driving forces of EMI, it is unsurprising that policy implementation varies widely. EMI provision is growing (backlash and a return to national languages does exist), but this growth, or policy implementation rather, is not universal. As Curle et al. (2020: 11) note:

> Factors which influence the implementation of EMI include the driving forces behind its introduction, language education policies, provisions for language support, and language proficiency requirements for students and staff. EMI programmes can also vary in terms of how much English is used for teaching and learning in the curriculum.

Some key driving forces behind EMI implementation, including policies and language use, have been kindled by (post-)colonialism and globalization. As the teaching of content in English in response to bottom-up EMI initiatives (such as in the Netherlands and northern Europe) or top-down EMI policy (in much of the rest of the world), it takes on different forms. EMI practices have been decontextualized from the Anglophone sphere and recontextualized in regions sometimes both socio-historically and socio-politically far removed from that sphere. As the influence of English as a global lingua franca persists, governments and educational institutions alike will continue to encourage younger generations to improve their English proficiency through EMI to equip them to compete in a global market (Rose and McKinley 2018). It is important, then, to explore what this encouragement means for putting EMI into practice in different regional contexts.

EMI practice relates to the goals of a programme. However, these are not always clear, and explicit policy implementation guidelines do not always exist. Language-learning objectives are also often implicit, making EMI appear, at the outset at least, different from other content-based approaches to teaching English, such as content and language integrated learning, or CLIL (Rose and Galloway 2019). EMI programmes also often require specific English proficiency levels for admission (e.g. McKinley et al. 2021), whereas CLIL programmes typically specify a requisite language proficiency level for graduation (e.g. Arnó-Macià and Mancho-Barés 2015). However, many EMI programmes, such as those in Southeast Asia (Galloway and Sahan 2021 forthcoming), also have such graduation requirements. It is a complex situation. Some universities are explicit with their goals, whereas others appear to assume that language skills are a 'by-product' of studying content in English (Taguchi 2014).

Several researchers have discussed EMI practice using Macaro's (2018) three models of EMI: the preparatory year, the institutional support and the pre-institutional selection model. In the preparatory year model, students take long, intensive English for Academic Purposes (EAP) courses before studying through the medium of English. In universities where language proficiency is assumed to be higher, the institutional support model offers modified content courses at the start, supported with EAP or ESP courses. Language support is reduced over time as students start to take more content courses in English. The pre-institutional selection model provides limited language support, using English-language entrance requirements to select students. More recently, Sahan et al. (2021) discovered four variations of EMI implementation, based on a study in Turkey, with varying levels of L1 and English-language use and interaction.

Other scholars have provided categorizations of types of EMI provision, such as Brown's (2014) six types of EMI programmes (based on how the programmes were organized and implemented), Kudo and Hashimoto's (2011) categorization of EMI programmes (based on the university's approach to internationalization), Richards and Pun's (2021) typology of EMI (based on fifty-one features across ten EMI curriculum categories) and Shimauchi's (2012, 2016) categorization of EMI implementation (based on the students served by the programmes). Others place EMI programmes on a continuum from English-language teaching to content instruction in English (Met 1998; Thompson and McKinley 2018; Galloway and Rose 2021; and others), which problematizes definitions of EMI and the implementation of top-down EMI policy in different contexts. These continuums are helpful in seeing how EMI policy is conceptualized in different ways: as a pedagogical approach to delivering subject matter in some contexts, and closely linked with goals to improve English proficiency in others.

These categorization schemes highlight diversity in EMI practice as to how EMI policy is being implemented, to exemplify different interpretations of implementing EMI in higher education. EMI policy implementation may be explored at the national/regional or institutional/classroom level using a variety of research tools (policy analysis, stakeholders' conceptualizations of EMI, observations of EMI in practice, context analysis). But there is an imbalance of research at these levels. The twenty-one chapters in this volume respond to this need for an equal examination of macro-, meso- and micro-level EMI implementation in different contexts. EMI policy implementation has struggled to avoid unrealistic expectations and disappointment. It is hoped that this volume will provide insights into context-specific problems that can inspire potential solutions.

Book organization

It is unsurprising that EMI policies and practices vary significantly given the global scale of EMI. We acknowledge that 'EMI practice' is very context dependent, and, as Macaro et al. (2021: 2) point out, this diversity in policy and practice is 'potentially a welcome situation given the complexity of the different contexts in which EMI is being promoted'. In this edited volume, our authors do highlight some commonalities in policy implementation, but the chapters mostly provide an in-depth understanding of evolving interpretations and current policies regarding EMI in higher education, showcasing how EMI practices vary widely.

Chapters focus on Europe (EMI strongholds Denmark and the Netherlands, but also Austria, Estonia, Italy and Poland), as well as growth areas in South, Southeast, Central and East Asia (Bangladesh, China, Hong Kong, Japan, Nepal, the South Caucasus and Vietnam), the Middle East and Africa (Ethiopia, Kuwait, South Africa, Tunisia and Turkey) and Latin America (Brazil, Colombia and Mexico). With seven chapters at each level, we cover a broad range of regional contexts. Each chapter includes an introduction to frame the chapter, an overview of EMI policy in context to highlight extant EMI research on the region and a focused analysis, which in the meso and micro chapters presents the studies conducted by the contributor(s). These chapters comprise a comprehensive volume of EMI in practice in different contexts, and each chapter ends with a discussion of implications for researchers and practitioners to consider in light of the whole volume.

Macro-level analysis of EMI

The macro-level chapters provide insights into moves towards EMI in diverse contexts considering English-/foreign-language policies and national-level EMI – or English taught programmes (ETP) and English medium education (EME) – initiatives through policy scans, questionnaires and interviews with senior management and Ministries of Education.

Hamid and Al Amin explore the dominance of EMI in higher education in Bangladesh, a context where EMI has been associated with colonial rule but has expanded in the past three decades with implementation in private universities. Through an overview of the implementation of EMI across public and private higher education sectors, they highlight educational, social and sociocultural consequences of EMI. The next two chapters are more recent EMI contexts in the largest countries in their regions, but they are starkly different. Martinez and Cibele Palma examine the rapidly growing EMI in Brazil. They provide a synthesis of EMI driving forces and posit what directions it may take, and why, based on existing policy, current demographics and emerging trends. Next, Zhou and Rose deliver a helpful overview of the vast EMI implementation in Mainland China, providing clarity around the issues associated with its exponential growth of EMI programmes, specifically learner development, needs and agency.

We then shift to the first of the two EMI stronghold contexts in our volume: Denmark. Hultgren explores the rise of EMI at universities in Denmark, clarifying its position as a pioneer of EMI practices. But Hultgren also argues that the rise of EMI in Denmark has been accidental, as a result of performance-based funding systems and the European harmonization project. It is an important note for emerging EMI contexts to not attempt to model EMI practices on such origin contexts as Denmark.

The next two contexts are infrequently mentioned in EMI literature, but they provide important bases for arguments around injustices of EMI. Simie, having grown up and been educated in Ethiopia, describes a complex, highly multilingual context where, although never colonized, English has been the medium of instruction since the first higher education institution started just over seventy years ago. Despite wide expansion of universities, poor proficiency continues to weaken the quality of education. Next, Sah, originally from and educated in Nepal, provides an overview of EMI in the South Asian country with a very similar timeline to Ethiopia for EMI in higher education. But in a postcolonial context, EMI expansion has led to different concerns. Through a socio-historical contextualization, Sah explains that neoliberal forces weigh heavily on EMI policy and practices with significant implications for local language ecology.

The macro section closes with the only national context outside of East Asia that has seen considerable investigation into EMI policy and, more recently, EMI practices. Sahan evaluates partial EMI programmes in Turkish higher education with consideration given to English proficiency and language support for teachers and students, comparing this with all-English EMI programmes. The implications for the two different models may be far-reaching, particularly for emerging EMI contexts.

Meso-analysis of EMI

Our meso-level analysis includes chapters focusing on EMI programme offerings at the institutional level in Austria, Colombia, Estonia, Italy, Poland, South Africa and Vietnam. Meso-level analysis may also include policy scans, website analysis, questionnaires and interviews (and other qualitative data collection techniques), not only with senior managers but also EMI programme coordinators and directors, as well as teachers and students.

The first two chapters in this section take critical perspectives of institutional-level EMI to reveal valuable insights. Starting in the 'heart of Europe', Smit and Komori-Glatz explore EMI policy at the institution level in Austria. Critical of a 'laissez-faire approach' of EMI in Austria at the macro-level, which sees the presence of English as an unquestioned reality, they highlight key examples in a range of institutions taking proactive approaches to EMI implementation. Next is the second of our three Latin American countries in the volume, the relatively underexplored context of Colombia. Miranda and Molina-Naar profile growing trends for EMI in Colombian universities. They explore EMI initiatives in public and private universities across four main cities in the country to provide a critical appraisal of the appropriateness of EMI in the Colombian higher education context.

Three diverse European contexts make up the next three chapters. Soler Carbonell delves into the ideological critiques of EMI to arrive at a more positive outlook for EMI in Estonia. By analysing the linguistic representations in recent public exchanges in different media on the question of language in Estonian higher education, he draws on the ongoing polarization of Estonian and English to reveal an evolution of the debates since 2012. Now aligning more with Nordic countries, developments in EMI in Estonia are in tandem with socio-political changes. We move then to Italy, and Costa and Grassi present their study of lecturer needs by exploring their perspectives before and after an EMI teacher training programme at an Italian university. Lecturer experiences highlighted in the chapter are illustrative of the context, offering potential insights for similar contexts. On to Poland, and Mikołajewska and Mikołajewska emphasize in their chapter the scarcity of research on EMI in Polish higher education. As such, they provide a useful overview of the current situation in Poland. Maintaining a focus on EMI practices, they illustrate the understanding and implementation of EMI at the institutional level.

Next, van der Walt explores the effectiveness of EMI at the institutional level in South Africa in preparing higher education students for their professions. She argues for the need to include African languages against the dominance of English but acknowledges considerable challenges, notably presented by students' negative attitudes towards other languages, although attitudes are known to improve in professional environments. She presents a strong argument for the inclusion of additional languages in EMI.

Closing out the section, Nguyen provides a systematic historical overview of EMI policy and practice in Vietnam. Although English has been the medium of instruction for some postgraduate degrees since the 1990s and undergraduate degrees since the 2000s, regulations in government legislation have lacked the specificity to inform practices. Examples of university responses to EMI policies show a range of approaches, with potential applications to contexts outside ASEAN.

Micro-analysis of EMI

In our final section, the authors analyse EMI as it is implemented in classrooms in the South Caucasus, Hong Kong, Japan, Kuwait, Mexico, the Netherlands and Tunisia.

The first three chapters in this section provide optimism towards EMI in rather different contexts. Covering Armenia, Azerbaijan and Georgia, Linn first outlines the relevant South Caucasus higher education context before providing an overview of his team's research into students', teachers', university administrators' and Ministry colleagues' experiences of EMI. The focus of the study is on the voices of students, recorded via free text questionnaire responses. The positive voices counter the often-negative tone of EMI research. Next, Siu and Lin highlight EMI students' and teachers' creativity and trans-semiotic agency in Hong Kong, thanks to allowances for translanguaging, drawing on multiple semiotic resources. We then move on to EMI success stories from Japan. Aizawa, Curle and Thompson provide evidence through student interviews of not only their EMI challenges but also their ability to gain content knowledge through EMI.

Concerns about content knowledge acquisition in EMI raise both problems and solutions. Alazemi and Alenezi establish an important argument concerning top-down EMI policy in Kuwait with directly transferable findings for similar contexts. In their investigation of EMI classrooms, they conclude that the policy fails to recognize students' limited comprehension in English lectures having studied solely in Arabic until entering university, limiting their acquisition of content knowledge. Offering a potential solution to such a problem, Escalona Sibaja and Zamarrón Pérez highlight the effectiveness of an immersion course developed for pre-sessional students at a bilingual international and sustainable university in Mexico. They conclude their study with recommendations for improving the EMI programme with implications for similar contexts.

Next, we move to the second of our two stronghold countries. In their study at a university in the Netherlands, Wilkinson and Gabriëls explore EMI glocalization, noting the Englishization of Dutch higher education as a result of the quick expansion of EMI. They argue that this Englishization reflects the impact of neoliberalism on higher education, particularly due to the commodification of education and research.

The final chapter of the volume considers the impact of EMI on employability in Tunisia. Badwan argues that EMI has many perceived benefits, but there are also uncertain consequences as it is unclear whether the skills developed are actually needed or valued in the job market, where Arabic and French are the dominant languages.

Final thoughts

This book stems out of our own first-hand experience working in EMI universities in Japan and our identification of the need for more research to strike a better balance of all three levels of analysis with key stakeholders. EMI growth worldwide is truly phenomenal, and our aim with this volume is to respond to the need for evolving understanding of current practices and conceptualizations of EMI policy in global contexts. The authors utilize a variety of methods in their studies, and, as such, this volume also aims to foster research. EMI is a complex, interdisciplinary field, and while the authors are all operating in the field of applied linguistics, it is also hoped that the volume will foster essential future interdisciplinary research on this growing global phenomenon. While provision is still outpacing research, the field of EMI continues to grow, with very different outcomes. Our book aims to highlight the complexities across contexts but also any common denominators in 'EMI in practice'.

We hope this volume can be a useful resource for the growing body of EMI researchers and for those operating in the fields of applied linguistics, EMI and the internationalization of higher education and language policy.

References

Arnó-Macià, E., and Mancho-Barés, G. (2015), 'The role of content and language in content and language integrated learning (CLIL) at university: Challenges and implications for ESP', *English for Specific Purposes*, 37: 63–73.

Brown, H. G. (2014), 'Contextual factors driving the growth of undergraduate English-medium instruction programmes at universities in Japan', *Asian Journal of Applied Linguistics*, 1 (1): 50–63.

Curle, S., Jablonkai, R. R., Mittelmeier, J., Sahan, K., and Veitch, A. (2020), English medium instruction: Part 1 literature review', in N. Galloway (series ed.), *English in Higher Education*, London: British Council.

Galloway, N., and Rose, H. (2021), 'English medium instruction and the English language practitioner', *ELT Journal*, 75 (1): 33–41.

Galloway, N. and Sahan, K. (2021). *An Investigation into English Medium Instruction in Higher Education in Thailand and Vietnam*. London: British Council.

Kudo, K., and Hashimoto, H. (2011), 'Internationalisation of Japanese universities: Current status and future directions', in S. Marginson, S. Kaur and E. Sawir (eds), *Higher Education in the Asia-Pacific*, 343–59, Netherlands: Springer.

Macaro, E. (2018), *English Medium Instruction*, Oxford University Press.

Macaro, E., Sahan, K., and Rose, H. (2021), 'The profiles of English medium instruction teachers in higher education', *International Journal of Applied Linguistics*: DOI: 10.1111/ijal.12344.

McKinley, J., Rose, H., and Zhou, S. (2021), 'Transnational universities and English Medium Instruction in China: How admissions, language support and language use differ in Chinese universities', *RELC Journal*, 52 (2): 236–52.

Met, M. (1998), 'Curriculum decision-making in content-based language teaching', in J. Cenoz and F. Genesee (eds), *Beyond Bilingualism: Multilingualism and Multilingual Education*, 35–63, Bristol: Multilingual Matters.

Richards, J. C., and Pun, J. (2021), 'A typology of English-medium instruction', *RELC Journal*: 0033688220968584.

Rose, H., and Galloway, N. (2019), *Global Englishes for Language Teaching*, Cambridge University Press.

Rose, H., & McKinley, J. (2018). Japan's English-medium instruction initiatives and the globalization of higher education. *Higher Education*, 75(1): 111–29.

Sahan, K., Rose, H., and Macaro, E. (2021), 'Models of EMI pedagogies: At the interface of language use and interaction', *System*, 101: 102616.

Shimauchi, S. (2012), 'Nihon ni okeru kotokyoiku no kokusaika to eigo program ni kansuru kenkyu' [Research on internationalization of higher education and EMIDP (English medium instruction degree programs) in Japan], *Kokusai Kyoiku [Journal of International Education]*, 18: 1–15.

Shimauchi, S. (2016), *Higashi Ajia ni okeru ryugakusei idou no paradaimu shifuto – Daigaku kokusaika to Eigo puroguramu no Nikkan hikaku* [Paradigm shift on international student mobility in East Asia: Comparative analysis on internationalization of higher education and English-medium degree programs in Japan and South Korea], Tokyo: Toshindo.

Taguchi, N. (2014), 'English-medium education in the global society', *International Review of Applied Linguistics in Language Teaching*, 52 (2): 89–98.

Thompson, G., and McKinley, J. (2018), 'Integration of content and language learning', in J. I. Liontas (ed.), *The TESOL Encyclopedia of English Language Teaching*, 1–13, Wiley Online Library.

Part I
Macro-analysis

English-Medium Instruction in Bangladeshi Higher Education: A Policy Perspective

Obaidul M. Hamid and Md Al Amin

Introduction

English-medium instruction (EMI) refers to the use of English for academic activities, including teaching, learning and research. EMI fits into the model of content teaching *for* language teaching (Mohan 1979), which means that although content teaching (e.g. business and sciences) is the explicit focus of instruction, language learning gain is also factored into policy goals. EMI in this sense is different from content and language integrated learning (CLIL), which exemplifies content teaching *and* language teaching (Mohan 1979). It is generally understood as being stronger in policy (the what) than in planning/pedagogy (the how) (Jones 2014). In other words, although the policy aims for changes in teachers' and students' language behaviours, there is limited discussion on how the change is managed and achieved.

As a global phenomenon, EMI has a strong presence in Bangladesh. Although it is available at all levels of education, higher education has become its main adopter. The origin of EMI is associated with British colonial rule which sought to educate the natives in English in the interest of colonial domination. This colonial legacy has subsequently been reshaped by the forces of globalization, which has established English as a global lingua franca. More critically, EMI has served as a tool for neoliberalization of higher education with all its anticipated and unanticipated consequences. Our aim in this chapter is to provide a critical overview of EMI in Bangladeshi higher education with reference to policy and policy motivations. We also outline policy implementation processes and educational and social outcomes of EMI.

EMI and higher education from a global perspective

The emergence of EMI as a global trend in higher education (e.g. Bowles and Murphy 2020) is not surprising in a neoliberal environment. First, the phenomenal spread of English in the past several centuries is unprecedented in history. Starting its global journey as a language of colonization, it has come to be known as the language of globalization. English has been the unrivalled language of science, technology, trade, commerce and diplomacy in a globalized world where global interdependence and connectivity have become the norm for individuals, communities and societies which can be facilitated by a global lingua franca. Pursuing education in English is increasingly seen as normal given that it is the main language for generating, preserving and disseminating knowledge. English is also considered an essential part of human capital and the set of skills that are demanded by the new economy dominated by transnational corporations (Ali and Hamid 2021). Underlying these essential processes is the dominance of neoliberalism which has come to shape almost every aspect of our life with its principles of market fundamentals, including privatization, commercialization and loosening of state regulation (Harvey 2005).

The emerging English-using global polity has responded to these global and neoliberal developments by introducing and investing in English. EMI has been one of the key policy strategies for many nations. To some extent, it has come to redefine nationalism as it demanded policy accommodation even in nations with a strong sense of nationalism demonstrated by national languages. For these nations, internationalization of higher education has become a key goal, which essentially means opening the sector to global challenges and opportunities. Internationalization has played out in different ways for different nations. If it has allowed more developed nations to attract international students and staff to their higher education thus giving them a share of the competitive international education market, for less developed nations it has at least helped to reduce the outbound flow of students to more developed and English-prominent nations (Hamid et al. 2013b). As a global academic lingua franca, English has been the obvious choice in this process of internationalization (Bowles and Murphy 2020).

EMI and higher education in Bangladesh

EMI in Bangladeshi higher education had two points of entry, nearly three-quarters of a century apart. The first entry was part of the colonial education policy during British rule in India (1757–1947). The debates between the Orientalists and the Anglicists about the best medium of education for the natives in the first quarter of the nineteenth century came to an end in favour of the Anglicists with the adoption of Macaulay's Minutes in 1835. This paved the way for English and English education in colonial India. The first university (the University of Dhaka) which had English as the only medium of instruction was established in the current Bangladesh territory in 1921. The other public universities that were established during Pakistani rule (1947–71) also had English-medium instruction demonstrating colonial continuity in education policy. However, the separation of Bangladesh from Pakistan as an independent nation in 1971 had a significant impact on medium of instruction policy. At the height of linguistic nationalism that sought to establish Bangla in all walks of life, including higher education, English lost its status as the exclusive medium of instruction. The position of English was further weakened by the Bengali Introduction Law, 1987, during the military rule which called for use of Bangla in all offices and institutions across the country.

The latest national education policy (Ministry of Education 2010: 24) states that 'English will remain as a medium of instruction in higher education along with Bangla'. It applies only to public sector higher education. Although this is a clear statement of the medium for teaching and learning, there are no further details on how the two languages will be used in the sector. In the absence of clarity – or regardless of what the macro-level policy says – it is important to consider the policy as practised by the forty-six universities constituting the public sector. The policy in practice appears to be more complex, as different institutions have different priorities, resources and constraints. Nevertheless, certain broad patterns can be identified. For example, specialist universities such as science, technology, engineering and medicine rely on English, as books and other resources are mainly available in English. General or comprehensive universities do not reflect uniformity in terms of medium of instruction (MOI) as arts, humanities and social sciences are taught mainly in Bangla while sciences and other specialist fields prefer English. Based on our experience of teaching and interacting with colleagues, it can be safely asserted that flexibility in language use is the norm.

The second entry point for EMI to higher education is more recent showing the influence of globalization and neoliberalism. As previously noted, MOI in the public sector shows some balance between English and Bangla reflecting the emphasis on nationalism and national identity on the one hand and exploiting the benefits of the global language on the other. However, the MOI in the private sector universities is heavily swayed towards utilitarian motivations rather than nationalist ideologies (Hamid and Baldauf 2014). It is on nationalist grounds that the University Grants Commission has recently imposed two compulsory courses on Bangla and the history of Bangladesh on all students in these universities.

Private universities are relatively recent entities which were first established in the early 1990s by the introduction of the Private University Act, 1992. So far there are 105 such universities, the majority of them located in Dhaka and other urban settings. Although there is no discussion of language or medium of instruction in the act, each university has adopted EMI by default. This is interesting because setting up a private university is a micro-level initiative by individual actors with interest, resources and entrepreneurship (Zhao 2011). However, since each university from its micro context has adopted the same language policy, EMI reflects what is called the 'macroization' of micro policy (Hamid and Baldauf 2014).

The neoliberal origin of private universities needs to be emphasized. First, they have privatized higher education, which had existed only in the public sector. They operate following corporate models to ensure quality, efficiency and accountability and compete with one another for market share of fee-paying students. These universities have also accomplished economization of education showing an alignment between the curriculum and job market demands. Consequently, each university curriculum focuses heavily on business, sciences and engineering fields with negligible presence of arts and humanities (Anwaruddin 2013). The rationale for opening these universities was also dominated by neoliberal arguments. Although the private sector was allowed to step in to compensate for the limited capacity of the public sector in meeting the growing demand for higher education, privatization was ultimately another choice for those who could afford higher education. Private universities sought to minimize the outbound flow of Bangladeshi students to foreign countries for higher education. EMI served as a key strategy in this process by fulfilling two purposes. It helped to introduce internationalization of higher education in the local context for prospective students to consider before they went abroad. It also provided a corrective to public sector failure in developing students' English-language proficiency demanded by the job market.

EMI actors, processes and motivations

The EMI policy discussed in this chapter reflects the institutional as well as individual nature of agency and corresponding policy processes and motivations

(Zhao 2011). EMI in the public sector was inherited as a colonial legacy. If the post-independence political elite did not abolish the colonial policy, they significantly undermined its hold being guided by nationalist sentiments. Without denying the role of English and its dominance as an academic lingua franca, a linguistic hierarchy was constructed in which English was not allowed to supersede the national language.

While EMI in the public sector seems to be regulated on nationalist grounds, its largely deregulated utilization in the private sector does not reflect such ideologies. As previously noted, Bangla has been imposed as a mandatory course on students only recently. The utilitarian approach to English and EMI adopted by private universities reflects postnational and neoliberal tendencies. The EMI actors of private universities are identifiable individuals. The vast majority of them are successful businesspeople whose desire for establishing universities may reflect the global direction of entrepreneurship and investment. If these actors are not people with power in a modern sense (Zhao and Baldauf 2012), they seek power and dominance by utilizing their capital and entrepreneurial desire in relation to education.

Since the individual actors who initiated the private university enterprises adopted the same language policy (i.e. EMI), it can be argued that they share the same neoliberal habitus and agency, at least in terms of language and language ideologies. As per this habitus, EMI is a default option for private universities. English is perceived to be central to the enterprise and its academic and organizational functioning. Other languages such as Bangla may have only an informal or peripheral role, if we ignore the recent imposition of the Bangla-language course.

Practices of EMI across public and private universities

Research on EMI in Bangladeshi universities is very limited, which does not allow for theorizing on EMI practice. Based on the few case studies that have been conducted (e.g. Hamid et al. 2013a; Rahman et al. 2020) and drawing on our experience of teaching and research, we will discuss major practices of EMI. We would argue that such practices reflect institutional divides between universities in the public and private sectors in terms of ideologies informing their origin, identity and operation.

The first characteristic of the practice of EMI is the accommodation of the two main languages, Bangla and English, and the linguistic hierarchy constituted by them. Bangla is dominant in public universities while it is English that dominates private universities. By extension, if English is the other language in the public sector, Bangla has been given this role in private universities. However, while English as an academic lingua franca has a functional and instrumental role in public universities, Bangla seems to have a negligible presence in private universities. This is so because Bangla is associated only with social life on campus with a minimal academic role. On public university campuses, boundaries between English and Bangla appear to be porous, as the languages seem to have some kind of coexistence. Such boundaries seem to be more pronounced in private universities. Policing language behaviours is unheard of in any public university which, however, is common in some private universities (Hamid et al. 2013a).

This divergent language ideology and management is associated with the projected identity of institutions and identity management. There is a silent competition between the two sectors. The majority of public universities were established long ago, and this has contributed to their prestige and reputation. Also, tuition is almost free in these universities. Private universities are faced with a phenomenal marketing challenge in luring prospective students in the prevailing social environment. This has called for a significant discursive investment. While public universities may not be keen on constructing a positive organizational self through websites and other semiotic resources, this identity construction is a strategic imperative for private universities. Construction of self-identity may inevitably refer to public universities, which are often represented as the other. This self-construction emphasizes several features to assert their distinction from public universities, including their alignment with global universities in terms of curriculum and pedagogy, use of English for teaching and learning, and prioritizing students' English proficiency development in preparing them for global and local job markets. Available research suggests that teachers and students of private universities are often engaged in such self-construction (Hamid et al. 2013a; Rahman et al. 2020).

What is important beyond such self-construction discourses is how EMI is managed in the two sets of universities. Student recruitment is a critical process that may ensure that students are admitted based on, among other requirements, language proficiency and academic skills. However, this process is characterized by lack of consistency and efficiency from a language point of view.

Students seeking places in higher education institutions for undergraduate studies have to take admission tests. These tests are extremely competitive in public universities given the limited number of places on the one hand and the growing demand for higher education on the other. The English language is included in the tests, but it is unclear what the test content seeks to assess and how this may relate to students' future study. This practice has been going on for decades suggesting that language as a medium of instruction may not be a question deserving policy or research attention. The language for learning has largely been an issue for students themselves who need to address it in their own ways. Some public universities may offer short-term language support programmes, but these are generally understood as being inadequate in meeting students' academic needs.

The language for learning in the public sector higher education does not seem to have presented an educational challenge because students either learn through the medium of their mother tongue or fall back on their mother tongue if English was dominant in their field of studies. This does not mean they do not face language challenges; many of them do, particularly those coming from rural areas (Hamid 2021) or those with ethnic minority backgrounds. However, these issues may not be prioritized in the context of more pressing questions facing the sector.

The question of English-language proficiency is critically important for universities in the private sector where English is the sole medium of instruction. Officially, all private universities recruit students based on admission tests, which include the English language. While some universities in the sector may ensure rigour in the process, others may be somewhat flexible so they do not lose students. Since EMI is used across the board, it may be expected that there would be uniform standards of English proficiency for recruitment purposes, although such standards have been unheard of. On the positive side, all private universities offer multiple English foundation courses focusing on speaking, listening, reading and writing as language support for their studies through English. However, the effectiveness of these courses in meeting students' academic language needs is an empirical question (Riya and Kabir 2019).

The question of how EMI is practiced for teaching and learning activities in the classroom may constitute the heart of the matter. Exclusive use of English in the classroom may be a rarity in public universities except in disciplines such as English (Hamid 2021). Although officially English is the only classroom language in private universities, the nature of actual language use may be different from the policy. While insiders of private universities, including teachers, may assert the exclusive use of English, those from outside may be sceptical about such assertions (Rahman et al. 2020). Whether English only or mixed with Bangla, both approaches may be problematic from different perspectives. Mixing

English with Bangla may help both teachers and students in maximizing their engagement in teaching and learning, but such practice may go against the policy. On the other hand, English only may meet policy expectations and help those teachers and students coming from English-medium schooling, but the majority of teachers and students may feel academically challenged due to their varying levels of ability for English use. Suspending Bangla from the classroom in which they have native proficiency may also be preposterous leading to a situation of sink or swim with English.

Educational and social implications of EMI

The global trend of EMI as reflected in higher education in Bangladesh may have mixed educational and social consequences. With EMI, we can see the potential of educational divides perpetuating social divides. Choosing English for teaching and learning may not be unrealistic when we consider the dominance of the language in all sectors of society, including information, education, research and knowledge. It may also be a realistic policy choice at a time when nations have to survive in a fiercely competitive global environment. However, the EMI policy, particularly in private universities, does not appear to be a neutral medium. While EMI means continuity for those students coming from English-medium pre-university education backgrounds, it is a disruption of MOI for Bangla-medium educated students who have to make a new beginning. EMI is generally appreciated by students and other stakeholders, but there are concerns about the possibility of one section of students benefitting more than others.

EMI has been deployed as a policy strategy with the potential for double gains: students learning the content while also enhancing their capacity for English use for educational, social and professional communication. Such gains can be achieved only when teachers and students are confident of their functioning in English in the academic domain. This operational proficiency in English is not equally distributed across the student population. As a consequence, some students may incur double losses in place of double gains. This loss or gain may not be restricted to campus life; students may carry it over to the job market where they may win or lose due to their learning experiences and outcomes.

As discussed in this chapter, the introduction of EMI during colonial rule aimed at continuing colonial subjugation by a divide-and-rule strategy (Jahan and Hamid, 2022). EMI was one such strategy, which sought to create a minority elite with pro-Western views and a majority with traditional views and ideals. This social divide along linguistic lines created during colonial rule has remained intact in postcolonial Bangladesh. EMI has been an exclusive educational pathway for the privileged class in society, different from other educational routes to the future (Jahan and Hamid 2019). Although the sector-wide adoption of EMI may be seen as undermining the elitist labelling, potentially it secures the privilege of those who come from EMI schooling background.

More problematic is the enactment of the social divide by student groups belonging to different mediums of instruction in their schooling. The choice of MOI is not simply a linguistic or educational question; this is associated with students' social backgrounds, identities and worldviews (Jahan and Hamid 2019). While private universities have brought an opportunity for students coming from different educational backgrounds to interact and study together, social belonging and friendship patterns of students may still be mediated by students' previous schooling backgrounds (Jahan and Hamid, 2022). This may affect students' life at university and beyond. These social and sociological questions may demand appropriate policy approaches beyond the provision of academic language support.

Conclusions and recommendations

The overview of EMI in Bangladeshi higher education undertaken in this chapter raises a number of critical issues. As argued, EMI has emerged as a dividing line between public and private universities, creating unhelpful debates in the sector. There is also an unmissable divide within private universities between students and staff coming from English-medium and Bangla-medium education backgrounds.

In terms of policy recommendations for moving forward, neither English-only nor Bangla-only can be a practical MOI choice. Perhaps a more reasonable and viable MOI strategy is a hybrid approach, which will take a flexible view of both languages to accommodate language backgrounds of students and staff and their future communication needs in a globalizing world. In that spirit, if private universities have to create more academic and social space for Bangla, public universities have to create more opportunities for academic and social communication in English. More critically, language and MOI policies in the whole sector need to be guided by an understanding that the two languages are not hostile neighbours; they are an essential part of individual and societal linguistic repertories. Students and staff should be welcome to freely shuttle between the two porous linguistic territories without travel documents.

References

Ali, M. M., and Hamid, M. O. (2021), 'English and human capital development', in S. Sultana, M. M. Roshid, Z. M. Haider, M. M. N. Kabir and M. H. Khan (eds), *The Routledge Handbook of English Language Education in Bangladesh*, 369–81, London: Routledge.

Anwaruddin, S. M. (2013), 'Neoliberal universities and the education of arts, humanities and social sciences in Bangladesh', *Policy Futures in Education*, 11 (4): 364–74.

Bowles, H., and Murphy, A. C., eds (2020), *English-Medium Instruction and the Internationalization of Universities*, Cham, Switzerland: Palgrave Macmillan.

Hamid, M. O. (2021), 'An autoethnography of a Musafir life exploring English language education', in S. Sultana, M. M. Roshid, Z. M. Haider, M. M. N. Kabir and M. H. Khan (eds), *The Routledge Handbook of English Language Education in Bangladesh*, 327–37, London: Routledge.

Hamid, M. O., and Baldauf, R. B. Jr (2014), 'Public-private domain distinction as an aspect of LPP frameworks: A case study of Bangladesh', *Language Problems & Language Planning*, 38 (2): 192–210.

Hamid, M. O., Jahan, I., and Islam, M. M. (2013a), 'Medium of instruction policies and language practices, ideologies and institutional divides: Voices of teachers and students in a private university in Bangladesh', *Current Issues in Language Planning*, 14 (1): 144–63.

Hamid, M. O., Nguyen, H. T. M., and Baldauf Jr, R. B. (2013b), 'Medium of instruction in Asia: Context, processes and outcomes', *Current Issues in Language Planning*, 14 (1): 1–15.

Harvey, D. (2005), *A Brief History of Liberalism*, Oxford: Oxford University Press.

Jahan, I., and Hamid, M. O. (2019), 'English as a medium of instruction and the discursive construction of elite identity', *Journal of Sociolinguistics*, 23: 386–408.

Jahan, I., and Hamid, M. O. (2022), 'Medium discourses and the construction of self and other in social media in postcolonial Bangladesh', in C. LaDousa and C. P. Davis (eds), *Language, Education, and Identity: Medium in South Asia*, 44–70, New York: Routledge.

Jones, J. M. (2014), 'The "ideal" vs. the "reality": Medium of instruction policy and implementation in different class levels in a western Kenyan school', *Current Issues in Language Planning*, 15 (1): 22–38.

Ministry of Education (2010), *National Education Policy*, Dhaka: Bangladesh.

Mohan, B. A. (1979), 'Relating language teaching and content teaching', *TESOL Quarterly*, 13 (2): 171–82.

Rahman, M. M., Singh, M. K. M., and Karim, A. (2020), 'Distinctive medium of instruction ideologies in public and private universities in Bangladesh', *Asian Englishes*, 22 (2): 125–42.

Riya, R. R., and Kabir, M. M. N. (2019), 'Usefulness of English foundation courses: A study on private universities in Bangladesh', *Manababidya Gabesanapatra (The Research Journal of Humanities)*, 3: 369–93.

Zhao, S. (2011), 'Actors in language planning', in E. Hinkel (ed.), *Handbook of Research in Second Language Teaching and Learning*, 905–23, New York: Routledge.

Zhao, S., and Baldauf, R. B. Jr (2012), 'Individual agency in language planning: Chinese script reform as a case study', *Language Problems & Language Planning*, 36 (1): 1–24.

2

Brazil Trying English-Medium Instruction On for Size: Emerging Trends and Policy

Ron Martinez and Ane Cibele Palma

Introduction: EMI 'window shopping' in Brazil

There is little to no record of English-medium instruction (EMI) occurring in Brazilian higher education prior to 2011 (Martinez 2016). While that clearly means that, relatively speaking, EMI is a newcomer to the country, what is important to understand, and of greater relevance to the present chapter, is what has motivated this rather recent emergence. A better understanding of what has given rise to the phenomenon of EMI in Brazil, we believe, can help inform better EMI policy going forward.

First, it is worth briefly noting what has motivated EMI in other regions where the practice is more well established, particularly Western Europe, where there are reports of classes being offered through English as early as the 1980s (e.g. Wilkinson 2012). Important political developments in subsequent years, most notably the Maastricht Treaty of 1992 that founded the twelve original member states of the European Union, followed by the Bologna declaration in 1999, which aimed to 'harmonize' the European higher education system (Huisman et al. 2012), had the effect of augmenting the prominence of English as an academic lingua franca (Jenkins 2013). After all, a degree programme in the Netherlands, if taught exclusively in Dutch, meant probably teaching students from that country alone. To offer the same programme through English carried the potential of drawing students not only from other neighbouring countries in the EU but even from other continents. Importantly, for many universities that also meant being able to attract more paying students and higher tuition fees (Wächter and Maiworm 2014).

In Brazil, by contrast, there is no real social, academic or linguistic counterpart to the movements that took place in Europe in the 1990s. While there have been recent and comparatively narrow attempts at reciprocal recognition and accreditation of diplomas across countries in South America (e.g. the ARCU-SUL accord), there is no Latin American version of the Maastricht Treaty or a process quite like that which took place in Bologna. Indeed, even if such treaties and processes did occur in and around Brazil, the linguistic effect would not be the same. The twelve original member states of the EU had (at least) twelve distinct national languages, making English, the most widely taught language, a likely default lingua franca in academic settings. By comparison, the predominant languages of the four member countries that make up the Mercosul South American trade bloc (Argentina, Brazil, Paraguay and Uruguay) are basically limited to two (Spanish and Portuguese), which are typologically close and often mutually intelligible – thus largely obviating any need to recur to a third language. And with respect to any financial incentive attached to EMI, unlike many universities elsewhere, higher education institutions (HEIs) in Brazil that offer classes through English are predominantly and increasingly the public ones (Gimenez et al. 2018) – 100 per cent tuition free (the highest-ranked universities in Brazil are public).

So how, and why, has EMI emerged in Latin America's largest country and economy? One apparent watershed seems to be the Brazilian student mobility programme Ciência sem Fronteiras, or Science without Borders (henceforth, SwB). Beginning in 2011, the SwB programme originally aimed to send over one hundred thousand college students to overseas STEM-related university programmes, the majority of which were English medium, for stays of around six months. SwB had the general purpose of helping increase the international profile of Brazilian student scholars, with potential intellectual and cultural gains that could ostensibly be shared once they were back in their home institutions. Unfortunately, the SwB programme was later criticized by some in Brazil (Rivas and Mullet 2016; Sá 2016) as having failed for a number of reasons. For one, there was no real mechanism built into SwB to institutionally reappropriate any competence or knowledge acquired by the outgoing students upon their return. Thus, the extent to which SwB fostered 'internationalization' by some of the more well-known definitions (e.g. Knight 2015) had been left open to interpretation and debate. Moreover, the programme was expensive and ran out of money in 2016, thereby shuttering the initiative indefinitely.

While SwB may be seen by some as having fallen short of its original objectives, there are other fruits, if unintended, that were born of it. One such fruit is the push to 'internationalize at home' (Beelen and Jones 2015), that is, to try to foment institutional practices and academic cultures that afford the same kinds of rewards to students in their home institution that can be had when going abroad – benefitting many rather than the relative few. After all, while SwB was able to ultimately send over ninety thousand Brazilian students to foreign universities, that number still represents a tiny fraction of the millions of college students in all of Brazil. There were many students that were able to take advantage of SwB but still far more that could not. The reasons those students were unable to participate in the SwB programme are myriad, but the most oft-reported impediments were practical ones: either a candidate did not possess the necessary proficiency in the language required by the destination programme/institution (Amorim Borges and Garcia-Filice 2016) or the student had important domestic responsibilities (e.g. employment ties, caregiver to a parent or child) that made it unrealistic to simply leave the country – or both (Feltrin et al. 2016).

At the same time, SwB did raise awareness of the benefits of having an international academic experience and seems to have been the impetus for more recent interest among universities to offer a more sustainable and inclusive *internationalized* experience for their students (Finardi and Archanjo 2018). One example is the Languages without Borders (LwB) programme, originally created in 2012 as a language support programme for SwB candidates. When funding for SwB ceased in 2016, LwB survived as a programme that offered a great diversity of extracurricular classes to practice foreign languages. A further example is the government PRINT programme (Programa Institucional de Internacionalização), which in 2018 offered funding to help institutions increase their international profiles, including incentives for offering classes through foreign languages. And while there was funding earmarked for international travel in the PRINT call, such travel would be limited almost exclusively to the maintenance and strengthening of specific international partnerships to encourage bidirectional exchange (i.e. Brazilian students and staff going abroad but also welcoming students at home). This is a notable shift from the SwB days of incentivizing only outgoing, individualized and mostly non-reciprocal international experiences at high budgetary cost. To wit, publicly available data from Brazilian Ministry of Education reveal that SwB cost the government some 2 billion reals per year to run; the total allotted annual budget for PRINT is 300 million reals – a fraction of the cost with a potentially broader impact.

At least at the time of writing, there seems to be no more government appetite for the relative largesse that characterized earlier pushes to internationalize, most emblematically represented by the now defunct SwB programme. Instead, the challenges now are perhaps less related to matters of finance and more to do with changes in institutional culture. An internet search for the terms 'EMI' and 'Brazil' prior to the years 2015 would produce almost zero relevant results. Then, starting in 2015, there is a sudden spike: the British Council helps sponsor lecturer EMI workshops at the University of Oxford; in early 2016, the very first EMI lecturer training courses are offered in Brazil, first by the British Council, then promoted at the Federal University of Paraná in partnership with tutors from the University of Oxford.[1] By 2017, a number of universities are beginning to offer classes through English, and the very first national EMI symposium in Brazil is launched in late 2018. What started with just two or three universities in Brazil with EMI offerings in 2011 (still not called 'EMI' at that stage locally) by late 2019 had blossomed to something closer to fifty (Gimenez et al. 2018).

Yet EMI in Brazil today is still nothing like what is called 'EMI' in many other countries in which it is more established. For example, while each year there are now hundreds of course options available at dozens of universities, there is still only a small handful of actual EMI programmes in the country. Furthermore, university administrations regularly report difficulty actually keeping track of how many EMI classes are being offered, since there is often no incentive or even mechanism for lecturers to report their EMI activities – a gap at least partly exacerbated by a general lack of EMI institutional policy in Brazilian institutions. And whereas the student body in EMI classes in Western Europe may often be multinational, English-medium classes in Brazil are still mostly attended by Brazilians.

Taken together, the brand of EMI that is taking shape in Brazil appears to be markedly distinct from EMI in many other countries. The origins of Brazilian EMI can be traced to a perceived need to promote more sustainable internationalization practices (i.e. internationalization at home), and that perception appears to have 'bottom-up' origins – starting with lecturers rather than institutional edicts. EMI practice in Brazil has therefore almost universally preceded corresponding policy. Part of the reason that Brazilian institutions were slow to show interest in fostering EMI is because the HEIs in which EMI has seen the most growth have been public universities, where the bulk of Brazilian research is produced (Sousa et al. 2019). Since there was no obvious financial incentive to support EMI in previous years, public institutions mostly left their EMI lecturers (if they were even aware of them) to their own devices. With programmes like PRINT – with a membership comprised almost entirely of public institutions – this has now begun to change.

EMI in Brazil – at least at the time of writing – can perhaps be best compared with a new kind of 'must-have' product or fashion accessory. There is a kind of 'buzz' surrounding this hot item, but the novelty is such that many are still unsure how to 'wear' it or what to do with it exactly. They have seen that it is all the rage abroad and do not want to be left out. Indeed, most Brazilian HEIs are still reluctant to commit to a purchase. Instead, they could be said to be still mostly 'window shopping', aware that they risk looking out-of-fashion if they do not buy soon but are perhaps unsure of which 'model' or 'brand' to spend their increasingly tight budget on.

It will be argued in this chapter that those holdouts may actually be making a wise choice in their careful browsing, as they may consider creating a confection better suited to their needs rather than buying into an imported model wholesale. Just like so many cultural phenomena that have found their way into Brazil and evolved into something special (American jazz to bossa nova, English football to the Brazilian jogo bonito …), it may be that the unique characteristics of Brazilian higher education may eventually produce a kind of EMI that is equally unique.

Brazilian EMI in the changing room

As the title of the present chapter suggests, it can be said that Brazil is currently 'trying EMI on for size'. What we mean by this is that, continuing with the 'fashion accessory' metaphor employed in the previous section, EMI can be seen as a novel product that HEIs in Brazil are unsure about how to wear, why they want it in the first place (beyond 'it's all the rage'), what the proper fit might be and how it will look to peers. However, instead of looking towards what 'products' are readily available to try to make them fit, it might be better to examine how EMI is already occurring and see how those practices can be institutionally supported. There may already be items in the home wardrobe that are better suited.

Because EMI has not been traditionally supported, officially, by Brazilian HEIs, university lecturers that have offered classes through English have mostly done so because they felt personally motivated to do it. This off-the-books EMI has a number of disadvantages, of course. It means that institutions are often unaware of the extent to which EMI may be happening within their walls. It further means that, unfortunately, having offered (lecturers) or taken (students) an EMI class does contribute officially to their academic careers. At the same time, the mostly laissez-faire attitude of Brazilian administrators towards EMI practices in their institutions has also allowed creativity to flourish, organically.

Conventional EMI policy conceived solely by university administration officials might assume, for instance, that for every EMI class there must be an assigned lecturer, who in turn must deliver a minimum number of hours to fulfil contractual obligations. There may even be 'English-only' requirements (e.g. Kirkpatrick 2014) and even minimum levels of proficiency for lecturers and students alike (Dimova 2020; O'Dowd 2018). In Brazil, such preconceptions have not yet taken hold. The motivated professors that offer their courses in English have enjoyed a kind of freedom not always encountered in other contexts and have therefore let their EMI practices be guided by what best suits them, their students and their particular disciplinary and pedagogical realities. In our EMI lecturer development courses that we have run for faculty teaching in at least eight different universities (Martinez and Fernandes 2020), the sheer spectrum of EMI delivery models is impressive. For example, it is common for lecturers to act as EMI 'convenors', who may be assigned to a particular class number but who share the course syllabus with several other professors who, in turn, are equally interested in 'trying on' EMI. Since the majority of EMI course offerings are electives, lecturers have also frequently reported thinking 'outside the box' entirely when it comes to teaching through English, offering intensive two-week courses rather than semester-long ones, for instance, and bringing in voices from overseas for mini-lectures over Skype and Zoom. Recently, the 'I' in EMI has been rethought at the Federal University of Paraná, for example, with a project-based cooperation between that institution and Penn State University, with no joint 'instruction' involved but instead collaborative project work that is carried out among students at both universities through English. And some of the more interesting EMI examples we have heard from lecturers have even rethought the 'E' in that acronym, holding so-called 'English Fridays' in their regular classes normally delivered in Portuguese, or assigning final assessments that involve delivering a presentation in English, just once in a semester.

These are just a few of the many examples of EMI that vary from what is most typically considered EMI, and these variations have emerged because the lecturers themselves – often without support from their own institutions – have felt so motivated to provide an internationalized experience for their students that they have incorporated English into their lessons in whatever ways they find best fit their particular contexts and learning needs. EMI practice is being actively created by Brazilian lecturers themselves, who often express fear that they might not be 'doing' EMI 'right'. Yet if the lecturers and students find that those practices are 'right' for them, who would dare question them?

While the freedom from institutional pressures to deliver EMI in accordance with prescribed policy has allowed less conventional EMI models to flourish, at some point Brazilian HEIs will need to commit to officially supporting EMI if they want to really see it move beyond being a mere fashion accessory. As mentioned earlier, there are very few actual full EMI degree *programmes* available in Brazil – and for good reason. So far, EMI has been limited to that proverbial changing room, not committing to any sort of 'purchase'. It has been convenient for HEIs in Brazil – particularly in the prestigious public institutions – to allow their more motivated lecturers to dabble in EMI whilst not having to support them or their students in any official capacity. The current overall lack of institutional pronouncement regarding important questions stunts EMI growth in Brazil and likewise means that only the most motivated teachers take the EMI plunge. For example, lecturers currently report being unsure if it is even legal for them to offer a course through English (it is). There are common questions concerning language (English only? Adequate level of proficiency?) that require official positions. Lecturers need a clearer answer to 'What's in it for me?' (as do students), starting with official acknowledgement. In the next section, we will conclude by making recommendations for what can help guide EMI policy decision-making in Brazil, which we see as a sine qua non if it is to flourish and reach its potential in the country.

From prêt-à-porter to made-to-measure

In the previous section we posed the issue of the current general lack of institutional EMI policy in Brazilian HEIs as having both positive and negative implications. On one hand, a paucity of policy has meant lecturers could exercise their EMI practices at their own discretions. On the negative side, however, a lack of EMI policy can mean both lecturers and students may feel unsupported; in addition, it means that – without financial incentives (the case in public universities in particular) – only the most confident and motivated staff will be likely to engage. It is, therefore, paramount that institutions finally move beyond 'trying on EMI for size' and actually make an official commitment to it. EMI is happening, regardless, and considering the push to internationalize at home, that should be seen as potentially beneficial to the institution and its academic community – but it must be supported to optimize its impact and ensure careful integration into institutional goals. By the same token, policy need not and should not look to traditions of EMI established outside Brazil to guide their policy. Instead of making a priori assumptions about which EMI model should be supported by the institution, administrators might consider looking at what practices have already been adopted by their faculty and even ask them how they – and those existing practices – can be better supported.

This is the general thrust of Ernesto Sirolli's well-known TED Talk entitled 'Want to help someone? Shut up and listen!' Sirolli, founder of an international non-profit that teaches leaders worldwide how to foster and maintain sustainable development, recounts how he learned early on that attempting to *impose* 'support' rarely, if ever, works. Instead, aid should only be offered where wanted and is most likely to meet with success if the local ecology and knowledge is respected and incorporated. That means, in practice, that instead of pronouncing 'all lecturers must possess X level of English', for instance (e.g. O'Dowd 2018), EMI lecturers who are already teaching successfully should be asked about what their thoughts are on levels of proficiency in their teaching context. It means that rather than establishing 'EMI means English at all times', current EMI lecturers be asked about how they use English in their current classes. The experience of these professors – grounded in their actual pedagogical and institutional home environment – is likely to provide important insights, ones that are more ecologically valid (Martinez et al. 2021). Moreover, the mere act of officially acknowledging their practice and consulting with them as a group may be conducive to attracting more lecturers and maybe even the eventual creation of a community of EMI practice among them.

It is our belief that the organic way in which EMI has emerged in Brazil, particularly in the public education sector where it has experienced the most rapid growth, has been chiefly driven by some of the best and most motivated staff. It is time for Brazilian HEIs to finally acknowledge the value of their practice by supporting it institutionally. This should mean, in our view, not deciding for them what the best EMI fit is but instead taking stock of the rather impressive array of comfortable and appealing EMI gear that may already be hanging in their own wardrobe.

Note

1 This was a special course delivered for the Universidade Federal do Paraná by Julie Dearden and Tom Spain of the Department of Education at the University of Oxford, who at the time were affiliated with the EMI Oxford research centre. In later

years, Julie Dearden also began running EMI courses through a company that she established with a similar name, but with no affiliation with the University of Oxford.

References

Amorim Borges, R., and Garcia-Filice, R. C. (2016), 'A língua inglesa no Ciência sem Fronteiras: Paradoxos na política de internacionalização', *Interfaces Brasil/Canadá*, 16 (1): 72–96.

Beelen, J., and Jones, E. (2015), 'Redefining internationalization at home', in *The European Higher Education Area*, 59–72, Springer International. Available online: https://doi.org/10.1007/978-3-319-20877-0_5.

Dimova, S. (2020), 'English language requirements for enrolment in EMI programs in higher education: A European case', *Journal of English for Academic Purposes*, 47: 15–32

Feltrin, R. B., da Costa, J. O. P., and Velho, L. (2016), 'Mulheres sem fronteiras? Uma análise da participação das mulheres no Programa Ciência sem Fronteiras da Unicamp: Motivações, desafios e impactos na trajetória profissional', *Cadernos Pagu*, 48: 81–97.

Finardi, K., and Archanjo, R. (2018), *Washback Effects of the Science without Borders, English without Borders and Language without Borders Programs in Brazilian Language Policies and Rights*, Cham, Switzerland: Springer. Available online: https://doi.org/10.1007/978-3-319-20877-0_5.

Gimenez, T., Sarmento, S., Archanjo, R., Zicman, R., and Finardi, K. (2018), *Guide to English as a Medium of Instruction in Brazilian Higher Education Institutions (2018–2019)*. Available online: https://www.britishcouncil.org.br/sites/default/files/guide_to_english_as_medium_of_instruction_2018-19.pdf (accessed 30 June 2020).

Huisman, J., Adelman, C., Hsieh, C.-C., Shams, F., and Wilkins, S. (2012), *Europe's Bologna Process and Its Impact on Global Higher Education*, Thousand Oaks, CA: Sage. Available online: https://researchportal.bath.ac.uk/en/publications/europes-bologna-process-and-its-impact-on-global-higher-education (accessed 11 June 2020).

Jenkins, J. (2013), *English as a Lingua Franca in the International University: The Politics of Academic English Language Policy*, Routledge. Available online: https://www.routledge.com/English-as-a-Lingua-Franca-in-the-International-University-The-Politics/Jenkins/p/book/9780415684644 (accessed 29 May 2020).

Kirkpatrick, A. (2014), 'A J A L the language(s) of HE: EMI and/or ELF and/or multilingualism?', *The Asian Journal of Applied Linguistics*, 1 (1): 4–15. Available online: http://caes.hku.hk/ajal (accessed 14 May 2020).

Knight, J. (2015), 'Internationalization: A decade of changes and challenges', *International Higher Education*, 50: 112–21.

Martinez, R. (2016), 'English as a medium of instruction (EMI) in Brazilian higher education: Challenges and opportunities', in K. Finardi (ed.), *English in Brazil: Views, Policies and Programs*, 191–228, Londrina: Eduel.

Martinez, R., and Fernandes, K. (2020), *Development of a Teacher Training Course for English Medium Instruction for Higher Education Professors in Brazil*, 125–52. Available online: http://doi:10.4018/978-1-7998-2318-6.ch007.

Martinez, R., Machado, P., and Palma, C. (2021), 'An exploratory analysis of language-related episodes (LREs) in an EMI context', in D. Lasagabaster and A. Doiz (eds), *Language Use in English-Medium Instruction at University: International Perspectives on Teacher Practice*, 11–33, Oxford: Routledge.

O'Dowd, R. (2018), 'The training and accreditation of teachers for English medium instruction: An overview of practice in European universities', *International Journal of Bilingual Education and Bilingualism*.

Rivas, R. M., and Mullet, S. (2016), 'Countervailing institutional forces that shape internationalization of science: An analysis of Brazil's Science without Borders program', *RAI Revista de Administração e Inovação*, 13 (1): 12–21.

Sá, C. M. (2016), 'The rise and fall of Brazil's science without borders', *International Higher Education*, 85: 17–18.

Sousa, P. J. L., da Silva, G. S., Sousa, O. D. S., and Souza, W. D. S. (2019), 'RANKING UNIVERSITÁRIO DA FOLHA 2017: o efeito moderador pesquisa na relação entre internacionalização e inovação', *Revista de Administração e Negócios Da Amazônia*, 11 (1): 17.

Wächter, B., and Maiworm, F. (2014), *English-Taught Programmes in European Higher Education: The State of Play in 2014*. Bonn: Lemmens Medien GmbH.

Wilkinson, R. (2012), 'English-medium instruction at a Dutch university: Challenges and pitfalls', in *English-Medium Instruction at Universities: Global Challenges*, 3–24, Channel View.

3

English-Medium Instruction in Mainland China: National Trends and Institutional Developments

Sihan Zhou and Heath Rose

Introduction

English-medium instruction (EMI) in Chinese higher education has been occurring in lockstep with the rapid internationalization of universities, which is usually operationalized with a more international curriculum, a strengthened international mobility of scholars and students and international technical assistance and cooperation programmes (see Zhang 2018). This internationalization is largely anchored at the macro level of policy planning to a string of higher education initiatives, including the highly funded '985' and '211' projects and the current 'Double First-class' initiative. The goal of these projects was to build world-class universities in a global context through the internationalization of education and research. A further example of China's internationalization efforts is the ongoing 'Belt and Road Initiative', which aims to improve the economic connectivity of China with other world nations. This initiative has forged university alliances to promote collaborative research and academic exchanges. Because internationalization and EMI are highly connected, these national policy initiatives have directly and indirectly propelled the growth of EMI in China. These macro-level developments have been joined by institutional developments that further promote EMI, which has resulted in EMI taking on a myriad of formats due to differing demands, needs and driving forces. This chapter provides an overview of implementation of EMI in higher education in Mainland China, synthesizing research on the drivers of curriculum Englishization and recent trends in EMI programme development. It explores the issues associated with exponential EMI growth and offers recommendations for macro-level policy planning.

Growth of EMI

EMI has expanded at an unprecedented rate in Chinese higher education over the past two decades. This acceleration has occurred in tandem with the internationalization of the nation's tertiary education sector. EMI, often discussed with reference to 'bilingual education' in China (Tong et al. 2020), gained momentum when the nation entered the World Trade Organisation (WTO) in 2001, after which time the cultivation of an English-proficient labour force became an urgent part of China's economic agenda (Beckett and Li 2012). A directive was then issued by China's Ministry of Education (MOE 2001) calling for 5–10 per cent of university courses to be delivered through English within three years. Since then, EMI provision has mushroomed across universities in Mainland China. By 2006, 132 out of 136 universities surveyed offered EMI courses (Wu et al. 2010).

In 2007, a bundle of policies further cemented the role of EMI in educational reforms and escalated its expansion nationwide (MOE and MOF 2007; MOE 2007a,b). In a proposal jointly promulgated by the MOE and the Ministry of Finance (2007) on 'undergraduate teaching quality and teaching reform projects in higher education', it encouraged the construction of bilingual curricula and promoted enhancing the English competence of Chinese university students to engage directly in academic research. This issue was then iterated in a subsequent guideline (MOE 2007a), which advocated introducing foreign experts or faculty with overseas experience into leading universities to teach disciplinary courses in English. With the role of EMI promoted within higher education reform, the MOE (2007b) announced their support for the building of five hundred model bilingual courses in Chinese universities from 2007 to 2010.

In the most recent decade (2010–20), the landscape of EMI in China has undergone more nuanced changes. Based on a policy analysis of ninety-three EMI-related documents from sixty-three universities in China, a recent report revealed a shift in policy away from bilingual models of EMI (where some Chinese use is mandated in the curriculum) towards English-only programmes (Rose et al. 2020). In a similar vein, Zhao (2020) reported that university offerings of full-English programmes picked up speed since 2010, a trend running in parallel to the growth of international student numbers in China. This observation aligns with a milestone national policy 'The National Outline for Medium and Long-Term Educational Reform and Development (from 2010 to 2020)', where English-taught disciplinary courses were considered a requisite for enlarging the quantity of inbound international students (MOE 2010). It thereby seems, within the recent ten years, that EMI in Chinese higher education has started to develop dual goals: for both cultivating globally competitive home students and attracting international students (also see Zhang 2018).

Drivers of EMI

From the discussion above it is clear that university internationalization and global competition for international students are clear drivers of EMI growth at a national level. Nonetheless, the driving forces behind EMI are complex and are manifestations of both top-down and bottom-up forces. In short, EMI is a response to meet the demands of top-down government initiatives but also the demands of numerous stakeholders (university presidents, deans, programme directors, teachers, students and parents).

An investigation of the stated top-down driving forces for EMI in sixty-five university policies in China revealed that the five most common dimensions were: 'cultivating talents' in local students; 'responding to globalisation and promoting internationalisation'; 'improving the quality of teaching and curricula'; 'implementing national and/or provincial policies'; and 'assisting the development of the university and of higher education' (Rose et al. 2020: 21). Another clear top-down driving force is linked with China's emphasis on raising the profile of Chinese universities in global university league tables, wherein the international profile of faculty and students and research output in international journals (predominantly English-medium) play a role in ranking criteria (Xu et al. 2019). Thus, EMI is seen by many top-down policymakers as a means to more closely align universities' teaching and research activities.

However, top-down policies only provide one perspective of EMI in China. In order to better understand the bottom-up forces fuelling EMI in East Asia, a study by Galloway et al. (2017) surveyed 579 students and interviewed 28 teachers at seven Chinese and five Japanese universities. They discovered the biggest driving force for students was to learn or improve their English. Other key reasons provided were a general interest in English and in the content. These driving forces tap into the common notion that EMI is a means to 'kill two birds with one stone', in that it is seen to give 'students a chance to increase their English proficiency skills and enhance their academic progress in other subjects at the same time' (6). Despite weak evidence of the efficacy of EMI for English-language development (for a review, see Macaro et al. 2018), this belief underpins much of the driving force of EMI at the institutional level in contexts like China. Indeed, many institutions in Asia purport that EMI is a relatively simple solution to solving the problems of internationalization and language proficiency (Hamid et al. 2013).

Students have also expressed instrumental motivations for undertaking EMI, which further fuel demand. These include a belief that partaking in EMI in higher education might lead to improved opportunities for employment and study abroad (Galloway et al. 2017). While it is true that the demand for English proficiency is growing in many professional sectors, there is not yet clear evidence that EMI programmes afford their graduates better access to future employment opportunities (Macaro et al. 2018). Some forms of EMI could, however, provide smoother pathways for study abroad in Anglophone contexts. Xu et al. (2021) observe that transnational education has been widely supported in Chinese higher education especially in the form of 'new turnkey-foreign style affiliated institutions'. One of the unique selling points of these dual-accredited degrees is that students are theoretically placed on equal footing with those earning the same degree at the foreign affiliate university, which might allow for smoother admission into future degrees that require a previous bachelor's degree to have been taught in English.

Current trends in EMI

EMI provision in Chinese higher education covers a great deal of variations in terms of languages used at the classroom level. Based on a systematic review of studies published on bilingual education in Chinese higher education within the past two decades, Tong et al. (2020) found the majority (85 per cent) of research that identified the type of bilingual model was carried out in 'immersion programmes', in which English was supposed to be used for instruction most of the time. However, the review later pinpointed a mismatch between the labels used and the actual language use in these programmes. For example, a programme labelled as 'immersion' might in reality be delivered in Chinese half of the time.

In a recent multilevel study, Rose et al. (2020) investigated EMI provision across twenty-nine universities in Mainland China. The sample covered a wide spectrum, ranging from 'double first-class' universities and disciplines to language-specialist, transnational and ordinary universities. Findings revealed that EMI in Chinese higher education was operationalized in diverse forms depending on the student body, including (but not limited to):

- Full English-taught programmes for *mainly domestic students* jointly delivered by Chinese and foreign institutions (often discussed as '中外合作办学' or transnational education). These programmes could be run at the level of universities, the second-tier affiliated colleges/departments or as degree programmes.
- Full English-taught programmes in Chinese universities for *exclusively international students*. These programmes were created to attract full-degree international students and were not available for local students, although local students could often take some of the same courses for credits towards their own degree programmes.
- Full English-taught courses in non-EMI programmes for *mainly non-degree international exchange students*, also available as elective courses for *local students*.
- Bilingual courses for *domestic students* who chose to learn some content courses in English. In these courses, textbooks, slides and readings were in English while classroom teaching usually involved the use of Chinese to varying degrees.
- Content courses (either full English or bilingual) for *English majors*. These courses varied in language use according to the proficiency of staff and students and often included language-related topics such as cultural studies, linguistics, area studies, translation, journalism and media studies.

Similar to what Tong et al. (2020) reported, Rose et al. (2020) also observed that the name of 'full English-taught' programmes or courses was not necessarily translated into an exclusive use of English in practice. During the interviews (n = 26), almost all lecturers and programme heads reflected that the use of Chinese was necessary to ensure that students comprehended difficult content. This was confirmed by a questionnaire with EMI lecturers (n = 88), where 80.24 per cent of the respondents favoured the use of both English and Chinese in classroom teaching. It seems, however, that the ratio of language use was very much contingent on factors such as the proficiency of students rather than how the course was labelled. For instance, some lecturers in a bilingual course at a top 'double first-class' university expressed that their use of Chinese was extremely limited because the English proficiency of students was already very high.

Issues associated with growth

Despite strong policy support and velocity in EMI expansion in Chinese higher education, issues in the quality of implementation have been noted. Hu (2008: 206) criticizes current academic discourse as painting a 'rosy picture' of the development of bilingual education in China while neglecting potential problems and challenges it incurs. Along this line, some studies have found that the majority of teacher questions and student responses in EMI classes were both linguistically and cognitively simple (Hu and Duan 2018; Hu and Li 2017). The findings have cast doubts on the proposed 'double gains' of EMI – that is, improved English competence on top of content learning.

At the institutional level, Huang (2006) notes an inconsistency in instructional language within the same major or even the same course, which greatly affects the quality of teaching. Several studies have also revealed that the extant incentive systems hardly match the substantial effort and time that teachers invest in EMI delivery (e.g. Hu et al. 2014; Rose et al. 2020). This, in the long run, would inevitably result in a demotivation among teachers to set up EMI courses or to ensure high-quality implementation. Further, the delivery of EMI has been constrained by the rather limited number of suitable EMI textbooks and teaching resources (Huang 2006; Zhang and Liu 2005). Huang (2006) describes the dilemma thus: on the one hand, there are very few domestically designed subject textbooks in English and on the other, introducing textbooks from abroad would require a high financial budget (see also Tong and Shi 2012). Concurrently, our researchers have cautioned that using exported textbooks exclusively without supplementary materials in Chinese would hinder an in-depth understanding of the subject, making students 'westernized' and detached from local perspectives (Zhang and Liu 2005: 76).

Another widely expressed concern in the successful implementation of EMI programmes is the paucity of qualified teachers (e.g. Fang 2009; Li 2011; Zhang and Liu 2005). Drawing on a shortage of nearly eight thousand teachers for a designated goal of building one hundred exemplary bilingual programmes in Shanghai by 2007, one study concludes that the scarcity of teachers has become the largest 'bottleneck' in curbing the growth of bilingual education (Fang 2009). It seems, nonetheless, that limitations arise not only from the quantity but also from the quality of teachers: English proficiency and pedagogical competence of EMI teachers have been major sources of scepticism (Fang 2009; Li 2011; Zhang and Liu 2005). In a university with 'double first-class' disciplines in Wuhan, it was reported that only 18.09 per cent of students enrolled in bilingual courses were satisfied with their teachers' English ability (Fang 2009). Inadequate English proficiency also downgrades teachers' pedagogical competence to a certain extent, where they tend to rigidly stick to textbooks and avoid improvised speech and interactions (Hu et al. 2014; Huang 2006; Zhang and Liu 2005). Although professional development training has been deemed important by teachers, it has not been sufficiently prioritized by universities (Macaro and Han 2020).

A further fundamental issue surrounds student proficiency to undertake university study in English. The majority of students might have not yet arrived at a requisite level of English proficiency to thrive in EMI classes (e.g. Han and Yu 2010; Hu et al. 2014). Han and Yu (2010), for instance, speculate that around 75 per cent students from leading universities and 80 per cent from ordinary universities might not be sufficiently proficient for EMI classes, even after two years into studies. It has hence been suggested that a minimum proficiency threshold be enacted to screen students into EMI courses (Tong and Shi 2012). In the study of Hu et al. (2014), a minimum threshold of 120 (80 per cent) in the national entrance exam (*Gaokao*) was stipulated as a criterion for admitting students into EMI courses. However, this criterion seemed inadequate – students still reportedly struggled to comprehend content delivered through English in class. As Hu (2019) later notes, the benchmark also falls far below the internationally used IELTS Band 6.5 criterion.

An important catalyst for the obstacles in learning through English is that the grammar-oriented English education in secondary school fails to prepare students for the academic English skills necessitated in university EMI contexts. Hence, researchers have called for strengthening support mechanisms to suit the learning needs of students. Such support may include embedding tailored English for Academic Purposes (EAP)/English for Specific Purposes (ESP) programmes into EMI programmes (Galloway and Ruegg 2020; Jiang et al. 2019), tightening collaboration between linguistic and content experts (Li 2019) and providing self-access language support such as a writing centre (Galloway and Ruegg 2020). Many of these measures require substantial English-language staff resources and a possible restructuring of programme curricula, meaning universities may be resistant to implementing them.

Conclusions: Recommendation for future policy

It is clear that the growth of EMI in China is unlikely to be abated in the foreseeable future due to ongoing macro-level policies and institutional developments which are inextricably wound up with internationalization efforts in higher education. It is also clear that developments in EMI have brought numerous language-related challenges for students, programme administrators and teachers. To address these challenges, some recommendations for future EMI policy planning in Chinese universities are offered.

First, future policy might consider how to structurally provide mechanisms for greater levels of language support for students entering EMI programmes. Research clearly shows that in many EMI contexts, students' English-language proficiency falls below recommended benchmarks and that the high-school English curricula do not prepare students for academic study in English. Policies could encourage systems of support for students in the form of tailored EAP/ESP, as recommended by a number of researchers (e.g. Galloway and Ruegg 2020). EAP programmes are common in many EMI contexts, including in Hong Kong higher education (Evans 2011), so Chinese mainland universities could adapt these established practices in their own policymaking to improve structured support for students' language development.

Second, to address the issue of teaching quality, macro-level policies could encourage greater engagement with teacher education. In recent decades some universities have promoted teacher development through the establishment of credentials required to take up a permanent academic position, such as postgraduate diplomas and certificates for teaching in higher education. Macaro and Han (2020: 230) suggest that the necessary momentum for promoting the implementation of such a system for EMI in China might only be possible if 'a national level certification is seen as an instrument for raising the status of Chinese universities'. In the absence of certification, policies could promote greater engagement with professional development opportunities to build either linguistic competencies for those teachers who want to develop their language abilities or EMI professional competencies for those teachers who want to improve their pedagogical practices.

Finally, to address issues surrounding challenges in curriculum development, policymakers might want to ensure the growth of EMI policy is not outpacing universities' ability to create quality programmes. Financial resources earmarked for EMI may need to be diverted to more centralized processes to help create teaching resources, incentivize curriculum development and evaluate the quality of the programmes that have already been created so they are continually revised and improved.

In conclusion, Mainland China's higher education sector is an area of dynamic and evolving policymaking, which has seen the emergence of numerous forms of EMI, each with their own contextualized issues. While there is no one-size-fits-all solution to these issues, future national-level policy could address some of the issues at a very broad political level to steer universities towards better quality, rather than more quantity, in their EMI provisions.

References

Beckett, G., and Li, F. (2012), 'Content-based English education in China: Students' experiences and perspectives', *Journal of Contemporary Issues in Education*, 7 (1): 47–63.

Evans, S. (2011), 'Historical and comparative perspectives on the medium of instruction in Hong Kong', *Language Policy*, 10 (1): 19–36.

Fang, Y. (2009), 'Lun gaoxiao shuangyu jiaoshi duiwu jianshe zhongde wenti ji duice [On the development of university bilingual teaching staff: Problems and solutions]', *Journal of Huazhong Agriculture University (Social Science Edition)*, 2: 106–9.

Galloway, N., Kriukow, J., and Numajiri, T. (2017), *Internationalisation, Higher Education and the Growing Demand for English: An Investigation into the English Medium of Instruction (EMI) Movement in China and Japan*, London: British Council.

Galloway, N., and Ruegg, R., (2020), 'The provision of student support on English medium instruction programmes in Japan and China', *Journal of English for Academic Purposes*, 45: 100846.

Hamid, M. O., Nguyen, H. T. M., and Baldauf Jr, R. B. (2013), 'Medium of instruction in Asia: Context, processes and outcomes', *Current Issues in Language Planning*, 14 (1): 1–15.

Han, J., and Yu, L. (2007), 'A study to determine Chinese college students' English proficiency required for bilingual education', *Modern Foreign Languages*, 30 (1): 65–72.

Hu, G. (2008), 'The misleading academic discourse on Chinese–English bilingual education in China', *Review of Educational Research*, 78 (2): 195–231.

Hu, G. (2019), 'English-medium instruction in higher education: Lessons from China', *The Journal of Asia TEFL*, 16 (1): 1–11.

Hu, G., and Duan, Y. (2018), 'Questioning and responding in the classroom: A cross-disciplinary study of the effects of instructional mediums in academic subjects at a Chinese university', *International Journal of Bilingual Education and Bilingualism*, 22 (3): 303–21.

Hu, G., and Li, X. (2017), 'Asking and answering questions in English-medium instruction', in J. Zhao and Q. Dixon (eds), *English-Medium Instruction in Chinese Universities: Perspectives, Discourse and Evaluation*, 184–203, Routledge.

Huang, Y. (2006), 'Gaoxiao shaungyu jiaoxue de wenti yu duice [Questions and countermeasures of bilingual instruction in higher education]', *Chinese Journal of Medical Education Research*, 5 (3): 242–4.

Jiang, L., Zhang, L. J., and May, S. (2019), 'Implementing English-medium instruction (EMI) in China: Teachers' practices and perceptions, and students' learning motivation and needs', *International Journal of Bilingual Education and Bilingualism*, 22 (2): 107–19.

Li, H. (2011), 'Waiyulei yuanxiao shuangyu jiaoxue he daxueyingyu jiaoxuede ziyuan zhenghe wenti fenxi [Analysis on the resource integration of bilingual instruction and college English teaching in foreign language colleges]', *Economic Research Guide*, 25: 312–13.

Li, Y. (2019), 'Language–content partnership in higher education: Development and opportunities', *Higher Education Research & Development*, 39 (3): 500–14.

Macaro, E., and Han, S. (2020), 'English medium instruction in China's higher education: Teachers' perspectives of competencies, certification and professional development', *Journal of Multilingual and Multicultural Development*, 41 (3): 219–31.

Macaro, E., Curle, S., Pun, J., An, J., and Dearden, J. (2018), 'A systematic review of English medium instruction in higher education', *Language Teaching*, 51 (1): 36–76.

Ministry of Education (MOE) (2001), '*Guanyu jiaqiang gaodeng xuexiao benke jiaoxue gongzuo tigao jiaoxue zhiliang de ruogan yijian* [Guidelines for improving the quality of undergraduate teaching]', 28 August. Available online: http://old.moe.gov.cn/publicfiles/business/htmlfiles/moe/moe_309/200412/4682.html (accessed 21 December 2020).

MOE (2007a), *Jiaoyubu guanyu jinyibu shenhua benke jiaoxue gaige quanmian tigao jiaoxue zhiliangde ruogan yijian* [Guidelines for further deepening the reform and improving the overall quality of undergraduate teaching], 17 February. Available online: http://www.moe.gov.cn/srcsite/A08/s7056/200702/t20070217_79865.html.

MOE (2007b), *Guanyu qidong 2007 niandu shuangyu jiaoxue shifan kecheng jianshe xiangmu de tongzhi* [Notice on launching the 2007 bilingual teaching model course construction project]. 29 August. Available online: http://www.moe.gov.cn/s78/A08/moe_745/tnull_25884.html.

MOE (2010), *Guojia Zhongchangqi Jiaoyu Gaige He Fazhan Guihua Gangyao (2010–2020)* [The National Outline for Medium and Long-Term Educational Reform and Development (from 2010 to 2020)], 29 July. Available online: http://www.gov.cn/jrzg/2010-07/29/content_1667143.htm.

MOE and Ministry of Finance (MOF) (2007), *Jiaoyubu caizhengbu guanyu shishi gaodeng xuexiao benke jiaoxue jiaoxue zhiliang yu jiaoxue gaige gongcheng de yijian* [Opinions of Ministry of Education and Ministry of Finance on implementing 'undergraduate teaching quality and teaching reform projects in higher education'], 22 January. Available online: http://www.moe.gov.cn/srcsite/A08/s7056/200701/t20070122_79761.html.

Rose, H., McKinley, J., Xu, X., and Zhou, S. (2020), *Investigating Policy and Implementation of English Medium Instruction in Higher Education Institutions in China*, British Council.

Tong, F., and Shi, Q. (2012), 'Chinese–English bilingual education in China: A case study of college science majors', *International Journal of Bilingual Education and Bilingualism*, 15 (2): 165–82.

Tong, F., Wang, Z., Min, Y., and Tang, S. (2020), 'A systematic literature synthesis of 19 years of bilingual education in Chinese higher education: Where does the academic discourse stand?' *SAGE Open*, 10 (2): 215824402092651.

Wu, P., Wang, S. G., Jiang, X., Zeng, D. J., Guan, Y. X., and Li, X. F. (2010), *Gaodeng Xuexiao Shuangyu Jiaoxue de Xianzhuang Yanjiu he Shijian Tansuo* [An exploratory study of bilingual education in Chinese higher education], Beijing: Higher Education.

Xu, X., Rose, H., and Oancea, A. (2019), 'Incentivising international publications: Institutional policymaking in Chinese higher education', *Studies in Higher Education*, DOI: 10.1080/03075079.2019.1672646.

Zhang, L., and Liu, X. (2005), 'Shuangyu jiaoxue: Gongshi, fenqi ji wuqu' [Bilingual education: Consensuses, controversies, and misconceptions], *Modern Education Science*, 6: 73–6.

Zhang, Z. (2018), 'English-medium instruction policies in China: Internationalisation of higher education', *Journal of Multilingual and Multicultural Development*, 39 (6): 542–55.

Zhao, W. S. (2020), 'The practice of quality assurance standards for English medium courses in Chinese universities – interpretation on standards of the selection of "branded English medium courses for international students"', Paper presented at the 2020 International Symposium on Quality Assurance of English Medium Higher Education (EMHE), October, Beijing.

4

English-Medium Instruction in Danish Universities: An Unintended Policy?

Anna Kristina Hultgren

What drives English-medium instruction in global higher education?

Research into English-medium instruction (EMI) has grown exponentially in recent years; yet to date, most of it has focused on the *consequences* of EMI.[1] Questions have included: What are the attitudes of lecturers and students to EMI? What are the consequences for local languages and cultures? How fair and equitable is EMI? How does it affect the quality of teaching and learning? Some research has sought to devise solutions to mitigate any adverse consequences, for example, language policies, teacher training programmes and student support mechanisms (Coleman et al. 2018; Dimova et al. 2015; Macaro 2018). Far less is known about the *causes* of EMI (for a review, see Galloway 2020), probably because applied linguists, who have been the main contributors to EMI research, have not seen it as within their remit. However, given that what we are witnessing is a language change of gigantic proportion, in Europe not seen since the adoption of Latin as a lingua franca in the thirteenth to eighteenth centuries, it is arguably a research priority of significant importance to uncover why and how precisely EMI comes about. As Macaro (2018: 290) asks:

> Why should a country decide to change its educational system from one in which its students are learning academic subjects through the home language to one where they are learning it through the medium of a second language ... Why would they make this momentous change, knowing full well that many students will struggle to understand what is being taught, and might engage less with the learning process as a result?

In the literature, EMI is often cursorily attributed to 'internationalization', and only few studies have explored the reasons for introducing EMI. Such studies report on institutional decision-makers being motivated by a desire to 'attract foreign staff and students', 'strengthen the international profile' and 'internationalise the curriculum' (Wächter and Maiworm 2014). Whilst such studies are valuable in terms of uncovering decision-makers' express motivations for introducing EMI, they assume that EMI is a deliberate policy, whereas, in fact, this may not always be the case. It is possible that EMI is at least partially an indirect result of higher education reforms that have nothing to do with language (Dafouz and Smit 2020; Hultgren 2014; Piller and Cho 2013). If EMI happens at least partially unintentionally, it seems important to devote some serious consideration to what actually brings it about.

Over the past few decades, higher education systems across the world have undergone momentous reforms, driven in tandem by international organizations, national governments and university management. These reforms have sought to reconceptualize universities as a driving force in the creation of a 'global knowledge economy' (Wright 2019). The reforms, undergirded by a neoliberal ideology, are premised on adopting 'new forms of managerialism, cost cutting and market competition purportedly copied from industrial corporations' (5). As Shear and Hyatt (2017: 2) put it:

> This neoliberal fantasy of unbridled market competition via the marketisation of knowledge provides the ideological terrain from which much of the education reform efforts in the past few decades have emerged

In Europe, relationships between universities and the nation state have changed; accountability has been strengthened, and universities are increasingly allocated government funding according to the attainment of targets (de Boer et al. 2008). Consequently, universities find themselves in an increasingly competitive marketplace and as part of a commodification of scientific knowledge. Reforms have sometimes been justified by many more people going to university today: 45 per cent of a generation on average in OECD countries where a generation ago, some 24 per cent went to university. This has inevitably put pressure on the system and necessitated alternative funding systems.

Insofar as EMI was never a goal in its own right, it is arguably important to probe into the nature of higher education reforms and the extent to which they bring about unintended linguistic consequences for polities, societies and cultures around the world. This is what I focus on in this chapter, using as a case study Denmark, a country which has been at the forefront in Europe in the provision of EMI. More specifically, the question I address in this chapter is: 'What have been the supranational, national and institutional drivers of EMI in Danish higher education?' I will argue that in many cases EMI has not been an explicit policy decision but rather an unintended and unforeseen outcome of a set of higher education reforms that have swept across the European higher education sector since the 1990s. In the final section of the chapter, I briefly consider the implications of this 'unintended' language shift for researchers.

Of course, the brevity of the chapter will only allow me to begin to address this momentous question, and it is important to bear in mind that drivers of EMI are likely to vary significantly according to different national and institutional contexts. I will begin by tweaking Macaro's important question above slightly and ask not '*why* should a country decide to change' but '*do* countries decide to change' to signal the possibility that nation states may not possess the degree of agency to make this decision. That said, we should not assume that global reforms, and their linguistic instantiation, are 'the work of a "universalistic logic" or reified "global forces"'; rather, they are produced by 'human actors who, through discursive and material practices, create regularised patterns and institutional systems that both enable and constrain them' (Wright 2019: 6, citing Rizvi 2004). In other words, to refer to an age-old sociological debate, higher education reforms – and EMI – arise in the interplay of structure and agency.

Before I begin, it is probably helpful to clarify the epistemological standpoint from which I write. Arguably, one of the greatest strengths of the EMI research community is its multifaceted and international composition. EMI is a topic that has brought together a diverse group of scholars who may not otherwise have interacted to a great degree: researchers in applied linguistics, sociolinguistics, TESOL, language learning, language-in-education, language policy, English as a lingua franca, content and language integrated learning and many others. Whilst they all share an interest in EMI, each brings to the debate their own questions, interests and theoretical assumptions. The field of EMI will be enriched by such diversity, as will each of the fields on their own; however, it puts the onus on all of us to make explicit the epistemological standpoint from which we are writing if we are to have fruitful discussions. My own standpoint is as a critical sociolinguist concerned with unpacking the precise relationship between the political and the linguistic spheres. To understand this, I share the view of those linguists who have argued for the need for linguists to direct attention towards the political economy (e.g., Block 2018; Saarinen 2020). For EMI researchers specifically, this means engaging with academic governance and higher education policy to a greater extent than what has been the case to date. In the next section, I briefly outline the EMI situation in Danish higher education.

EMI in Danish higher education

Denmark, a small country in Northern Europe with just under six million inhabitants, has long been at Europe's forefront in the delivery of EMI in higher education (Dimova et al. 2015; Hultgren et al. 2014; Wächter and Maiworm 2014). Seen from a European perspective, Denmark comes in at second place, just after the Netherlands, in the delivery of English-taught programmes in European higher education (Wächter and Maiworm 2014). An early survey found that 20 per cent of programmes at Danish universities are delivered in English, with 26 per cent at graduate and 6 per cent at undergraduate level (Hultgren 2013a). Whilst this shows that the vast majority of teaching still happens in the national language, Danish, studies replicated over time have demonstrated a growth in the use of EMI in Denmark and across Europe over the past fifteen years (Maiworm and Wächter 2002; Wächter and Maiworm 2007, 2014).

Having said this, observational and ethnographic research has shown that communicative practices at Danish university campuses are often far more multilingual, multicultural and multimodal than a quick count of the number of programmes taught in English allows us to capture (Hultgren 2013b; Mortensen 2014; Hultgren et al. 2014). Mortensen (2014), for example, shows how Danish university students draw on English and Danish in an interwoven repertoire, whilst Hultgren (2013b) shows how lecturers' talk transcends not only linguistic but also modal boundaries, for example, when they incorporate print educational material in English into their spoken lectures in Danish. Such multilingual and inter-semiotic interaction – often disrespectful of traditional language and modal boundaries – has been amply described in recent sociolinguistic work under what Pennycook (2016) labels the 'trans-super-poly-metro movement'. In the EMI literature, it is reflected in a conceptual shift and a suggested replacement of the term 'EMI' with 'EMEMUS' (English-medium education in multilingual university settings) to highlight the intrinsic plurality of languages and educational activities in contemporary university settings (Dafouz and Smit 2020). Far from replacing other languages, then, it could be argued that English enables, enhances and visibilizes linguistic pluralism. As de Swaan (2020: 208) puts it, 'The more languages, the more English.'

Whilst the focus in this chapter is on the extent to which higher education reforms have unintentionally driven the rise of EMI in Danish higher education, it is important to contemplate that there may also be some pre-existing country-specific factors that have made Denmark particularly susceptible to adopting EMI, with the caveat that the distinction between pre-existing factors and policy drivers is not always clear-cut. In the next section, I start by considering some country-specific features of Denmark which may have contributed to making this country particularly receptive to EMI.

Country-specific factors making Denmark conducive to EMI

One factor that may have made Denmark particularly receptive to EMI – and its counterpart: intensified multilingualism – is a high pre-existing level of English-language proficiency in the country. Although Danish, a Northern-Germanic language, is the official language in Denmark, with Faroese, Greenlandic and German recognized as regional languages, the status and importance of English has been steadily growing since the period after the Second World War. According to the English First (EF) global ranking of English skills, Denmark boasts the second highest English-language proficiency in the world, topped only by the Netherlands (EF 2020). According to the latest Eurobarometer, 86 per cent of Danes declare themselves being able to hold a conversation in English (for comparison, the proportion for Spain is 22 per cent) and 44 per cent would rate their English as 'very good' (second place in Europe after Malta where English is an official language alongside Maltese) (European Commission 2012).

Other factors that may make Denmark particularly prone to adopting EMI are its small population combined with its ambition to be a key player in the globalized knowledge economy (Hultgren 2014). Where requisite skills have been unavailable within the country's borders, national policy has sought to recruit skilled migrants, and the University of Copenhagen has targets in place for the recruitment of international staff (Hultgren 2014). Denmark's strong reputation in research and high living standards make it an attractive destination for skilled migrants, and 18 per cent of new appointments at Danish universities were non-Danish in 2007–9 (Hultgren 2013a). Similarly, for students, Denmark's reputation for high-quality, low-cost education makes it one of the most popular destinations in Europe in which to study with around 15 per cent of the student body estimated to be international (OECD 2020). There is anecdotal evidence of British students choosing to study in Denmark to avoid the high tuition fees in the UK, and EMI allows them to do so. In addition to such country-specific drivers, there are other drivers which may be shared by other contexts. These are discussed in the next section focusing, in turn, on the supranational, national and institutional levels.

Drivers of EMI at the supranational, national and institutional levels

At the supranational level, a key driver of EMI in Danish (and European) higher education is likely to have been the creation of a common European Higher Education Area (EHEA), which started with the signing of the Bologna Declaration in 1999. Whilst there is nothing quite equivalent to the EHEA in other places of the world, there are tendencies towards regionalization in Asia, Africa and elsewhere. The declared aim of the Bologna process was to standardize degree structures in order to facilitate mobility within the region, on the assumption that cross-border mobility enhances the quality of higher education. However, the rationale was also to make the EHEA more competitive (EHEA 2020). Whether one places the emphasis on cooperation or competition in the creation of an EHEA, the key observation here is that not a single word in the Bologna Declaration is devoted to 'language' or 'English' (Phillipson 2006); yet it is a given that in order for cross-border mobility to work, a shared language is needed. In today's linguistic ecology, this shared language tends to default to English.

At the national level, a key driver of EMI in Danish higher education may have been a shift to accountability and performance-based funding structures, encoded in new university laws. Thus, since 2010, universities in Denmark have been allocated state funding in relation to how well they perform on four indicators: (1) number of publications, with more funding allocated to publications in more prestigious channels; (2) number of students completing a year of study; (3) value of external grants captured; and (4) number of PhD degrees awarded in any given evaluation cycle. These key performance indicators play out very clearly at the institutional policy level, to which I now turn, where they indirectly, albeit to different degrees, may contribute to driving the use of English.

At the institutional level, rewarding publications in high-ranking journals is likely to encourage publishing in English-medium channels, which, all being equal, will have greater prestige. It is interesting to note that the Danish bibliometric policy does not explicitly mention that outputs should be in English; just that they should be of a certain standing, confirming that English is an indirect outcome of bibliometric policies (Hultgren 2013a). Funding criterion 2, number of students completing a year of study, might pull in the opposite direction, that is, towards a greater use of Danish to ensure that domestic students, who still constitute the vast majority, complete their studies and do not drop out. However, it is also the case that Danish universities recruit widely and have many students from the Nordic countries and Europe and that this necessitates a shared language, which tends to default to English. Some universities may also wish to complement scarce and competitively allocated state funding by tapping into the more lucrative, fee-paying non-EU student market, which also leads to English being used as a lingua franca. While the final two criteria, allocating funding on the basis of external grants captured and PhDs awarded, may not in and of themselves drive English, they may fuel universities' competitive spirit and encourage them to widen their pool of recruitment both of staff and students. The University of Copenhagen, for example, has targets for the recruitment of international faculty based on the logic that a global pool of candidates enables universities to recruit 'the best' (Hultgren 2013a). The presence of international faculty and students on university campuses necessitates a shared language which in today's linguistic ecology tends to default to English. In this way, English comes to be used on university campuses and for scholarly publications without there necessarily being an official English-language or EMI policy.

What I am suggesting, in other words, is that English may, at least to a certain extent, be the indirect outcome of a complex interplay of policy reforms centred on international competition, collaboration and competitively allocated public funding that plays out at the global, national and institutional level. In this increasingly diverse context, English becomes 'the most cost- and hassle-free choice' (Coleman 2013: xiv). As Fabricius et al. (2017: 589) put it: 'If communication of knowledge is the transaction, it can only be carried out in one currency, English.' This is not to say that language policies explicitly advocating English in Danish higher education do not exist: they do. Or rather, all Denmark's eight universities have some sort of language policy in place which advocates 'parallel language use' (i.e. the dual use of English and Danish). However, it might also be argued that 'parallel language use' is a post-hoc description of an increasingly multilingual university context, rather than it playing a significant role in actually driving the use of English (Hultgren 2014). Certainly, when the concept was originally proposed in the Nordic communities around the turn of the millennium, it was primarily intended as a way to safeguard the national Nordic languages against a perceived encroachment from English. Since then, it has been appropriated by some Danish universities to mean 'more English', thus justifying further expansion of English and subverting the original and intended meaning of the concept. Clearly, some courses are also strategically marketed in English to facilitate international recruitment of students.

Implications for EMI researchers

Above, I have tried to argue, using Denmark as a case study, that EMI may not be first and foremost a deliberate policy but that it can be driven covertly by educational reforms that are not primarily language-related at the supranational, national and institutional levels. This does not mean, of course, that EMI cannot *also* be explicitly driven by a dedicated policy, and it certainly seems possible that nation states and institutions across the world may look to what goes on elsewhere and decide to implement an EMI policy. 'Policy borrowing' is a well-known phenomenon in educational and other policy domains, which refers to the way in which policymakers imitate or copy policies from one nation state or context to another (Burdett and O'Donnell 2016). It also seems possible that introducing an EMI policy, far from actually driving EMI, may sometimes be a post-hoc response to events that have already taken place.

In terms of what this means for researchers, I would suggest that there is still considerable work to do when it comes to understanding how EMI comes about. Hence there is a need for EMI researchers to engage with academic governance and higher education policy. This means redirecting attention to university decision-makers alongside lecturers and students, who have been the predominant focus of research to date. Even for EMI researchers who do not see their remit as establishing the causes of EMI, it seems important to be attuned to the possibility that EMI may not always be a deliberate policy decision. This will have a bearing on research questions and on how projects are carried out. When discussing the consequences of EMI for teaching and learning, for example, it will be useful to keep an eye not only on the language-related changes, such as having to work in several languages, but also on the underlying issues of working and learning in increasingly neoliberally governed organizations. For those researchers working on finding solutions to EMI, whether this is content and language integrated learning initiatives, language policies, teacher training programmes or something else, it will similarly help to be cognizant that policymakers themselves may not always have deliberately decided to implement EMI, nor that it features centrally on their radar. This may be one reason why despite the abundance of very promising, localized initiatives to deal with some of the challenges of EMI, these have not always been implemented and sustained on a large institutional scale. One way to increase the possibilities of this happening is to engage more directly with decision-makers at supranational, national and institutional levels in order to raise their awareness.

The field of EMI is sometimes criticized for a lack of criticality. I would argue, however, that there is and should be room for neutral, constructive and critical scholarship in the EMI research field. Whilst this distinction is not clear-cut, neutral approaches to EMI seek to describe the phenomenon and identify and examine any challenges that may result from using EMI. Constructive approaches, meanwhile, seek to alleviate any challenges by devising solutions that can help address any perceived challenges. Critical approaches, finally, might explore the underlying drivers of EMI, some of which I have proposed in this chapter. The field of EMI is wide enough to house researchers who are critical, neutral and constructive at one and the same time. Collectively, it is perfectly possible, indeed desirable, for us to neutrally and constructively identify and seek solutions to some of the challenges that have been reported by EMI stakeholders, while at the same time critically approaching the underlying causes which – perhaps unintentionally – drive EMI.

Note

1 This chapter was funded by UK Research and Innovation (grant reference: MR/T021500/1).

References

Block, D. (2018), 'The political economy of language education research (or the lack thereof): Nancy Fraser and the case of translanguaging', *Critical Inquiry in Language Studies*, 15 (2): 1–21.

Burdett, N., and O'Donnell, S. (2016), 'Lost in translation? The challenges of educational policy borrowing', *Educational Research*, 58 (2): 113–20.

Coleman, J. (2013), 'Foreword', in A. Doiz, D. Lasagabaster and J. Sierra (eds), *English-Medium Instruction at Universities*, xiii–xv, Bristol: Multilingual Matters.

Coleman, J., Hultgren, A. K., Li Wei, Cheng-Fang Tsui, C., and Shaw, P. (2018), 'Forum on English-medium instruction', *TESOL Quarterly*, 52 (3): 701–20.

Dafouz, E., and Smit, U. (2020), *ROAD-MAPPING English Medium Education in the Internationalised University*, London: Palgrave McMillan.

de Boer, H., Jongbloed, B., and Enders, J., eds (2008), *Progress in Higher Education Reform across Europe Governance Reform Volume 1: Executive Summary Main Report*, European Commission.

de Swaan, A. (2020), 'The unequal exchange of texts in the world language system', in C. Vigouroux and S. Mufwene (eds), *Bridging Linguistics and Economics*, 203–23, Cambridge: Cambridge Univiersity Press.

Dimova, S., Hultgren, A. K., and Jensen, C., eds (2015), *English-Medium Instruction in European Higher Education*, Berlin: De Gruyter Mouton.

EF (2020), *The World's Largest Ranking of Countries and Regions by English Skills*. Available online: https://www.ef.com/wwen/epi/.

EHEA (2020), *History*. Available online: http://www.ehea.info/pid34248/history.html.

European Commission (2012), *Europeans and Their Languages*, European Commission.

Fabricius, A. H., Mortensen, J., and Haberland, H. (2017), 'The lure of internationalization: Paradoxical discourses of transnational student mobility, linguistic diversity and cross-cultural exchange', *Higher Education*, 73: 577–95.

Galloway, N. (2020), *English in Higher Education – English Medium Part 1: Literature Review*, London: British Council.

Hultgren, A. K. (2013a), *Parallelsproglighed på danske universiteter: en status rapport 2013* [Parallellingualism at Danish Universities: A status report 2013], Copenhagen: Centre for Internationalisation and Parallel Language Use.

Hultgren, A. K. (2013b), 'Lexical borrowing from English into Danish in the sciences: An empirical investigation of "domain loss"', *International Journal of Applied Linguistics*, 23 (2): 166–82.

Hultgren, A. K. (2014), 'Whose parallellingualism? Overt and covert ideologies in Danish university language policies', *Multilingua*, 1–2 (33): 61–87.

Hultgren, A. K., Gregersen, F., and Thøgersen, J.,eds (2014), *English in Nordic Universities: Ideologies and Practices*, Amsterdam: John Benjamins.

Macaro, E. (2018), *English Medium Instruction: Language and Content in Policy and Practice*, Oxford: Oxford University Press.

Maiworm, F., and Wächter, B. (2002), *English-Language-Taught Degree Programmes in European Higher Education*, Bonn: Lemmens.

Mortensen, J. (2014), 'Language policy from below: Language choice in student project groups in a multilingual university setting', *Journal of Multilingual and Multicultural Development*, 35 (4): 425–42.

OECD (2020), *Education at a Glance 2020: OECD Indicators*, Paris: OECD.

Pennycook, A. (2016), 'Mobile times, mobile terms: The trans-super-poly-metro movement', in N. Coupland (ed.), *Sociolinguistics: Theoretical Debates*, 201–16, Cambridge: Cambridge University Press.

Phillipson, R. (2006), 'English, a cuckoo in the European higher education nest of languages?', *European Journal of English Studies*, 10 (1): 13–32.

Piller, I., and Cho, J. (2013), 'Neoliberalism as language policy', *Language in Society*, 42 (1): 23–44.

Rizvi, F. (2004), 'Theorizing the global convergence of educational restructuring', in S. Lindblad and T. Popkewitz (eds), *Educaitonal Restructuring. International Perspectives on Traveling Policies*, 21–41, Greenwich: Information Age Publishing.

Saarinen, T. (2020), *Higher Education, Language and New Nationalism in Finland Recycled Histories*, London: Palgrave.

Shear, B. W., and Hyatt, S. B. (2017), 'Introduction: Higher education, engaged anthropology and hegemonic struggle', in Susan Brin Hyatt, Boone W. Shear and Susan Wright (eds), *Learning under Neoliberalim: Ethnographies or Governance in Higher Education*, 2–29, New York: Berghahn.

Wächter, B., and Maiworm, F. (2007), *English-Taught Programmes in European Higher Education: The Picture in 2007*, Bonn: Lemmens.

Wächter, B., and Maiworm, F. (2014), *English-Taught Programmes in European Higher Education: The State of Play in 2014*, Bonn: Lemmens.

Wright, S. (2019), 'Introduction: An ethnography of university reform', in S. Wright, S. Carney, J. B. Krejsler, G. Bykærholm Nielsen and J Williams Ørberg (eds), *Enacting the University: Danish University Reform in an Ethnographic Perspective*, 3–24, Dordrecht: Springer.

5

Policy Analysis of English-Medium Instruction in Ethiopian Higher Education

Tolera Simie

Background

Ethiopia is a multilingual and multicultural country that has over eighty-five languages. Among the SSA states, it is the only country with its own scripts and written language that has been used in traditional schooling for thousands of years beginning from the Axumite civilization in the fourth century. It has a recorded history of indigenous education systems associated with the Ethiopian Orthodox Church that has influenced the political and social life of the country for so long.

Although religious-based education has existed for centuries, modern education in Ethiopia is only a century old. The first modern primary school was introduced by Emperor Menelik in 1908 serving mainly as a language school in which European languages, including French, English and Italian, were taught to the few elite students at the time. Long after the introduction of modern schooling, the emperor introduced the first higher education institution, University College of Addis Ababa, in 1950. English was adopted as a medium of instruction, at the inception of the new university, by the expatriates who were mandated by the emperor to run the new institution (Murphy and Mengistu 2020). Since then, English remains the medium of instruction in all secondary and higher education institutions, whereas Amharic (the lingua franca of the country) is used as the medium of instruction across primary schools. However, with the introduction of new Education and Training Policy (ETP) in 1994, a multilingual education policy was adopted for primary education where over fifty-two local languages have been used as the medium of instruction (Ministry of Education 2015). The English-medium instruction (EMI) policy was reaffirmed in the 1994 ETP and subsequent higher education proclamation documents released by the government in 2003, 2009, 2019 and 2020.

It is important, however, to note that the adoption of EMI policy in most low- and middle-income countries is linked with colonial legacy that favours the English language. The situation in Ethiopia is different. There are certain characteristics that make the introduction of EMI policy to higher education in Ethiopia distinct. Firstly, Ethiopia has a well-developed language with its own scripts and writing system that has been used in traditional education for centuries. Secondly, it has no colonial legacy, except for a five-year Italian occupation. Thirdly, the adoption of EMI was not a deliberate decision to benefit from globalization or for its pedagogical values. According to Woldegiorgis (2020), EMI policy was introduced in Ethiopia to escape from the centuries long traditional education system and modernize the education system through English education.

However, in the absence of past colonial influence, the adoption of EMI policy has been considered a kind of self-colonization by some Ethiopian scholars (e.g. Ramadikela et al. 2020; Woldegiorgis 2020). The association of English with modernity and the Westernization of Ethiopian education have been regarded as a violence on the indigenous epistemic system implying that both the content of the curriculum and the language of instruction disengage students. Negash (2006: 33) argues that teaching all academic subjects in English at the cost of one's native language 'is tantamount to the wholesale adaption of the culture that the English language represents'. As a result, in the academic discussions there have been increased calls for the replacement of EMI policy with Ethiopian languages.

Conversely, emphasizing the significant role of English in education, development and communication in Africa, Negash (2011) argues that no major African languages, other than English, can connect African communities with one another and with the wider world. Similarly, Yadete (2017) points out that Ethiopia cannot afford to ignore education through English without which sharing political, economic and social issues with the outside world is impossible. Scholars who are in favour of the EMI policy argue for a balanced language policy approach in which English and indigenous languages can be used as dual mediums of instruction. In summary, to educate its student population through English and for the country to benefit from globalization, policymakers need to democratize access to and improve proficiency in English language, which is central in the debate of adopting EMI policy, as briefly discussed in the next section.

Literature review

The status of English in Ethiopia

English was introduced to the Ethiopian education system by Emperor Haile Selassie during the Second World War. Since then, it has been taught as a subject and used as a medium of instruction and research publication; however, its use outside educational institutions is still limited to the elitists in the country. As a result, unlike in the streets of most SSA countries, English has no dominance over the national or local languages in the streets of cities and towns in Ethiopia. Until the 1990s, public access to English was limited to one official newspaper, *The Ethiopian Herald*, one television programme and one radio programme both limited to an hour per day to broadcast in English (Negash 2011). Despite limited access to English and the small number of proficient users, Yadete (2017) observes the eagerness of many – especially the young generation – to speak in English. Thus, English is highly regarded as a language of opportunity for higher education and employability, and it has never, unlike in some SSA contexts, been stigmatized as a colonial language in Ethiopia.

Owing to globalization, the use of English in public and private organizations has now become increasingly visible in the country. Over the past couple of decades, Ethiopia has attracted a significant number of foreign investors and tourists (Mognhode and Woldemariam 2015), which has increased the demand for learning English and its use in public spaces. Most private companies and federal government websites as well as street signages are published in English along with the national language, Amharic. This suggests that despite the absence of historical connection to the socio-economic aspects of Ethiopian societies, English has now emerged as a relatively dominant force not only in the education system of the country but also in commerce, politics and job markets. However, the position of English has not yet been stated in the constitution of the country.

EMI policy and practices

EMI can be defined as 'an educational system where content is taught through English in contexts where English is not the primary, first, official language' (Rose and McKinley 2018: 4). This definition seems to be relevant in the Ethiopian context as English is a second or third language for most students and teachers in the country. That said, the spread of English as an international language has led to an exponential rise of EMI programmes in higher education institutions (HEIs) across the globe. The exponential growth of the EMI phenomenon has been characterized as an 'unstoppable train' (Macaro 2018) that has already left its station. However, research about the benefit of adopting EMI policy has not yet been conclusive.

There seems to be two schools of thought about its use as a language of instruction. On one hand, many scholars maintain the belief that English is key to increasing economic competitiveness and gaining advantages from globalization (Macaro 2018) and internationalization of higher education (Rose and McKinley 2018). Such presumed advantages of adopting EMI centre on the belief that education through the medium of English can enhance graduates' English proficiency, individuals' mobility and competitiveness in an international job market (Rose and Galloway 2019). On the other hand, scholars in SSA countries (e.g. Kamwangamalu 2013; Romaine 2015) argue that the use of EMI can impede the quality of education holding back development. Kamwangamalu (2013) argues that in SSA contexts most students do not acquire a level of proficiency in English to move up the social ladder, which suggests that learning academic content and educational outcomes can be obstructed by students' lack of competence in English. Additionally, Romaine (2015: 263) states that adopting English as the sole medium of instruction 'will not guarantee the supposed benefits of participation in the global economy for the majority of African students'. In support of Romaine's views, Ferguson (2013) highlights that EMI policy generally favours students from more affluent socio-economic backgrounds as they are more likely to have access to quality education through English that prepares them for better employment opportunities.

A significant body of literature indicates that knowledge of and proficiency in English in EMI settings is a requirement for academic success and economic development (Ghenghesh 2014; Rose et al. 2019). Therefore, the perceived benefit of EMI policy appears to be influenced by students' and teachers' abilities in the language of instruction, which suggests that individual success in education and societal development depends on good mastery of English language. In many contexts, including HEIs in Ethiopia, where students have insufficient proficiency in English, learning remains at a surface level, and teachers often resort to code-switching to facilitate learning. As Rose and Galloway (2019) indicate the English-only policy in multilingual HEIs has been challenged and the pedagogical value of code-switching has been receiving recognition among

EMI researchers. However, in some settings code-switching can be the source of educational inequality. In the Ethiopian context, students of diverse linguistic backgrounds are unlikely to benefit from code-switching as they may not share the same first language with their EMI teachers. Drawing on the debate about the role of linguistic competency in implementing EMI policy, the next section discusses language-related challenges in the implementation of the policy in Ethiopian HEIs.

Challenges in EMI policy implementation

Language-related challenges

Ethiopian higher education policy is highly centralized by the Ministry of Education. For instance, placement of students to university programmes can only be processed by the ministry. Universities have no authority over recruiting students to their institutions but can only assign, according to students' interest and spaces available, to EMI programmes on their campuses. To enrol for higher education programmes, students need to pass university entrance exams taken at the end of secondary education.

However, the standard of higher education has been undermined by the lack of quality students being prepared at the pre-tertiary level (Ministry of Education 2015) attributed partly to students' poor competency in English. Having studied all academic subjects through the medium of English for four years in secondary schools, students enter HEIs based on the assumption that those who pass university entrance exams have sufficient proficiency level to cope with the demand of university education through English. However, a comprehensive study commissioned by the government to review the standard of education (Teferra et al. 2018) highlighted that university students' poor command of English has been impacting the quality of teaching and learning in HEIs. To maximize students' English proficiency level, universities offer compulsory English-language courses along with other academic disciplines, such as the concurrent support model described by Macaro (2018), to all first-year undergraduate students. The courses lasting over two terms focus on developing students' writing and communication skills.

However, since the courses are offered irrespective of students' field of study, there appears to be lack of integration between students' language needs and their subject of studies. A case study that investigated English-language needs of business students at Adama Technology University and medical students at Haramaya University reported that the gap between students' language needs and the English courses offered remain wide as students still struggle to accomplish academic tasks while studying EMI contents (Gelan et al. 2015; Mognhode and Woldemariam 2015). To mitigate students' linguistic challenges, the government introduced English-language improvement programme in which universities identify struggling students and offer English-language support outside normal contact hours. However, the impact of the programme on the students' proficiency level has not been investigated and the language proficiency problem persists.

As discussed in the previous section, proficiency in the language of instruction appears to play a vital role in the quality of academic achievements (Ghenghesh 2014). In line with Ghenghesh, other studies (e.g. Rose et al. 2019) have shown that in English taught programmes general English-language proficiency appears to be a significant predictor of students' academic performance. However, despite a relatively long history of EMI in higher education in Ethiopia, students' and teachers' lack of competence in English has been partly blamed for the deteriorating quality of learning outcomes for the graduates (Negash 2006; Taye 2019). Traditional teaching methods and lack of resources combined with lack of opportunities for the students to practise their English outside educational institutions have contributed to poor competency in English. As a result, despite the official policy line that stipulates English as a sole medium of instruction in HEIs, code-switching has been a common classroom practice in the rapidly expanding HEIs in Ethiopia.

The impact of massification policy

Within the context of widening participation and increasing economic competitiveness, massification of higher education has become a worldwide phenomenon in the past thirty years. A similar trend has been observed in SSA countries where enrolments for university education have grown faster than in any other region in the world (Akalu 2016). Similarly, as Ethiopia has embarked on an ambitious plan to alleviate poverty and align itself with lower-middle income countries by 2030 (Teferra et al. 2018), it has expanded its HEIs to provide the economy with skilled human capital. Thus, the government has increased the number of public universities from 2 to 50 since the expansion began in 2000 (Tamrat 2020). The private HEIs have also expanded to over 250 colleges and 4 major universities. The overall number of students in HEIs has significantly increased with average enrolment standing at 13.8 per cent in 2020 compared to only 0.8 per cent before 2000. Currently, over one million students attend university education in both public and private HEIs. As a result, higher education in Ethiopia has moved from a small elite to a mass system in the past twenty years.

However, the efforts to expand higher education come with great opportunities for the development of skilled human capital in the country as well as challenges that have undermined the quality of quantitatively expanding EMI programmes across HEIs (Semela 2011). Universities must teach through English – a foreign language mostly limited to education – presenting myriad issues as most students, especially in rural Ethiopia, have limited English proficiency. Along with the massification policy, the government adopted a special admission (affirmative action) policy for students from historically deprived federal states (Akalu 2016) to maximize their participation in university education. However, a qualitative study conducted to investigate the experience of these group of students at Addis Ababa University reported the academic and social challenges they face during the first year of their studies 'due to lack of preparation at high school and absence of special support system in the university' (Shimekit 2018: 39). As Galloway and Ruegg (2020) and Milligan, et al. (2016) have highlighted provision of academic and language support for students on different EMI programmes can significantly enhance their academic performances, which does not appear to be the case in the Ethiopian context. This implies that despite the positive discrimination policies, students from disadvantaged backgrounds are unlikely to succeed in their university education due to lack of language support.

Consequently, the focus on expansion policy has overshadowed the focus on quality of provision. The decline in the quality of educational outcomes for the new graduates has been extensively documented (Akalu 2016; Ministry of Education 2020; Semela 2011). Graduates' lack of communication skills, inability to read and produce written report in English are cited as evidence of poor educational outcomes. By implication, Ethiopia's ambitious plan of lifting its citizens out of poverty is dependent partly on students' strong command of English for successful completion of university education with the skills and knowledge that enable them to meet the demand of the twenty-first-century job markets. Thus, higher education massification policy alone does not guarantee economic growth without research into the effectiveness of EMI programmes and provision of adequate resources to support its implementation.

EMI research reports

Unlike primary education where positive correlation between the multilingual education policy and students' strong learning outcomes have been observed, there seems to be a mismatch between the expansion policy and quality of students' academic performance in Ethiopian HEIs. The implementation of EMI policy can be characterized mainly by a lack of quality in educational outcomes for the graduates. For instance, when the Ministry of Education recruited ten thousand new university graduates for the newly established universities' teaching position in 2015, the sweeping majority of the candidates failed to pass qualifying exams in their specialist subjects (Woldegiyorgis 2018). The causes of poor performance can be attributed to different factors, including low proficiency levels in English. Existing EMI studies on Ethiopia HEIs generally report on students' language-related challenges. A few selected research reports will be discussed in this section.

A mixed method study conducted at Hawassa University to investigate students' level of difficulty in comprehending lectures reported that only 4 per cent of the respondents were able to comprehend 90 per cent of lecture contents delivered through English, while 77 per cent of them were able to comprehend only up to 50 per cent of the lecture content (see Aberra 2016). Although, deficiency in English has been highlighted for students' difficulty in lecture comprehension, language support available to the students has not been discussed in the report. Similarly, a quantitative study that investigates students' attitude to code-switching at Bahir Dar University has reported that 90 per cent of students in the study have indicated they were in favour of teachers' switching from English to Amharic to aid their comprehension of the content (Teklesellassie and Boersma 2018), which implies students' lack of proficiency to comprehend EMI content. Additionally, a qualitative study that interviewed graduate-level lecturers to explore factors affecting quality of education at Addis Ababa University echoed a similar experience. In his findings, Akalu (2016) reports that students' lack of participation in classroom interaction is not because of a lack of ideas but a lack of proficiency in English. The study, like a study by Teklesellassie and Boersama (2018), reveals that students' comprehension and participation increase when teachers switch to Amharic. As Kirkpatrick (2014) points out, unless the learner has sufficient proficiency in the English language, complex tasks cannot be successfully understood in EMI content learning; thus, the first language is an appropriate medium for such learning. Although students can benefit from code-switching as it helps gain content knowledge, it can also be the sources of educational inequality in multilingual Ethiopian universities classrooms, as highlighted in the next research report.

A qualitative study conducted through interviewing EMI students of diverse linguistic backgrounds at Kotebe Metropolitan University reported that students from non-Amharic-speaking backgrounds 'suffer passivity' in classrooms (Taye 2019) when teachers code-switch to Amharic to describe complex concepts. As students receive primary education in their local languages, and Amharic is taught as a subject only from grade five with little interest to teach and learn the language, many students lack the required level of proficiency in Amharic when they get to universities. This language policy has led to lack of a common language for interethnic communication which has also resulted in frequent violent clashes among ethnically rival university students (see the Guardian 2020). There is strong evidence that HEIs in the country face increasing challenges due to language barriers linked with linguistically diverse student population. As a result, many scholars call for policymakers to review the current monolingual EMI policy and consider flexible language-in-education model to foster unity and facilitate learning at all levels of education.

Conclusion

This chapter presents the overall picture of EMI policy and practice in Ethiopian HEIs focusing on language related challenges and the impact of the expansion policy on the implementation of EMI policy. Despite research evidence about the challenges in the medium of instruction neither the government nor universities have a comprehensive language policy to improve students' deficiency in English-language skills. Additionally, owing to the expansion of universities in all federal states in the country, the gap in academic success among university students seems to be widening as students from more affluent socio-economic backgrounds get better access to English-learning resources thereby improving their chances of success in university education.

Education plays an important role in promoting development in a society, and language is essential to facilitate it. However, Ethiopian HEI expansion to increase access and participation in university education does not take the country out of poverty unless there is a change in the standard of the language of instruction across its HEIs. Future research may be able to explore strategies on how students' English proficiency levels can be improved and supported to enhance the quality of EMI provision.

References

Aberra, M. (2016), 'The students' level of English language proficiency in ensuring quality education with particular reference to Hawassa University', *Research Journal of English Language and Literature*, 4 (1): 1–12.

Akalu, G. A. (2016), 'Higher education "massification" and challenges to the professoriate: Do academics' conceptions of quality matter?' *Quality in Higher Education*, 22 (3): 260–76.

Ferguson, G. (2013), 'The language of instruction issue: Reality, aspiration and the wider context', in McIlwraith, H. (ed.), *Multilingual Education in Africa: Lessons from the Juba Language-in-Education Conference*, 17–22, London: British Council.

Galloway, N., and Ruegg, R. (2020), 'The provision of student support on English medium instruction programmes in Japan and China', *Journal of English for Academic Purposes*, 45: 100846.

Gelan, B., Degago, A., and Nelson, D. (2015), 'English for university students in Ethiopia: Implications of the needs analysis at Haramaya University, Ethiopia', *American Journal of Educational Research*, 3 (1): 86–92.

Ghenghesh, P. (2014), 'The relationship between English language proficiency and academic performance of university students – should academic institutions really be concerned?' *International Journal of Applied Linguistics & English Literature*, 4 (2): 91–7.

The Guardian (2020), *Suspicion and Fear Linger as Ethiopia's Campus Wars Go Quiet*. Available online: http://www.theguardian.com/global-development/2020/apr/15/suspicion-and-fear-linger-as-ethiopia-campus-wars-go-quiet.

Kamwangamalu, N. M. (2013), 'Effects of policy on English-medium instruction in Africa', *World Englishes*, 32 (3): 325–37.

Kirkpatrick, A. (2014), 'The language(s) of HE: EMI and/or ELF and/or multilingualism?' *Asian Journal of Applied Linguistics*, 1 (1): 4–15.

Macaro, E. (2018), *English Medium Instruction*, Oxford: Oxford University Press.

Milligan, L. O., Clegg, J., and Tikly, L. (2016), 'Exploring the potential for language supportive learning in English medium instruction: A Rwandan case study', *Comparative Education*, 52 (3): 328–42.

Ministry of Education (2015), 'Education Sector Development Programme V – policies and strategies', Ministry of Education, Addis Ababa.

Ministry of Education (2020), 'Higher education policy and strategy', Ministry of Science and Higher Education, Addis Ababa.

Mognhode, T., and Woldemariam, H. Z. (2015), 'The English language needs of business students at Adama Science and Technology University, Ethiopia', *Nawa Journal of Language and Communication*, 9 (1): 150–93.

Murphy, A., and Mengistu, M. (2020), 'The challenges of internationalization of EMI tertiary education in Ethiopia', in Bowles, H. and Murphy, A. C. (eds),

English-Medium Instruction and the Internationalization of Universities, Switzerland: Springer Nature.

Negash, T. (2006), 'Education in Ethiopia: From crisis to the brink of collapse', *Nordiska Afrikainstitutet Discussion Paper*, 33: 1–56.

Negash, N. (2011), 'English language in Africa: An impediment or a contributor to development?' in Coleman, H. (ed.), *Dreams and Realities: Developing Countries and English Language*, 1–26, London: British Council.

Ramadikela, P., Msila, V., and Abera, T. (2020), 'Decolonising epistemologies: The paradoxes of a self-colonised state', in Msila, V. (ed.), *Developing Teaching and Learning in Africa: Decolonising Perspectives*, 185–202, Stellenbosch: African Sun Media.

Romaine (2015), 'Linguistic diversity and global English: The Pushmi-Pullyu of language policy and political economy', in Ricento, T. (ed.), *Language Policy and Political Economy: English in a Global Context*, 252–75, New York: Oxford University Press.

Rose, H., and Galloway, N. (2019), *Global Englishes for Language Teaching*, Cambridge: Cambridge University Press.

Rose, H., and McKinley, J. (2018), 'Japan's English-medium instruction initiatives and the globalization of higher education', *Higher Education*, 75 (1): 111–29.

Rose, H., Curle, S., Aizawa, I., and Thompson, G. (2019), 'What drives success in English medium taught courses? The interplay between language proficiency, academic skills, and motivation', *Studies in Higher Education*, 1–13. Available online: https://doi.org/10.1080/03075079.2019.1590690.

Semela, T. (2011), 'Breakneck expansion and quality assurance in Ethiopian higher education: Ideological rationales and economic impediments', *Higher Education Policy*, 24 (3): 399–425.

Shimekit, T. (2018), 'Emerging regions students' first year experience at Addis Ababa University', *Research and Reviews: Journal of Educational Studies*, 4 (3): 39–46.

Tamrat, W. (2020), 'The nuts and bolts of quality assurance in Ethiopian higher education: Practices, pitfalls, and prospects', *Journal of Education Policy*, 0 (0): 1–18.

Taye, B. A. (2019), 'The medium of instruction in Ethiopian higher education institutions: Kotebe Metropolitan University case study', *African Journal of Teacher Education*, 8: 1–24. Available online: https://doi.org/10.21083/ajote.v8i0.4367.

Teferra, T., Asgedom, A., Oumer, J., Hanna, T. W., Dalelo, A., and Assefa, B. (2018), *Ethiopian Education Development Roadmap*, Ministry of Education, Addis Ababa: Education Strategy Centre..

Teklesellassie, Y., and Boersma, E. (2018), 'Attitudes towards code-switching in an English-medium content classroom', *PASAA*, 55: 55–77.

Woldegiyorgis, A. (2018), 'The vicious circle of quality in Ethiopian higher education', *International Higher Education*, 90: 18–19. Available online: https://doi.org/10.6017/ihe.2017.90.10001.

Woldegiorgis, E. T. (2020), 'Decolonising a higher education system which has never been colonised', *Educational Philosophy and Theory*, 53 (9): 1–13. Available online: https://doi.org/10.1080/00131857.2020.1835643.

Yadete, N. (2017), 'A journey with English: Reexamining the pragmatic stance towards the language of globalisation', in Borjian, M. (ed.), 50–100, New York: Taylor & Francis.

6

English-Medium Instruction as Neoliberal Endowment in Nepal's Higher Education: Policy-Shaping Practices

Pramod K. Sah

Introduction

Higher education (HE) policies are often shaped by macro-level political, ideological and economic agendas, local-global tensions and socio-historical contexts, and all of these are relevant to the Nepali context. In the current global structure, HE is largely considered as an economic *investment* (at both individual and societal levels) with a goal of improved symbolic and economic *returns*; for example, a nation state seeks its national economic boosts, while individuals aspire to well-paid jobs. This ideology of investment and returns has guided the selection of language to be used as a medium of instruction (MoI). The processes of such selections are currently guided by the state's neoliberal policies in HE that appropriate the use of a commodified language such as English in different forms: teaching English as an academic/specific language and using English as the MoI (Piller and Cho 2013).

Some scholars have claimed the rapid adoption of English-medium instruction (EMI) as 'global' (Dearden 2015) and 'unavoidable' with uncertainty (Macaro 2017), which analogously has received dire attention among researchers to understand its flows, policies, practices and discourses (Sah, 2022a). While most research has focused on exploring the practices of EMI programmes, there has been less focus on unpacking its policy landscape, especially concerning the ways macro-level politics have shaped EMI policies in South Asian polities (cf. Sah, 2022b). In low-income countries (e.g. Nepal), where national-level policy processes are compromised, for example, by the neoliberal policies of donor agencies (Regmi 2016), it is critical to explore the ways other political phenomena (e.g. neoliberalism) have shaped the EMI policy, practices and discourses.

Nepal is a multilingual South Asian country with over 130 languages, although Nepali is the state's only official language. In both K-12 schools and higher education, Nepali and English are predominantly taught as compulsory language subjects and also used as the MoI. Although Nepal's HE is at the initial stage of development in the global market in terms of its world ranking and visibility, with only eleven universities so far and most established after the 1990s, EMI has existed ever since the establishment of its first HE institution in 1918. However, the discourse of EMI policy development and practices in HE is rarely documented. About forty years ago, Subba (1980) surveyed the use of EMI in HE institutions in Nepal, and, thereafter, the investigation of EMI policy practices has surprisingly been ignored, while an increasing amount of research on EMI in the K-12 context has been done recently (e.g. Baral 2015; Sah and Li 2018; Sah and Karki 2020, to name a few).

To fill this void, this chapter provides a macro-level analysis of political and economic changes and the ways these changes have shaped and reshaped the EMI policy practices in HE vis-à-vis Nepal's multilingual ecology. It demonstrates the ways MoI policies in Nepal's HE have undergone a series of roller-coaster changes over decades, scuffling between the nationalist ideology (for the promotion of the Nepali language) and the neoliberal ideology (the English language), and further discusses the factors (re)shaping the EMI policy and its models. Drawing on the analysis, I argue that the EMI policy is a neoliberal endowment for Nepal's HE that has been developed through the state's policies and dispositions of privatization, internationalization and capitalism, creating a discourse of a market-driven education system that appreciates commodified languages and social semiotics and undermines local realities.

EMI as maiden policy in Nepal's higher education: An influence of quasi-colonialism

The beginning of both school and tertiary education was founded on the ideology of English as an elite language in Nepal (Phyak 2016; Sah 2021). The first school (i.e. Darbar School) in Nepal was English medium, which was opened for children from the contemporary ruler's families (the Ranas) in 1854. The use of EMI at Darbar School was partly because of the intention of Janga Bahadur

Rana, the then prime minister, to associate with the British colonizers in India. Later, the first institution of higher education, Tri-Chanda College, which also adopted EMI, was established in 1918 to house the graduates of Darbar School. Although, like Ethiopia (see Chapter 5 in this volume), Nepal has never been colonized and, hence, there is no direct colonial affiliation of English in Nepal's education system (Sah 2021), it can be argued that the maiden introduction of EMI was part of (i) quasi-colonialism, (ii) resource appropriation and (iii) elite ideology.

Until the mid-twentieth century, the educational institutions in Nepal were mainly designed to serve the elite population. Since this group was ideologically motivated towards English-medium education following the influence of the British-led Indian education system, EMI was envisioned as ideal for Nepal's HE. Therefore, what I call 'quasi-colonialism' is the process through which the colonial legacy of English-medium education in colonized India was imbued in Nepal's education system although the Nepali state never experienced any direct colonial control. Besides, the EMI policy was created as part of the 'resource appropriation', mainly in terms of teachers and curriculum. It was obvious that at the onset of HE institutions in Nepal, the state did not have human resources as well as teaching materials. Hence, it hired HE teachers from India who were either Hindi-English bilingual Indian citizens or educated Nepali-speaking citizens of Nepal. Meanwhile, since there were no printing presses and experts to design curriculum and teaching materials, English-dominated Indian curricula and teaching materials were adopted (NNEPC 1956). The initial EMI policy did not only restrict access to HE for those who had their schooling in vernacular languages but also created opportunities for exclusive elites who had received English-medium education from Indian institutions. So, I argue that the foundation of Nepal's HE was built on the 'elite ideology' that resulted in class-based social fragmentation through the EMI policy and its practices.

The roller coaster of MoI policy: From nationalist to elitist ideologies

The choice of language as MoI has not been static in Nepal; rather, it has been a case of roller coasters. In the mid-1990s with the collapse of the Rana regime and the establishment of democracy, the maiden use of EMI was resisted as the process of redesigning the nation on Nepali-language-based nationalism. The promulgation of Nepal National Education Planning Commission (NNEPC), the first formal policy initiative in Nepal, in 1956 recommended that

> the medium of instruction should be the national language [Nepali] in primary, middle, and *higher education institutions* ... In the same way *English*, which is merely taught as a foreign language *cannot be considered as an important medium of instruction* in educational institutions. (NNEPC 1956: 53, emphasis added)

The NNEPC stated that Nepali as MoI would 'bring equality among all classes of people' (53) and 'promote national unity and strength' Nepali nationality (216). For higher education, however, the NNEPC was a bit liberal towards the use of English. Although Nepali was recommended for 'classroom discussion, lectures, and other verbal exchanges', the 'reading competency in English and Hindi' was considered as essential 'to keep abreast of world development' (134).

During this period of overhauling the nation with nationalist intentions and policies, educational institutions (public-funded) serving poor and minoritized groups adopted Nepali-only instruction while several private and missionary institutions (serving elite students) continued English-medium education, which demonstrates the ways elitism has the power to downplay the state's policies (Gaige 1975). Given the pressure from private institutions and elite groups, the National Education System Plan (NESP) (1971–6) later declared that 'Nepali will be the medium of instruction up to the secondary school and will, in general, be *replaced by English in higher education*' (NESP 1971: 9, emphasis added).

Subba (1980) conducted a survey to map out what languages were used as MoI at HE institutions, which concluded that (i) English was never the exclusive MoI for class lectures; (ii) students had the option to use either Nepali or English in examinations, except for those in science, medicine and some branches of engineering who had to use English; and (iii) Nepali was predominantly used in subjects like social sciences, education, law and commerce, while it was alternatively used with English in class lectures of science, medicine, engineering, forestry and agriculture. However, on most occasions, 'the use of English [was] limited to textbooks and question and answer scripts in science courses' (82). Subba also observed that the students found English textbooks 'too difficult' to understand; however, they preferred EMI 'in the hope of getting a scholarship to study abroad' (84).

Hence, English-Nepali bilingual instruction was a de facto policy at HE institutions. With the changing political context in the 1990s, the National Education Commission (1992) concluded that the intention for implementing

Nepali as MoI had not become successful because of 'the slackness of implementation, the ambiguity at the stage of planning and direction, the proliferation of English-medium schools, and the use of English textbooks' (GoN, 1992: 219). The commission favoured Nepali-only as the MoI and, accordingly, recommended the development of reading materials in Nepali and even making it a 'language of science and technology with a sufficient number of textbooks written in that language' (219). Regardless of this de jure context, English-Nepali bilingual instruction continued. In response to this, the 'Medium of Instruction Roadmap' (2014) suggested English and/or Nepali as MoI in HE (MoEST, 2014). Seel et al. (2015: 59), in a joined commissioned paper of Ministry of Education and USAID, asserted that 'an option to use Nepali and English together as MoIs ... as more feasible than English-only' formalize and strengthen 'what is already being practice in an ad hoc manner'. Although the de facto use of Nepali-English bilingualism has been rightly recognized in the commissioned paper and the Medium of Instruction Roadmap, the ministry has not developed any specific policy guidelines for such instructional practices at the micro level.

Neoliberalism as agenda-setting for the EMI policy in Nepal

So far, the socio-historical analysis has demonstrated the roller coaster of MoI policies in Nepal's HE – fluctuating between Nepali and English along with the changing political contexts of quasi-colonial influences, nationalist ideology and elitism. This section furthers the analysis of EMI policy development in the contemporary HE landscape in Nepal. The macro-level EMI policy in Nepal's current HE is shaped by different but interdependent and interrelated discourses: (i) privatization of higher education, (ii) internationalization of HE, (iii) emphasis on STEM (science, technology, engineering and mathematics) disciplines and information technology, (iv) symbolic and linguistic capital of English and (v) transition from schools to HE (Figure 6.1).

Primarily beginning in the 1980s when Nepal adopted a free-market economy policy, the private-public partnership was initiated as a national agenda to provide educational services. The current Higher Education Policy (HEP) (2016) has also aimed that 'for the development of higher education, public, community, and private institutions will be promoted' (GoN 2016: 5). Consequently, out of 1,276 HE institutions, 751 are private colleges, 429 are community-based colleges

Figure 6.1 Neoliberal agendas shaping the EMI policy in Nepal.

and 96 are affiliated colleges of Tribhuvan University (GoN 2016). In Nepal, privatization has been suggested by foreign donors like the World Bank (Regmi 2016), and its consequent adaptation has allowed private agencies to engage with policymakers to influence policies in their favour. Therefore, the adoption of EMI in Nepal is a result of consistent pressure from private institutions and their agents to institutionalize their instructional practices (i.e. the use of EMI). In Nepal, almost all private schools and the majority of private HE institutions have adopted EMI to largely house the graduates of English-medium schools from elite and middle-class families.

Within this discourse of privatization, the internationalization and marketization of higher education have emerged recently at both de fact and de jure levels. At the de facto level, HE institutions have begun to offer, for example, A-Level courses accredited by foreign institutions, and some of them (e.g. Islington College and The British College) even offer international bachelor's and master's degrees. Similarly, many of such institutions have adopted Western names (e.g. Texas International College, Thames Int'l College, White House, Oxford College, Cambridge International College, Liverpool College, Pentagon College) to commodify their names to attract students. The HE landscape has become an open competitive market, in which institutions have adopted internationalization and EMI as a symbolic tool to attract students. EMI has become parallel to internationalization in the local market (Sah and Li 2018), and, therefore, as Tupas (2018: 107) argues, English in EMI is 'Market English', rather than a second or foreign language, constructing EMI as a Discourse in Nepal.

Besides this de facto EMI policy resulting from privatization, marketization, and internationalization, the Nepali state's current intentions for developing Nepal as an international education hub implicitly support EMI. The National Education Policy (2019) overtly states that 'Nepal will be developed as an educational hub that provides world-class education in specific subjects' (MoEST 2019: 35), aligning with the Higher Education Policy's (2016) specific focus on technical fields, for example, forestry, computer science, engineering and medical science. As part of the government's intentions to internationalize the HE landscape, the educational policies have emphasized STEM disciplines and commodified courses to attract international students as well as prepare Nepali students to sustain themselves in the global economy. To develop Nepal as an international education hub, the National Education Policy (2019) has also emphasized the use of information technology, while changing teaching methodology, curriculum and instructional approaches. The state's plans for accentuating STEM disciplines and information technology implicitly endorses EMI. Elsewhere (Sah 2021), I have argued how the goal of utilizing information technology, believing that all information technologies are available in English, has endorsed EMI as de facto policy, similar to Helm's (2020) contemplation of how the use of MOOCs (massive open online courses) has contributed to the promotion of EMI.

Another factor influencing the EMI policy in HE is the discourse of transition from schools to HE. Almost all private K-12 schools teach through English and, more recently, a large number of previously Nepali-medium schools have adopted EMI, serving elite and middle-class students (Sah 2021). It is a complex phenomenon whether the use of EMI in HE has shaped the school-level EMI policy or vice versa, but the research on EMI in schools (e.g. Sah and Li 2018; Sah and Karki 2020) has indicated easy transition to HE as one of the motivations for choosing English-medium schools. For example, the Medium of Instruction Roadmap (MoEST, 2014: 3) stated that 'to make it easier to study in higher education ... such subjects [e.g. science, mathematics, computer] should be taught through English in community schools'. It is believed that HE is always English-medium or high English proficiency is needed to study higher education. There is another side of the coin that 'the majority of school graduates pursue HE and [hence] there is an increasing trend to introduce English medium instruction in Nepalese universities' (Shrestha 2018: 52). It refers to the fact that the majority of school graduates in Nepal are from English-medium schools, which has created a demand for English-medium HE institutions.

In addition, the aspiration to the acquisition of symbolic and linguistic capital of English has shaped the EMI policy practices. There are different facets of such symbolic and linguistic capital. First, there is a widespread narrative in Nepal and elsewhere that credentials from English-medium education not only develop English literacy skills but also open up doors for jobs in international markets (Phyak 2016; Rana and Sah, in press). Second, there is an increasing trend among Nepali students to go abroad for further study (Linn, et al., 2021). Unlike many other Asian contexts (e.g. Japan; see Aizawa and McKinley 2020) where the incoming of international students has shaped the EMI policy, the outgoing of Nepali students for study abroad – which is linked to upward socio-economic mobility – has fuelled the EMI phenomenon in Nepal. Driven by the prospects of higher-quality education and improved career, there is a marked trend towards going to English-speaking countries, such as Australia, the USA, Canada and the UK, for higher education, which require Nepali students to prove English proficiency through international tests like IELTS or TOEFL. Hence, after graduating from schools in grade 10, many students join English-medium colleges for their 10+2 and bachelor's degrees with the hope that they will develop English proficiency.

Finally, in the centre of all these factors shaping the EMI policy in Nepal's HE remains neoliberal logic. The interlocking connections between state-regulated privatization, policies of internationalization in the capitalist world, commodified courses and disciplines of study, and individual desires of upward socio-economic mobility on the terrain of English are naturalized through neoliberal processes of HE. For a national economic boost, the government of Nepal has considered HE 'as a mechanism to produce human power' by helping students 'develop international-level competitive knowledge and skills' for national and international job markets (GoN 2016: 5–6). Such a neoliberal policy then 'imposes English as a natural and neutral medium of academic excellence' (Piller and Cho 2013: 24). Seel et al. (2015: 28) claimed that politicians and ethnic organizations believe that 'local languages cannot contribute to globalization' and exemplify that 'Singapore started from English and developed tremendously'. Therefore, neoliberalism has become a hidden agenda for the development of EMI since 'English is prioritized as the language of education stemming from the neoliberal ideology of commodification of English education as international, global and quality' (Sah and Karki 2020: 3).

The EMI model in Nepal's higher education

Now, I turn to a brief discussion of the EMI model in practice. There could be different EMI models at institutional levels but, by and large, the EMI model looks like the one illustrated in Figure 6.2.

Analogous to Subba's study forty years ago, there is a partial model of EMI in Nepal's higher education, in which English and Nepali are flexibly used for different activities. In terms of classroom instruction, it is rarely English-only but a combination of English and Nepali. As Paudel (2010) reports on an EMI programme, students often used Nepali to ask questions and teachers replied in English and Nepali, while lectures were in English with frequent switching to Nepali. The instructional practices are, however, discipline-specific in Nepal. Shrestha (2008) confers that, at Tribhuvan University, in disciplines such as medicine, engineering, agriculture and veterinary and forestry, English-only practice is more dominant. Further, at Nepal's HE institutions, there is a standardized examination system in which question papers are in English and students (mainly from social sciences and humanities) can write in both English and Nepali, but STEM students need to write in English only.

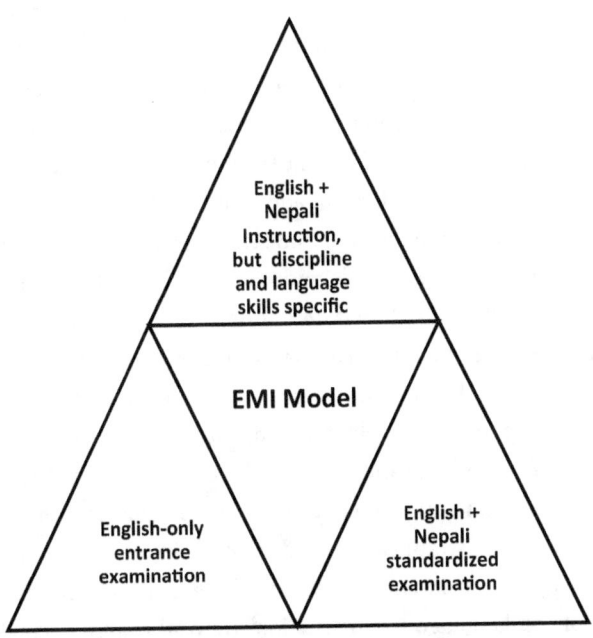

Figure 6.2 The model of EMI in Nepal's higher education.

Similarly, technical institutes, science and medical colleges and some faculties/institutes at universities require students to pass entrance tests, a merit-based competition, which are strictly English-only. In such tests, as reported in UNESCO (2007: 46), 'the students from public schools [Nepali-medium] are poor in that [English] language and score low marks in entrance tests'. This practice functions as a gatekeeper, reproducing marginalization and discrimination against economically poor students who have not attended English-medium schools and 'cannot afford to pay for expensive bridge courses to help them do well at the [English-medium] colleges' (46). Shrestha (2008: 198) analogously argues that students 'with fewer skills in English are denied access to Science and Engineering courses, which are often perceived as respectable [an indicator of symbolic capital] in Nepalese society'. Therefore, the entanglement between the ideology of specific disciplines that have more commodification values and the selection of EMI once again demonstrates a neoliberal construct.

Conclusion and implications

In sum, regardless of the policy roller coaster for the use of languages as media of instruction, EMI has always existed in the history of Nepal's HE as a form of elite reality. The analysis of recent policies, practices and discourses has revealed neoliberal ethos as the hidden agenda of HE that has promoted EMI as an appropriate instructional model, but often in the form of Nepali-English elite bilingualism, simultaneously subjugating the scope of local languages other than Nepali. The agendas of privatization, internationalization and communication of STEM (or technical) disciplines, in addition to the discourses created by the desire for economic and symbolic mobilities through HE, have contributed to the development of EMI as a neoliberal endowment in Nepal. The overarching goals of developing human capital based on national and international competition and performance, aligning with national developmental agendas of economic boosts, have become a default mechanism shaping the EMI policy.

Therefore, I argue that neoliberal language policy and discourse have considered HE as a tool of capital accumulation and national and individual prosperity, creating fundamental conditions for language hierarchies, language mineralization, social stratification and commodification of English-Nepali bilingualism. In this context, concerned bodies must reconsider (i) the 'indigenization of language of instruction' (Shrestha and Khanal 2016: 52) that values the self, identity, local and re-envisions an ecological approach to instruction (ii) challenging cultural hegemony of specific disciplines in HE and the language policy of entrance examinations to such programmes that have relational meanings to shaping MoI at the school level; and (iii) closing social-class-based inequalities stemming from the MoI policies. I also call for educational and applied linguistic researchers to conduct research that empirically informs EMI policy practices at the institutional level, given that the ad hoc adaptation of EMI has become widespread in response to the nation's neoliberal intentions recently.

References

Aizawa, I., and McKinley, J. (2020), 'EMI challenges in Japan's internationalization of higher education', in H. Bowles and A. C. Murphy (eds), *English-Medium Instruction and the Internationalization of Universities*, 27–48, London: Springer.

Baral, L. N. (2015), 'Expansion and Growth of English as a Language of Instruction in Nepal's School Education: Towards Pre-conflict Reproduction or Post-conflict Transformation', master's thesis in Peace and Conflict Transformation, Arctic University of Norway, Tromsø, Norway.

Dearden, J. (2015), *English as a Medium of Instruction – a Growing Global Phenomenon*, London: British Council.

Gaige, F. (1975), *Regionalism and National Unity in Nepal*, London: University of California Press.

Government of Nepal (GoN) (1992), *National Education Commission Report*, Kathmandu: Government of Nepal.

GoN (2016), *Higher Education Policy*, Kathmandu: Government of Nepal.

Helm, F. (2020), 'EMI, internationalisation, and the digital', *International Journal of Bilingual Education and Bilingualism*, 23 (3): 314–25.

Linn, A., Shrestha, P., Bezborodova, A., and Hultgren, K. (2021), *Current Practice in English-Medium Education in Higher Education: Case Studies from Kazakhstan, Turkmenistan, Bangladesh and Nepal*, London: British Council.

Macaro, E. (2017), 'English medium instruction: Global views and countries in focus', *Language Teaching*, 52 (2): 231–48.

MoEST (Ministry of Education, Science, and Technology) (2014), *The Roadmap of Medium of Instruction in Schools Education*, Kathmandu: Government of Nepal.

MoEST (2019), *National Education Policy*, Kathmandu: Government of Nepal.

NESP (National Education System Plan) (1971), *National Education System Plan 1971–1976*, Kathmandu: MOE, GON.

NNEPC (Nepal National Education Planning Commission) (1956), *Education in Nepal: Report of the Nepal Education Planning Commission*, Kathmandu: His Majesty's Government.

Paudel, P. P. (2010), 'Teaching English in multilingual classrooms of higher education: The present scenario', *Journal of NELTA*, 15 (1–2): 121–33.

Phyak, P. (2016), 'Local-global tension in the ideological construction of English language education policy in Nepal', in R. Kirkpatrick (ed.), *English Language Education Policy in Asia*, 199–217, Cham, Switzerland: Springer International.

Piller, I., and Cho, J. (2013), 'Neoliberalism as language policy', *Language in Society*, 42: 23–44.

Rana, K., and Sah, P. K. (in press), 'Motivations of developing English as a medium of instruction policy at a higher education institution in Nepal', in P. K. Sah and F. Fang (eds), *English-Medium Instruction and Linguistic Diversity in Asia Universities: Unsettling Critical Edges*, New York: Routledge.

Regmi, K. D. (2016), 'World Bank in Nepal's education: Three decades of neoliberal reform', *Globalisation, Societies and Education*, 15 (2): 188–201.

Sah, P. K. (2022a), 'A research agenda for English-medium instruction: Conversations with scholars at the research fronts', *Journal of English-Medium Instruction*, 1 (1): 124–36. https://doi.org/10.1075/jemi.21022.sah.

Sah, P. K. (2022b), 'English medium instruction in South Asian's multilingual schools: Unpacking the dynamics of ideological orientations, policy/practices, and democratic questions', *International Journal of Bilingual Education and Bilingualism*, 25 (2): 742-55. DOI: 10.1080/13670050.2020.1718591.

Sah, P. K. (2021), 'Reproduction of nationalist and neoliberal ideologies in Nepal's language and literacy policies', *Asia Pacific Journal of Education*, 41 (2): 238–52. DOI: 10.1080/02188791.2020.1751063.

Sah, P. K., and Karki, J. (2020), 'Elite appropriation of English as a medium of instruction policy and epistemic inequalities in Himalayan schools', *Journal of Multilingual and Multicultural Development*, DOI: 10.1080/01434632.2020.1789154.

Sah, P. K., and Li, G. (2018), 'English medium instruction (EMI) as linguistic capital: Promises and realities', *International Multilingual Research Journal*, 12 (2): 109–23.

Seel, A., Yadava, Y. P., and Kadel, S. (2015), *Medium of Instruction and Languages for Education (MILE): Ways Forward for Education Policy, Planning and Practice in Nepal*, Kathmandu: USAID.

Shrestha, I. M., and Khanal, S. K. (2016), 'Indigenization of higher education: Reflections from Nepal', in J. Xing and P. Ng (eds), *Indigenous Culture, Education and Globalization*, 137–57, New York: Springer.

Shrestha, P. (2008), 'ELT, ESP & EAP in Nepal: Whose interests are served?', in M. Krzanowski (ed.), *EAP and ESP in Developing Countries: State of Play vs Actual Needs and Wants*, 191–210, Canterbury: IATEFL (ESP SIG).

Shrestha, P. (2018), 'English language examination reform: international trends and a framework for Nepal', in D. Hayes (ed.), *English Language Teaching in Nepal: Research, Reflection and Practice*, 13–34, Kathmandu: British Council.

Subba, S. (1980), 'The medium question in Nepalese higher education', *Contribution to Nepalese Studies*, VII (1–2): 71–95.

Tupas, R. (2018), 'Market English as medium of instruction: Education in neoliberal times', in R. Barnard and Z. Hasim (eds), *English Medium Instruction Programmes: Perspectives from South East Asian Universities*, 104–15, London: Routledge.

United Nations Educational, Scientific and Cultural Organization (UNESCO) (2007), *Advancing Policy Options for Higher Education, Improving Transition and Access to Higher Education in Nepal*, Kathmandu: UNESCO.

7

Provision for Partial English-Medium Instruction Programmes in Turkish Higher Education: All or Nothing?

Kari Sahan

Introduction

Due to trends such as the internationalization of higher education and the use of English as an academic lingua franca, the number of universities offering English-medium instruction (EMI) programmes has increased exponentially in recent years (Macaro et al. 2018). Although the growth of EMI has been called an 'unstoppable train' (Macaro 2015: 7), EMI implementation varies across countries and geographical regions (Curle et al. 2020a; Macaro 2018). In some contexts, the introduction of EMI is accompanied by explicit or implicit policies promoting English-only instruction, often grounded in the belief that an immersion setting will promote language development – a belief which Moncada-Comas and Block (2019: 2) criticize as 'based on a naïve theory of second language acquisition, according to which language learning takes place by osmosis'. Nonetheless, monolingual ideology remains pervasive in many contexts and has contributed to policies and practices which discourage the use of the local language or the students' first language (L1) in EMI classrooms. However, an English-only approach is not the only model of EMI implementation: although they remain under-researched, bilingual or partial, EMI programmes are common in many regions, as illustrated in the different chapters in this volume. This chapter attempts to address this need for research by contextualizing partial EMI programmes in Turkey through an examination of macro-level policies.

Turkey is no exception in the global trend towards EMI. Although the history of EMI in Turkish higher education dates back to the 1950s, researchers have noted the incredible growth in EMI in recent years (Kırkgöz 2009; Selvi 2014). More than a decade ago, Kırkgöz (2009) argued that the implementation of EMI programmes in Turkey was motivated by a desire to gain access to scientific knowledge published in English, and that motivation continues even today. Although in Turkey 'the exact number of EMI programs and courses are unknown' (Karakaş 2019: 207; for an overview, see also Sahan 2020a), the growth of EMI programmes in recent years has accompanied an expansion of the higher education sector over the past two decades. Through a government-led effort to increase enrolment in higher education, the number of higher education institutions (HEIs) in Turkey doubled from 2005 to 2010 (Günay and Günay 2011) and has continued to increase since. Many of the new universities opened through this government-led initiative offer full or partial EMI programmes, representing a shift away from EMI as historically associated with elite education (Selvi 2014).

While partial EMI programmes remain under-researched and largely undefined in the literature, Turkey offers a unique example due to the presence of macro-level policy regulating higher education. By examining macro-level policies, this chapter provides an overview of partial EMI programmes in Turkey. The chapter evaluates policy provisions for English proficiency and support, drawing comparisons with provisions for full EMI programmes. It then discusses '30 Percent Partial EMI' programmes as a model for EMI education. In doing so, it offers a point of comparison for other EMI contexts and provides implications for researchers, practitioners and policymakers.

Overview of EMI policy in context

Universities in Turkey are regulated by the Council of Higher Education (Yükseköğretim Kurulu, YÖK), a central government agency connected to the Ministry of Education. Founded in 1981, YÖK regulates processes such as the establishment of new universities and university programmes as well as the hiring of staff. It also regulates matters concerning the medium of instruction and language support at Turkish universities. To introduce an EMI programme, a university must seek the approval of YÖK and meet national requirements in terms of staff qualifications and language support (Law no. 29662).

National regulations establish three types of medium of instruction at Turkish HEIs: full instruction in a foreign language, partial instruction in a foreign language and full Turkish-medium instruction (TMI). These regulations are laid forth in Law no. 29662, entitled 'Regulations Concerning the Principles for Foreign Language Teaching and Teaching in a Foreign Language at Higher Education Institutions', which was published in the National Gazette on 23 March 2016 and replaced previous regulations by the same name. Although the regulations describe 'foreign language' medium of instruction, the vast majority of these programmes are taught in English, with a select number of programmes offered in French and German (Sahan 2020a).

According to these regulations, 'partial EMI programmes' are defined as 'education in which at least 30 percent of the total credits of the classes given in the program are given in a foreign language' (Article 4, Law no. 29662). In other words, for a degree programme requiring ten equal credit-bearing classes, at least three classes must be taught in English. The remaining seven classes could be taught in Turkish, although the number of English-taught classes may exceed the 30 per cent threshold. Partial EMI programmes are therefore taught bilingually, meaning some classes are offered in English and others in Turkish, while full EMI programmes are those in which 100 percent of classes (e.g. total credits) are taught in English.

Although partial EMI programmes are bilingual, macro-level policies define language use in terms of credit-bearing classes. As such, policies for partial EMI programmes in Turkey do not envision a situation of parallel language use (Airey 2012; in Sweden) or bilingual programmes in which English and the L1 are used simultaneously (Mazak and Herbas-Donoso 2014; in Puerto Rico). Rather, partial EMI programmes are those in which a minimum of 30 per cent of classes are taught in English and the remaining classes are taught in Turkish.

Although a policy distinction is made between full and partial EMI programmes, the processes for admission and enrolment are the same for each form of education. University entrance is determined based on students' score rankings from a national university entrance exam. Although full EMI programmes often require higher university entrance exam scores than partial EMI programmes (ÖSYM 2020), the admissions process is the same for both types of programmes, and English language proficiency is not assessed in the university entrance exam, unless students are applying to a department in which the programme content is directly related to language, such as English-language teaching or English literature. For full and partial EMI programmes in a subject such as engineering, psychology or biology, there is no English-language assessment on the university entrance exam. As such, language proficiency is not a requirement for entry although macro-level policies establish language proficiency requirements that students must meet after enrolling on their EMI programmes. The following sections contextualize macro-level policies for partial EMI programmes with respect to language proficiency.

Student proficiency and language support

Macro-level policy stipulates the same English proficiency requirements and language support provisions for students enrolled in both full and partial EMI programmes. National policy establishes a preparatory model of language support (see Macaro 2018) for all EMI programmes in Turkey. The English preparatory programme (EPP) is a one-year intensive English-language programme offered to students before their EMI content classes. Completion of the EPP is required for students enrolled in full and partial EMI programmes, unless they meet the exemption criteria, which include passing a placement exam administered by their university.

Although YÖK regulations require that universities establish an EPP and conduct a placement exam at the beginning of the academic year, national regulations do not provide a minimal threshold of English proficiency required for EMI study. Rather, universities determine their own minimum English proficiency standards for EMI programmes. As such, a university may decide to set different proficiency requirements for full and partial EMI programmes, or it may establish the same minimum requirement for both programmes. While the EPP is a mandatory component of all EMI programmes, specific standards of English proficiency are not provided in macro-level policy documents, nor are curriculum guidelines specified with respect to the EPP (e.g. whether it should offer general English, English for academic purposes (EAP) or English for specific purposes (ESP) classes). These decisions are left to the university.

National regulations stipulate no additional language support following the EPP, although research has suggested that students face language-related challenges in their EMI classes (Başıbek et al. 2014; Kamaşak et al. 2021; Kırkgöz 2014). National policies also do not distinguish between the type of language support that students in full or partial EMI programmes might need. Instead, national provisions for EPPs are identical for both types of EMI programmes.

Teacher proficiency and language support

In addition to establishing the EPP, national regulations (Law no. 29662) outline the English proficiency requirements for lecturers teaching on EMI programmes. According to YÖK regulations, EMI classes 'should be given in this language

[English] and by teaching staff who have command of this language' (Law no. 29662, Article 8, Clause 7). While 'command of this language' does not specify the competencies required for EMI teachers, the regulations outline the criteria that lecturers must meet to teach content classes in English. There are four ways through which content teachers can meet the English proficiency criteria for EMI programmes (Article 8, Law no. 29662):

1. English exam: Teachers can submit an acceptable English exam score from a national language test (Yabancı Dil Sınavı, YDS) or an international test recognized by YÖK (such as TOEFL or the Cambridge English Proficiency exam).
2. Study abroad: Teachers who have completed their degrees in a country in which English 'is spoken as a native language' are qualified to teach on EMI programmes, although the regulations do not specify what qualifies as a 'native-speaking' country.
3. Work abroad: Teachers who have taught for at least one year at an HEI in a country in which English is an official language are qualified to teach on EMI programmes.
4. Native language: Teachers who are 'native-speakers' of English are qualified to teach through English, although the regulations do not define what is meant by 'native-speaker'.

These language proficiency criteria apply to lecturers teaching on both full and partial EMI programmes. However, a key policy distinction between these EMI programmes concerns the number of qualified teaching staff required for each programme. For full EMI programmes, every member of the teaching staff in the department must fulfil the English proficiency criteria. For partial EMI programmes, a minimum of four lecturers must be qualified to teach through English. In other words, to accommodate a curriculum in which 100 per cent of courses are offered through EMI, every lecturer must be qualified to teach through English. However, because partial EMI programmes offer up to 70 per cent of courses in Turkish, it is not necessary for every lecturer to meet these language requirements.

National policies provide no provisions for teacher training, professional development or support. Aside from the English proficiency requirements described above, no additional requirements are specified for lecturers on EMI programmes. Although EMI lecturers are required to meet a certain level of English proficiency, macro-level policies do not provide provisions for language support to help teachers achieve this standard of proficiency.

Process of teaching and learning

National policy provides little direction in terms of how processes of teaching and learning should be conducted in partial EMI classrooms. Policy only implies that one language should be used at a time in each classroom. While 30 per cent of courses should be taught in English, macro-level policies do not specify how partial EMI curricula should be arranged at the programme level. In other words, students are not required to take a certain number of EMI courses per semester (e.g. 30 per cent of credits per semester) but could reach the overall 30 per cent threshold by taking a few semesters of all EMI courses.

Guidelines for classroom-level practices are not specified in macro-level policy, aside from indicating that EMI classes should be taught in English. Although macro-level policy establishes bilingual programmes through the 30 Percent Partial EMI model, it does not envision bilingual instruction in the classroom. Instead, macro-level policies perpetuate a model of one-language-at-a-time instruction, which is supported through provisions for language proficiency that do not distinguish between full and partial EMI programmes, except with respect to the number of teaching staff required. Because macro policy envisions the English-taught classes in 30 Percent Partial EMI programmes to be delivered entirely in English, it does not make concessions for the needs of students and teachers on partial compared to full EMI programmes. While the 30 Percent Partial EMI model is bilingual at the programme level – as an overall percentage of credits for students' degree – it does not offer a model of flexible bilingualism through which English and Turkish may be used simultaneously, despite research suggesting that such classroom practices are common (Sahan 2020b).

30 Percent programmes as an EMI model

This section evaluates 30 Percent Partial EMI programmes as a model of EMI implementation, drawing comparison to other models of partial or bilingual EMI programmes in different country contexts.

The Turkish model of 30 Percent Partial EMI programmes might address a number of limitations arising as universities transition to EMI, including limitations in the number of staff qualified to teach through English, concerns over students' English proficiency or a desire to offer students the opportunity to experience EMI without going abroad. National policies allow for partial EMI programmes to be established with a minimum of four qualified teaching staff members, which may provide more flexibility to lecturers in terms of deciding the medium of instruction for their classes. Previous research has suggested that some lecturers feel pressure when teaching in English (Tange 2012) or do not feel confident in their English abilities (Kim et al. 2018). Theoretically, in partial EMI programmes, only those teachers interested in teaching through English would offer EMI classes.

Despite these advantages, more research is needed to evaluate micro-level processes and learning outcomes on partial EMI programmes. While research on partial EMI programmes in Turkey is scarce, one study found that lecturers on partial EMI programmes supported the implementation of EMI at their universities but had concerns about students' English proficiency and believed that students learned content more easily through TMI (Başıbek et al. 2014. Another study investigating the role of English at Turkish universities concluded that 'there is little evidence that [partial EMI] courses actually improve students' English in any way, and they almost certainly impede their academic progress' (British Council and TEPAV 2015: 67). However, this study relied on interview data from stakeholders across the higher education sector, including those who were not actively engaged in partial EMI programmes, and it did not measure learning outcomes in partial EMI programmes, making it unclear how the researchers arrived at their conclusions.

A study conducted on a partial EMI economics programme in Turkey found that academic success in EMI, measured as students' grade point average (GPA) from final scores in EMI classes, was significantly predicted by academic success in TMI classes, measured as students' GPA from final scores in TMI classes (Curle et al. 2020b). From this finding, the authors conclude that learning content in Turkish had a facilitative effect on EMI learning outcomes. However, further research is needed to investigate whether learning in Turkish supported students' outcomes in EMI classes or whether other factors such as academic aptitude, study habits and teaching practices may have contributed to these findings. In other words, research is needed to evaluate whether partial EMI programmes support students' learning in English or whether students are academically successful due to other factors.

My own research has suggested mixed perspectives on the effectiveness of EMI programmes for teaching and learning, supporting the findings from Başıbek et al. (2014). In interviews from a larger study (Sahan 2020a), some EMI engineering lecturers stated that partial EMI programmes negatively affected students' language and content learning, while other lecturers believed that these programmes were effective for developing bilingual engineers. Some students in focus groups also expressed concerns about the effectiveness of partial EMI programmes in terms of learning technical terminology in English due to a lack of exposure to English vocabulary across courses. These comments suggest that students in partial EMI programmes may benefit from ongoing ESP support throughout their studies.

To recapitulate, although partial EMI programmes in Turkey represent a bilingual model of EMI implementation, macro-level policies envision a one-language-at-a-time model of instruction. This stands in contrast to other models of multilingual or partial EMI implementation, in other country contexts, in which multiple languages may be actively used and acknowledged in the classroom. Chou (2018: 612) described partial EMI programmes in Taiwan as those 'in which the course books and examinations are in English, but the translation of concepts and codeswitching in lectures is allowed'. In their case study at a university in Japan, Aizawa and Rose (2019) found that courses were labelled according to how much of each language was used, meaning that courses could be categorized as English-only (E), Japanese-only (J) or a mix of English and Japanese (E/J or J/E). In contrast, macro-level language policy in Turkey does not allow for language mixing and does not recognize bilingual classes within the EMI curriculum – regardless of how common L1 use in EMI classes might be (Sahan 2020b). Moreover, neither Chou (2018) nor Aizawa and Rose (2019) noted a specific minimum threshold in terms of how many EMI classes must be offered within a degree programme. As such, the Turkish model of 30 Percent Partial EMI may be less flexible at the meso and micro levels compared to the other models of partial EMI implementation which allow for bilingual instruction. For example, Mazak and Herbas-Donoso (2014) found that EMI practices at a bilingual university in Puerto Rico were characterized by flexible language use through which English materials were used for teaching but lectures and discussions were conducted in Spanish. Similarly, Wang and Curdt-Christiansen (2019) concluded that macro-level policies recognizing bilingual education at universities in China provided institutional support for the multilingual practices that they observed in classrooms. In contrast, macro-level policies in Turkey do not support bilingual teaching pedagogies.

Nonetheless, the strengths and weaknesses of the 30 Percent Partial EMI model should be considered with respect to the aims of an EMI programme in its local context. If an aim of EMI is to attract international students, the 30 Percent Partial EMI model might be limited in terms of enrolling full-time international students, since these students would be required to complete up to 70 per cent of their courses in the local language. In Turkey, this problem is often addressed through a Turkish-language preparatory programme, modelled after the EPP. However, for universities which envision an 'internationalization at home' (Galloway and Rose 2015) situation, the 30 Percent model could make EMI courses more accessible to students who might not have the opportunity or means to study abroad. The 30 Percent Partial EMI model may also be helpful in supporting students' transition to EMI through content learning in the L1, as suggested by Curle et al. (2020b), although more research is needed to evaluate learning outcomes on these programmes, as well as to compare how partial EMI programmes might be implemented in terms of course arrangement.

Implications for researchers and practitioners

This chapter has evaluated macro-level policies for partial EMI programmes in Turkey and compared 30 Percent Partial EMI programmes with full EMI programmes and other models of bilingual EMI implementation. It now offers implications for researchers and practitioners.

In the Turkish context, more research is needed at the meso and micro levels to understand how this national policy is implemented in practice, particularly in terms of how EMI courses are distributed to comprise 30 per cent of programme curricula. Research in this area may suggest best practices in terms of how partial EMI programmes might support students' transition into EMI as well as support their English-language development. More research is also needed to compare students' experiences and learning outcomes in partial and full EMI programmes.

At the beginning of this chapter, I noted that EMI policy is often underpinned by a monolingual ideology which discourages language mixing in the classroom. Although 30 Percent Partial EMI programmes offer a form of a bilingual education, this chapter has demonstrated how macro-level policy in Turkey envisions a one-language-at-a-time mode of instruction for partial EMI programmes. Given that students enrolled in partial EMI programmes are bilinguals capable of following course content in both English and Turkish, macro-level policies fall short of embracing an integrated, flexible form of bilingual instruction.

For programme administrators and policymakers across contexts, the 30 Percent Partial EMI model might seem promising in terms of its ability to offer an 'internationalization at home' experience to domestic students without straining staff resources. It could also provide a stepping stone for programmes transitioning to EMI, since a partial EMI model would allow programme administrators to increase EMI provision gradually without flipping a switch to full EMI overnight. However, practitioners should consider the needs of teachers and students in their own local contexts when deciding on an approach to EMI implementation. A more flexible model of partial EMI may be better suited for students' needs. While the 30 Percent Partial EMI model supports L1-medium education through the majority of the curricula, this particular model does not encourage bilingual classroom practices, which may detract from teachers' and students' ability to utilize the linguistic resources available to them most effectively (Mazak and Herbas-Donoso 2014).

In evaluating the 30 Percent Partial EMI model, the aim of this chapter 'is not to suggest that there is a one-size-fits-all approach' (Galloway and Ruegg 2020: 12). Rather, approaches to EMI will differ based on policy objectives and local dynamics, and comparative research is needed to investigate partial EMI implementation across cultural contexts.

References

Airey, J. (2012), '"I don't teach language": The linguistic attitudes of physics lecturers in Sweden', *AILA Review*, 25: 64–79.

Aizawa, I., and H. Rose (2019), 'An analysis of Japan's English as medium of instruction initiatives within higher education: The gap between meso-level policy and micro-level practice', *Higher Education*, 77 (6): 1125–42.

Başıbek, N., Dolmacı, M., Cengiz, B. C., Bür, B., Dilek, Y., and Kara, B. (2014), 'Lecturers' perceptions of English medium instruction at engineering departments of higher education: A study on partial English medium instruction at some state universities in Turkey', *Procedia – Social and Behavioral Sciences*, 116: 1819–25.

British Council and TEPAV (2015), *The State of English in Higher Education in Turkey: A Baseline Study*, British Council. Available online: https://www.britishcouncil.org.tr/sites/default/files/he_baseline_study_book_web_-_son.pdf.

Chou, M. H. (2018), 'Speaking anxiety and strategy use for learning English as a foreign language in full and partial English-medium instruction contexts', *TESOL Quarterly*, 52 (3): 611–33.

Curle, S., Jablonkai, R., Mittelmeier, J., Sahan, K., and Veitch, A. (2020a), 'English medium part 1: Literature review', in N. Galloway (ed.), *English in Higher Education* (Report No. 978-0-86355-977-8), British Council. Available online: https://www.teachingenglish.org.uk/article/english-higher-education-%E2%80%93-english-medium-part-1-literature-review.

Curle, S., Yuksel, D., Soruç, A., and Altay, M. (2020b), 'Predictors of English medium instruction academic success: English proficiency versus first language medium', *System*. Available online: https://doi.org/10.1016/j.system.2020.102378.

Galloway, N., and Rose, H. (2015), *Introducing Global Englishes*, Abingdon: Routledge.

Galloway, N., and Ruegg, R. (2020), 'The provision of student support on English medium instruction programmes in Japan and China', *Journal of English for Academic Purposes*, 45. Available online: https://doi.org/10.1016/j.jeap.2020.100846.

Günay, D., and Günay, A. (2011), '1933'den Günümüze Türk Yükseköğretiminde Niceliksel Gelişmeler' [Quantitative developments in Turkish higher education since 1933], *Yükseköğretim ve Bilim Dergisi*, 1 (1): 1–22.

Kamaşak, R., Sahan, K., and Rose, H. (2021), 'Linguistic challenges and learner characteristics in English-medium university programs', *Journal of English for Academic Purposes*, 49: 1–16. Available online: https://doi.org/10.1016/j.jeap.2020.100945.

Karakaş, A. (2019), 'A critical look at the phenomenon of "a mixed-up use of Turkish and English" in English-medium instruction universities in Turkey', *Journal of Higher Education and Science/Yükseköğretim ve Bilim Dergisi*, 9 (2): 205–15.

Kim, J., Kim, E. G., and Kweon, S. (2018), 'Challenges in implementing English-medium instruction: Perspectives of humanities and social sciences professors teaching engineering students', *English for Specific Purposes*, 51: 111–23.

Kırkgöz, Y. (2009), 'Globalization and English language policy in Turkey', *Educational Policy*, 23 (5): 663–84.

Kırkgöz, Y. (2014), 'Students' perceptions of English language versus Turkish language used as the medium of instruction in higher education in Turkey', *Turkish Studies*, 9 (12): 443–59.

Macaro, E. (2015), 'English medium instruction: Time to start asking some difficult questions', *Modern English Teacher*, 24 (2): 4–7.

Macaro, E. (2018), *English Medium Instruction: Content and Language in Policy and Practice*, Oxford: Oxford University Press.

Macaro, E., Curle, S., Pun, J., An, J., and Dearden, J. (2018), 'A systematic review of English medium instruction in higher education', *Language Teaching*, 51 (1): 36–76.

Mazak, C. M., and Herbas-Donoso, C. (2014), 'Translanguaging practices and language ideologies in Puerto Rican university science education', *Critical Inquiry in Language Studies*, 11 (1): 27–49.

Moncada-Comas, B., and Block, D. ([2019] 2021), 'CLIL-ised EMI in practice: Issues arising', *The Language Learning Journal*, 49 (6): 686–98. Available online: https://doi.org/10.1080/09571736.2019.1660704.

ÖSYM (2020), *2020 Yükseköğretim Kurumları Sınavı Kılavuzu* [2020 Higher education institutions exam manual]. Available online: https://www.osym.gov.tr/TR,19226/2020-yuksekogretim-kurumlari-sinavi-yks-kilavuzu.html.

Sahan, K. (2020a), 'Variations of English-medium instruction: Comparing policy and practice in Turkish higher education', PhD diss., University of Oxford, Oxford, UK.

Sahan, K. (2020b), 'ELF interactions in English-medium engineering classrooms', *ELT Journal*, 74 (4): 418–27. Available online: https://doi.org/10.1093/elt/ccaa033.

Selvi, A. F. (2014), 'The medium-of-instruction debate in Turkey: Oscillating between national ideas and bilingual ideals', *Current Issues in Language Planning*, 15 (2): 133–52.

Tange, H. (2012), 'Organising language at the international university: Three principles of linguistic organisation', *Journal of Multilingual and Multicultural Development*, 33 (3): 287–300.

Wang, W., and Curdt-Christiansen, X. L. (2019), 'Translanguaging in a Chinese–English bilingual education programme: A university-classroom ethnography', *International Journal of Bilingual Education and Bilingualism*, 22 (3): 322–37.

Part II
Meso-analysis

8

English-Medium Education in Austria: General Trends and Individual Initiatives in Institutional Policy

Ute Smit and Miya Komori-Glatz

Introduction

With its imperial heritage, its location at the heart of Europe and a reputation for high quality of life, Austria has a somewhat paradoxical parallel tradition of being both strongly German speaking and – particularly with regard to its capital city Vienna – highly international. This is reflected in its higher education (HE) landscape. Like most European countries, Austria has experienced a wave of English-medium programmes (EMPs) in the past thirty years since it kicked off in the 1990s. The number of new EMPs increased remarkably in the early years of this millennium (Wächter and Maiworm 2014), while recent years have seen a slower push for more such programmes. With this rise in EMPs came, as in other European countries, a rise in research into English-medium education (EME) from which general trends can be extrapolated.

This chapter thus aims to provide an overview of and key insights into EME in Austria. It starts by sketching the Austrian HE landscape and draws on extant research to identify general trends and sometimes surprising policy patterns. It then highlights two diverse institutions to illustrate how these have implemented EME and finishes with some brief conclusions.

Austrian higher education landscape

Situated in central Europe, Austria presently has nine million inhabitants, which makes it a middle-sized member of the European Union.[1] While a monolingual self-image is generally encountered in official Austria (Cillia and Vetter 2013), there is a high level of multilingualism among individuals, especially in the larger cities of Vienna, Linz and Graz. HE has a long-standing history, with the University of Vienna – founded in 1365 – being among the oldest universities in Europe and the oldest still active German-speaking university in the world. Since then, many other research universities have been founded in various Austrian cities, resulting in twenty-two such universities at the time of writing. All of these are publicly funded and cater to 76 per cent of the present student population of almost 3,49,000. The next biggest share of students – 55,000 or 16 per cent – attend one of the twenty-one Universities of Applied Sciences (UAS), which leaves smaller numbers for the fourteen teacher education institutions (4 per cent) and twenty private institutions that, together, host 3.5 per cent of Austrian students.[2] Given the aim of our chapter, we will focus on the two largest HE strands, that is, research universities and UAS.

As illustrated by the basic information covered in Table 8.1, the two main strands of Austrian HE differ in a few fundamental ways. Research universities cover all educational levels – from bachelor to PhD – and do so in a wide range of academic specializations. UAS, on the other hand, offer bachelor and master programmes that fall into four main areas of direct relevance to the world of work. More precisely, UAS, founded in the 1990s, aim to offer the kinds of diversified HE qualifications required for the increasingly professional specializations found in industry and society more generally. Additionally, UAS also run part-time programmes and are thus characterized by fixed timetables and catering for lifelong learning (Gaisch and Aichinger 2018).

While graduate employability and professional experience are becoming more relevant for research universities as well, traditional HEIs are still primarily driven by a fundamentally academic interest in building up knowledge at an individual level as well as contributing to extant research (see Chapter 3 in this volume for a related discussion of EMI in China). This is not only visible in the wide range of academic areas in which they offer education up to PhD level (and beyond) but also in the relevance given to economically less marketable areas, such as humanities and arts, as well as the non-applied natural sciences.

Despite these general differences, both HE strands reveal a good deal of similarity with regard to the role of language in their activities. Most importantly, there are no explicit language policy (LP) regulations or documents. Information related to language(s) is typically integrated in internationalization strategies and the universities' 'development plans'. These documents are issued regularly as the basis for budgetary talks but are also made available publicly on the

Table 8.1 Overview of Austrian Higher Education Institutions (HEIs)

		Research universities	Universities of Applied Sciences
Students	Total	2,64,945	55,203
	Female/male (in %)	53.6/46.4	49.8/50.2
Study programmes	Total	1,125	496
	BA	363	258
	MA	599	238
	BA+MA jointly	42	–
	PhD	121	–
	Part-time	–	177
Main fields of study (by frequency of programmes)		Humanities and arts	Economics and social sciences
		Natural sciences	Technology and engineering
		Technology end engineering	Applied sciences
		Economics and social sciences	Health sciences
		Law	
		Medicine	

Source: Based on Dannerer et al. (2021: 287–8).

institutional websites. As such, they provide a useful proxy for examining HEIs' attitudes towards and concrete policies relating to language. The next section summarizes previous research investigating such policy documents to identify some key language-related trends in Austrian HEIs.

General trends in Austrian EME

As a small country, research into EME in Austria has been relatively concentrated on a handful of institutions, although interest has blossomed in recent years. Smit's (2010) seminal work was the first Austrian study analysing English as the medium of classroom interaction in a post-secondary tourism college that was one of the earliest institutions to run EME. Following this, Unterberger's (2014) dissertation project investigated the macro level of policy, this time at one of the country's research universities, WU Vienna of Economics and Business. This study focused on the implementation of EMPs, including a policy analysis of national and institutional documents and interviews with the university management (Unterberger 2012; Unterberger 2014; Unterberger and Wilhelmer 2011). This was complemented by Komori-Glatz's (2017b) doctoral thesis, which examined interaction in EME at the same institution (see also Komori-Glatz 2017a, 2018, under review; Komori-Glatz and Schmidt-Unterberger 2018 2021). In the UAS sector, Gaisch has examined EME in the context of internationalization and quality management (Gaisch 2014, 2016; Gaisch and Aichinger 2018).

Indeed, internationalization has emerged as highly relevant across all these institutions, taking on an important role in the universities' development plans. In the resulting internationalization processes, EME plays a significant part and is likely to do so for some time to come (Austrian Federal Ministry of Education, Science and Research 2020). At the same time, it is commonly regarded as the means for effecting internationalization, rather than an end in itself. This is often manifested in numerous references to internationalization with an underlying assumption that this requires EME, but relatively few explicit references to EME itself (Saarinen and Nikula 2013; Unterberger 2014).

On the other hand, there is also a clear trend across the institutions for the maintenance of German as the main medium of instruction (Dannerer 2020). Despite the attention given to EME in Austria, the proportion of all students enrolled in EMPs was only 1.8 per cent in the latest ACA survey (Wächter and Maiworm 2014). Though this figure has certainly risen in the past few years and EMPs are still being introduced at individual institutions, there can be no doubt that the vast majority of students in Austria still study primarily in German. These trends may be due to the historic monolingualism typical of Austria but also the economic power of the German-speaking DACH (Germany, Austria, Switzerland) region, as many international students wish to take advantage of studying in a German-speaking country. This applies both to German L1 speakers from Germany and Italy, who comprise approximately 13 per cent of the international student body in Austria,[3] and to students coming from the Central and Eastern European countries, who hope to gain a foothold in the German-speaking labour market and who jointly make up the second largest group of international students.

A recent analysis of Austrian HEI strategy and development plans (Dannerer et al. 2021) revealed that languages are generally mentioned rarely, but, when they are, they reflect the HEIs' own interpretations of internationalization, referring to (i) mobility and exchange, especially to incoming students and staff that do not speak German; (ii) study programmes, especially at master's level, that are offered in English, intending to offer quality education to local students; or, if at all, (ii) employability, in support of either German as relevant for students' later job opportunities and/or English as a prerequisite for the international world of work and of research. Across all these instances, it is striking that the notion of language, and English in particular, is positioned as a 'tool' rather than an end in itself, for example, by highlighting the role of the EMPs in facilitating internationalization-related aims. This in turn reflects the commodification of education, since introducing EME is perceived as an affordance to attract more and better international students, be included or improve their position in university rankings and accreditation schemes and stand out from the competition (Bonacina-Pugh et al. 2020; Komori-Glatz and Schmidt-Unterberger 2021).

This lack of critical awareness regarding language in general is also mirrored in a lack of systematic and systemic infrastructure for assessing and nurturing English-language proficiency in Austrian EME (Dannerer et al. 2021). While confirmation of English proficiency (usually by means of presenting certificates such as TOEFL, IELTS, etc.) typically performs a gatekeeping function at admission, there are generally minimal or no structures to support students or content lecturers throughout the programme and no exit requirements. In contrast to, for example, Denmark, where teachers are also required to present (sometimes rigorous) confirmation of a certain level of language proficiency (Dimova and Kling 2020), teachers at Austrian HEIs are both permitted and expected to be able to cope with their teaching according to their own assessment of their ability to teach in English, often without a reduction in their course load. Likewise, once admitted to the programme, students at research universities rarely receive language support or explicit language teaching. At UAS, however, language courses are frequently offered at bachelor's level, even on EMPs; this perhaps reflects the different level of responsibility the HEIs take for ensuring their students complete their programmes successfully.

Finally, although overall numbers may appear to heavily favour German-medium instruction, a more differentiated examination of the distribution of EME at the institutional level reveals that it is highly concentrated within certain disciplines. There is also some difference between types of institution, with UAS offering EMPs at both bachelor's and master's levels, while the research universities tend to focus on master's and PhD programmes. In both types of institution, the arts and humanities (apart from English and American studies programmes) largely continue to be taught through German, while the natural sciences, technical disciplines and business studies are broadly, sometimes entirely, taught in English.

To summarize, German still plays a major role in Austrian HE and is unlikely to be superseded by English any time soon. Nevertheless, EME is widely perceived as a key tool in internationalization processes, and, as in many other countries, is here to stay, particularly in certain disciplines such as the natural and technical sciences as well as business. At the same time, the conceptualization of English as a tool, rather than an end in itself, points at a lack of critical awareness towards language and thus both teachers and students are confronted with an extremely laissez-faire approach to using English as the medium of teaching and learning. In the next sections, we will present two individual institutions in more detail to illustrate how these general trends are manifested in practice.

WU Vienna University of Economics and Business

WU Vienna University of Economics and Business (WU) is a publicly funded business university in Austria's capital city, Vienna. In the 2019/20 academic year, WU counted 21,489 students, including 6,078 international students and approximately 1,000 incoming and 1,000 outgoing exchange students. A range of individual subjects and a handful of specializations, such as 'cross-functional management', 'international business' and 'international business communication', are offered in English at the undergraduate level. The university also has three bachelor's degree programmes, one of which is fully and exclusively taught in English, and fifteen master's programmes, of which eight are taught in English; a ninth will be offered as of 2021/22. Additionally, it has doctoral degrees in five disciplines, two of which are solely in English, and one in German with English tracks (WU Vienna University of Economics and Business 2020). Located on a single campus purpose-built in 2013, WU is a classic research university which caters primarily to full-time, traditional students. Its business focus does mean it is somewhat more oriented to professional practice than some of the other research universities, but it still places a high value on its research output and, increasingly, third mission. The university is keen to highlight its international orientation, with five incidences of the word 'international' on its brief 'About WU' page[4] and a full section in its latest development plan devoted to 'International orientation, mobility, cooperation, and networks' (WU Vienna University of Economics and Business 2019).

Founded in 1898 as the Imperial Export Academy, WU positions itself as having a tradition of being both international and innovative, presenting its beginnings as a 'new type of higher education institution, offering a comprehensive education in the field of international trade'.[5] Since 2000, EME has been the linchpin between these two characteristics. WU was one of the earliest Austrian adopters of the Bologna system and the first state university to introduce a fully English-taught business studies programme (a PhD in Finance, in 2005; Unterberger 2014). This was followed by a flurry of English-taught master's programmes in 2009–13, including joining the international CEMS alliance with its joint degree programmes, and rivalled only by the University of Innsbruck (Unterberger 2014). These new programmes accompanied a drive to obtain the prestigious 'triple crown' accreditation (EQUIS, AMBA and AACSB), for which English-taught courses were a requirement. In 2019, WU introduced the first fully English-taught bachelor programme in an Austrian research university, cementing its identity as a pioneer and shifting the university's strategic focus from establishing a recognizable brand and catching up with its competitors to honing its profile – and its competitive advantage – as a leader and innovator in the sector (Komori-Glatz and Schmidt-Unterberger 2021).

University of Applied Sciences Upper Austria (FH Upper Austria)

The 'Fachhochschule Oberösterreich', University of Applied Sciences Upper Austria (FH Upper Austria for short), is a regionally funded university of applied sciences.[6] It is highly involved in international research and has the strongest research output and accumulated research funds amongst Austrian UAS (Sabbatini and Kastner 2020). Founded in 1993 to provide high-quality, inclusive tertiary education in the province of Upper Austria, FH Upper Austria combines full-time and part-time studies and offers diverse specializations that are both 'practice-orientated and research-intense'.[7] It presently caters to almost six thousand students attending sixty-nine different bachelor's and master's programmes, offered on four campuses situated in the province. These campuses are not only different in location but also in terms of their specializations. The campus in Linz, the regional capital, focuses on medical engineering and applied social sciences. The campuses in Steyr and Wels, two middle-sized towns with strong industrialized traditions, specialize, respectively, in business studies and management, and in technology, engineering and applied natural sciences. The

Hagenberg campus, situated in a village close to Linz, focuses on informatics, communication and media studies.

FH Upper Austria positions internationalization as 'one of the most important pillars ... [and] a core goal in ... prepar[ing] students for careers in globally active businesses and institutions'.[8] Thanks to its 260 international partners in more than fifty-five countries worldwide, FH Upper Austria supports student mobility on an impressive scale, with more than five hundred incoming students and five hundred outgoing students, even under the Covid-19 restrictions of 2020. While all campuses have some incoming and outgoing students, the numbers reflect a relation between discipline and mobility, with lower numbers in healthcare and social studies than, for instance, technology and engineering.

Among regular students, the share of non-Austrians is 15 per cent. As a third of those are German nationals, this leaves 10 per cent or roughly 580 international students whose first language is presumably not German. This can be attributed to the two bachelor's-level and nine master's-level EMPs. While each campus offers at least one of the EMPs, the technological specializations in Wels and Hagenberg comprise the majority of eight EMPs. Additionally, there are twenty double degrees and about three hundred English-medium courses that are integrated in the German-speaking programmes, resulting in a share of English-medium courses of between 9 and 30 per cent of all courses. This offer is explicitly understood as supporting internationalization at home for all students, especially those who, for personal reasons, cannot gain study or work experience abroad. Such an inclusive approach, catering to all students and their educational success, means that some compulsory English-language teaching is included in all programmes at the bachelor's level and some at the master's level. By doing so, FH Upper Austria recognizes that, as the main lingua franca of academia, technology and industry, English is important for all students and alumni.

Conclusion

Drawing on key studies conducted over the past decade and spanning research universities and UAS, this chapter has identified general trends in Austrian EME and revealed how they are manifested in individual institutions and initiatives. As in many European countries, Austrian HE has experienced a surge in EME over the past thirty years. Numbers suggest that this rise has now reached a plateau, and English will not replace German as the general language of education, although certain disciplines such as business, applied sciences and technology continue to become increasingly dominated by English. At the same time, German also plays an important role in attracting international students to both EME and non-EME courses. While EME is perceived as a valuable tool for increasing mobility and internationalization processes, Austrian HEIs tend to see it as that rather than as an end in its own right. This is largely the case for both types of institutions, reflected in a general lack of gatekeeping and support for teachers, although there is more language teaching support for students at UAS than at the traditional research universities. A further difference can be seen in the motivations behind the internationalization processes themselves, where the FH Upper Austria's implementation of EME focuses on developing students' employability through high levels of mobility and offering internationalization at home to students unable to spend extended time abroad, whereas WU Vienna tends to see EME and internationalization as strategic moves to enhance its competitiveness on the international HE market.

While the institutions in focus can be said to be generally representative of the vast majority of Austrian HEIs, the nature of Austrian HE means there are still some niche areas that merit further research. For example, the country's strong reputation for music has a long tradition of attracting international students, which might be expected to go hand in hand with EME. Yet there has been little research into these specialist institutions to date, with preliminary investigations suggesting that these are still officially German-medium (Smit and Komori-Glatz, in progress). Similarly, the small proportion of private universities includes institutions with an explicit international orientation, such as cross-border institutions like the Central European University. In a similar vein, there is scope for further research into initiatives at a lower institutional level (e.g. individual English-medium courses offered within a German-medium bachelor's programme). There is some indication that EME may be frequently associated with more interdisciplinary subjects (as is the case at WU Vienna), and it would be interesting to see if this is the case across various institutions.

Notes

1 https://worldpopulationreview.com/countries/austria-population (last accessed 20 January 2021).
2 All numbers from February 2020; https://www.bmbwf.gv.at/Themen/HS-Uni/Hochschulsystem.html (last accessed 20 January 2021).

3 https://oead.at/fileadmin/Dokumente/oead.at/KIM/Downloadcenter/Publikationen/Zeitschriften_und_Periodika/oead.news_106_Internatonalisierung_der_Hochschulen.pdf (last accessed 20 January 2021).
4 https://www.wu.ac.at/en/the-university/about-wu (last accessed 9 January 2021).
5 https://www.wu.ac.at/en/the-university/about-wu/history (last accessed 9 January 2021).
6 Many thanks to Martina Gaisch who provided us with the necessary facts and figures.
7 https://www.fh-ooe.at/fileadmin/user_upload/fhooe/international/allgemein/docs/fhooe-international-folder-general.pdf (last accessed 20 January 2021).
8 https://www.fh-ooe.at/en/international/ (last accessed 20 January 2021).

References

Austrian Federal Ministry of Education, Science and Research (BMBWF) (2020), *National Mobility and Internationalization Strategy for Higher Education 2020–2030*.
Bonacina-Pugh, F., Barakos, E., and Chen, Q. (2020), 'Language policy in the internationalisation of higher education in Anglophone countries: The interplay between language policy as "text", "discourse" and "practice"', *Applied Linguistics Review*. https://doi.org/10.1515/applirev-2019-0148.
Cillia, R. de, and Vetter, E. (2013), *Sprachenpolitik in Österreich: Bestandsaufnahme 2011*, Frankfurt am Main: Peter Lang.
Dannerer, M. (2020), 'The university as a terrain for hidden language conflicts? German, English and the silence beyond them', *Sociolinguistica*, 34 (1): 131–54.
Dannerer, M., Gaisch, M., and Smit, U. (2021), 'Englishization "under the radar": Facts, policies and trends in Austrian higher education', in R. Gabriëls and R. Wilkinson (eds), *The Englishization of Higher Education in Europe*, 281–305, Amsterdam: Amsterdam University Press.
Dimova, S., and Kling, J. (2020), *Integrating Content and Language in Multilingual Universities*, Cham, Switzerland: Springer International.
Gaisch, M. (2014), 'Affordances for teaching in an international classroom', PhD thesis, University of Vienna, Vienna.
Gaisch, M. (2016), 'Internationalisation of second-tier higher education institutions: A look at universities of applied sciences in Austria', in Fachhochschule des BFI Wien (ed.), *Brücken bauen – Perspektiven gestalten: für Wirtschaft, Hochschule und Öffentlichkeit*, 1–9, Vienna: Fachhochschule des BFI Wien.
Gaisch, M., and Aichinger, R. (2018), 'Second-tier higher education institutions and the diversity challenge: Structural components adopted through a Germanic lens', in R. Latiner Raby and E. J. Valeau (eds), *Handbook of Comparative Studies on Community Colleges and Global Counterparts*, 217–33, Cham, Switzerland: Springer International.

Komori-Glatz, M. (2017a), '(B)ELF in multicultural student teamwork', *Journal of English as a Lingua Franca*, 6 (1): 83–109.

Komori-Glatz, M. (2017b), 'English as a business lingua franca in multicultural student teamwork: An EMEMUS study', PhD thesis, University of Vienna, Vienna.

Komori-Glatz, M. (2018), '"Cool my doubt is erased": Constructive disagreement and creating a psychologically safe space in multicultural student teamwork', *Journal of English as a Lingua Franca*, 7 (2): 285–306.

Komori-Glatz, M. (Under review), 'A first step on the road to EMEMUS: Using ROAD-MAPPING at an Austrian business university', in E. Dafouz and U. Smit (eds) *English-Medium Education across Multilingual University Setting: Applications and Critical Evaluations of the ROAD-MAPPING Framework*. London: Routledge.

Komori-Glatz, M., and Schmidt-Unterberger, B. (2021), 'From profiling to pioneering: The drivers behind English-medium education at WU Vienna', *European Journal of Language Policy/Revue européenne de politique linguistique*, 13 (2): 239–58.

Komori-Glatz, M., and Schmidt-Unterberger, B. (2018), 'Creating the international managers of tomorrow, today? Stakeholder perspectives on English-medium business education', in T. Sherman and J. Nekvapil (eds), *English in Business and Commerce: Interactions and Policies; English in Europe Volume 5*, 310–34, Boston: De Gruyter.

Saarinen, T., and Nikula, T. (2013), 'Implicit policy, invisible language: Policies and practices of international degree programmes in Finnish higher education', in A. Doiz, D. Lasagabaster and J. M. Sierra (eds), *English-Medium Instruction at Universities: Global Challenges*, 131–50, Bristol, Buffalo: Multilingual Matters.

Sabbatini, G., and Kastner, J. (2020), 'Forschung & Entwicklung an Fachhochschulen in Österreich: Leistung und Erfolgsgeschichte trotz herausfordernder Rahmenbedingungen?', *e & i Elektrotechnik und Informationstechnik*, 137 (1): 3–10.

Smit, U. (2010), *English as a Lingua Franca in Higher Education: A Longitudinal Study of Classroom Discourse*, Berlin: Mouton de Gruyter.

Smit, U., and Komori-Glatz, M. (2022), *EME in Music: International Higher Education of a Different Kind? 7th ICLHE Conference*, Maastricht, October, 18–22,

Unterberger, B. (2012), 'English-medium programmes at Austrian business faculties: A status quo survey on national trends and a case study on programme design and delivery', *AILA Review*, 25: 80–100.

Unterberger, B., and Wilhelmer, N. (2011), 'English-medium education in economics and business studies: Capturing the status quo at Austrian universities', *ITL – International Journal of Applied Linguistics*, (161): 90–110.

Unterberger, B. J. (2014), 'English-medium degree programmes in Austrian tertiary business studies', PhD thesis, University of Vienna, Vienna.

Wächter, B., and Maiworm, F. (2014), *English-Taught Programmes in European Higher Education: The State of Play in 2014*, Bonn: Lemmens Medien.

WU Vienna University of Economics and Business (2019), 'Strategic plan of WU (Vienna University of Economics and Business)'. Available online: https://www.

wu.ac.at/fileadmin/wu/h/strategy/documents/Entwicklungsplan_EN_ab_1.6.2019.pdf (accessed 9 January 2021).

WU Vienna University of Economics and Business (2020), 'Facts and figures'. Available online: https://www.wu.ac.at/fileadmin/wu/h/structure/about/publications/aktuelle_Brosch%C3%BCren/Facts-Figures_web.pdf (accessed 9 January 2021).

9

Profiling English-Medium Instruction in Colombian Universities: Policies and Practices

Norbella Miranda and Mario Molina-Naar

Introduction

Colombia is one of the most linguistically diverse countries in Latin America, with more than sixty Indigenous languages and two Creoles, in addition to members of the Deaf and Romani communities (Valencia Giraldo et al., forthcoming). Although it is considered a fast-growing upper-middle-income country (World Bank 2019), the divide between the rich and the poor still remains, with inequality rates persistently high (Alvaredo et al. 2017), making it difficult for many to pursue university studies. Higher education in Colombia is provided by the public and private sectors and has a total enrolment of 17.9 per cent of the 18- to 24-year-old population (OECD and the World Bank 2012).

The current legislation for undergraduate programmes demands that curricula incorporate the development of foreign-language communicative competence (MoE 2010), particularly English, as a strategy for internationalization (CESU 2014). Consejo Nacional de Educación Superior[1] (CESU) guidelines also include 'offering subjects in a second language' (139), understood as English, in all academic programmes, officially opening the door to English-medium instruction (EMI) in the country. Similar to Latin America and other regions where it is attached to internationalization (Bowles and Murphy 2020; Dafouz and Smit 2020; Tejada-Sánchez and Molina-Naar 2020), EMI seems to be gaining supporters in Colombian higher education. In countries such as Spain, research shows that some academic programmes are offering most of their courses in English as an internationalization at home (IaH) strategy (Escobar Urmeneta 2020), while in Brazil (Martínez 2016) and Mexico (Escalona Sibaja

2020), initiatives have been adopted through government-sponsored projects at the national level.

The Colombian educational policy for language teaching and learning, the National Program of Bilingualism (NPB) issued in 2004, has also privileged English in all levels of education as a means to 'insert the country into universal communication processes, in the global economy and in cultural openness, with internationally comparable standards' (MoE 2006: 6). This policy is in line with the Organization for Economic Cooperation and Development (OECD) and the World Bank's (2012) recommendation to promote the acquisition of competence in a second language to be better prepared for a competitive labour market which is increasingly global. The inclusion of an English component in the national exit test for undergraduates, Saber Pro, and its alignment with the Common European Framework of Reference (CEFR) (Council of Europe 2002) attest to the relevance of the English language in Colombian higher education. Nevertheless, the results of the Saber Pro exam do not match the policy goals. Benavides (2021) found that 19 per cent of senior university students are reaching the pre-intermediate B1 competence level recommended by the CESU and 8 per cent obtain the intermediate B2 level signalled in the NPB. According to Céspedes Gómez and Laverde Montero (2020), factors associated with students' results in nursing programmes included their financial resources, academic overload and lack of time to attend the courses offered by their institutions, besides their proficiency level at the start of the programme.

Research on English-language teaching in Colombian higher education has not particularly centred on EMI. Some of the EMI-related studies have focused on the implementation of content-based instruction and collaboration between faculty language and content professors (e.g. Sierra and Tamayo 2016) and the implementation of content and language integrated learning (CLIL) for the internationalization of the curriculum (IoC) (Montoya and Salamanca 2017) and at home (Corrales et al. 2016). We have also seen a recent concern for acknowledging the multilingual nature of the country in higher education (Araujo Quiroz 2013), addressing pedagogy and internationalization from a critical intercultural and decolonial perspective (Ortiz et al. 2020), and a critical analysis of the discourses around internationalization and institutional language policy creation (Miranda et al. 2016). Similar to other contexts where EMI is emerging, there is a need for more evidenced-based research (Bowles and Murphy 2020) to analyse the current status of EMI at the meso level of universities where initiatives are taking place. This chapter addresses this gap by looking at two questions:

1. What institutional policies promote EMI in Colombian universities?
2. What practices at the institutional level allow for the implementation of EMI in Colombian universities?

The study

Setting and participants

This research was conducted in six higher education institutions located in four main cities in Colombia. Selection criteria included a balance between public and private universities – that all six universities were offering EMI courses and that they were accredited by the MoE (see Table 9.1). Participants included professors involved in EMI initiatives or teaching from each university (see Table 9.2). Spanish is the first language of all participants, and they self-reported a C1 or C2 English proficiency level according to the CEFR.

Data collection and analysis

Data were collected using semi-structured interviews and institutional documents during the second semester of 2020. Participants were contacted through email and WhatsApp. Interviews were conducted in Spanish, via Zoom and Google Meet platforms, and recorded in agreement with the participants, who signed a consent form and completed an online survey with their socio-demographic information. We transcribed all interviews in Spanish and translated to English the relevant excerpts for publication. Methods for the policy analysis were similar to those of Rose and McKinley's (2018) investigation in EMI in Japan, where documents were downloaded from the webpages of the universities. We analysed the institutional internationalization and language policies and other documents with relevant information, such as the development plans (see Table 9.1).

We analysed the data using qualitative content analysis (Selvi 2020), which involved building a coding frame with main categories and subcategories. Our main categories were based on Dafouz and Smit's (2020) six dimensions of their ROAD MAPPING framework: Roles of English, Academic Disciplines, Management, Agents, Practices and Processes, and Internationalization and Glocalization. Our subcategories were partly driven from the theory and mainly from the data. Examples of emergent subcategories are 'Students' levels of English'

Table 9.1 Colombian Universities and Documents Analysed

University	Location	Type	Documents Analysed and Conventions
U1	Bogota	Private	• Internationalization Guidelines 2016–20 (U1.D1) • Development Plan 2016–20 (U1.D2) • Foreign Language Requirements 2016 (U1.D3)
U2	Medellín	Public	• General Statute 2011 (U2.D1) • Development Plan 2017–27 (U2.D2) • Foreign Language Competence Policy for undergraduate students 2014 (U2.D3)
U3	Medellín	Private	• Institutional Education Project 2020 (U3.D1) • International Relations Office ORI webpage (U3.D2) • Spanish and Foreign Language Policy 2016 (U3.D3)
U4	Cali	Public	• Internationalization Policy 2014 (U4.D1) • Development Plan 2015–25 (U4.D2) • Institutional Program for the Promotion, Teaching and Development of Bilingualism 2014 (U4.D3) • Reglamentation of Curriculum Policy 2017 (U4.D4)
U5	Barranquilla	Private	• Development Plan 2018–22 (U5.D1) • Second and Third Language Regulations 2013 (U5.D2)
U6	Barranquilla	Public	• Development Plan 2009–19 (U6.D1) • Policy for Teaching, Learning and Assessment of Foreign Languages with an emphasis on English, for undergraduate and graduate students 2018 (U6.D2)

and 'Institutional support for EMI practices'. The coding frame was revised and piloted with some of the interviews and then refined and used with the rest of the data. After each interview and document was analysed, we triangulated results.

One inconvenience that we experienced during the data collection process was the number of participants. We planned to interview two participants in each university: an administrator and a content expert; however, due to the multiple occupations of other potential participants, augmented by the Covid-19 pandemic, we worked with one participant from each institution. In spite of this, the information gathered was enough to answer the research questions, particularly because in several cases participants were both teachers and administrators.

Table 9.2 Participants (EMI Professors; One from Each Colombian University)

Participant	Position	Age	EMI Experience
P1	Professor at the School of Business	38	4
P2	Professor at the School of Economics	34	5
P3	Professor and head of the International Business Department	50	20
P4	Professor and director of the Language Teacher Education Programme	44	23
P5	Professor and director of the Department of Foreign Languages	52	10
P6	Professor and coordinator of the Foreign Language Teacher Education Programme	58	25

Findings

In what follows, we present our findings in two sections following the research questions. For each section, we discuss two salient trends. Our findings show that EMI has been in practice for more than two decades in some of the participating universities, but these practices have not always been ruled in official policies. A central issue, markedly in public institutions, is that students' English proficiency levels partly determine the actions taken at the institutional level to support EMI.

Understanding EMI from institutional policies

The analysis of policy documents shows that internationalization and languages, particularly English, are key to universities' medium-term plans. Not all universities have overt and explicit institutional language policy documents containing a rationale, definition of terms, staffing matters, the role of different languages or guidelines for EMI. However, they present issues related to EMI, internationalization and languages in documents of other kinds, such as universities' development plans and language requirements for graduation. In all cases, these documents have been produced by collective agents: the University Senate, the Academic Council and the academic unit in charge of language teaching. Two main findings in institutional documents are: the 'natural' link between internationalization and languages, and the tension between multilingualism and English.

The 'natural' link between internationalization and languages

All universities surveyed see languages as a natural means to achieve internationalization goals. According to U6, 'The internationalization of the curriculum, interculturality and IaH ... require an increasingly high communicative competence in foreign languages from undergraduate and graduate students' (U6.D2, p. 3).[2] Similarly, U5 states that consolidating student mobility is a challenge that will be faced through 'the strengthening of programs for multilingualism' (U5.D1, p. 33), among other strategies. Furthermore, U4's internationalization policy includes 'subjects with an international component and taught in a second language' (U4.D1, p. 6) as a deliberate planned action for increasing IaH.

In the same vein, some universities' language policy goals name their contribution to the 'international knowledge networks' (U4.D3, p. 2) or 'the need of a gradual transformation to curriculum approaches that facilitate flexibilization and IoC, as well as international mobility' (U6.D2, p. 2). Other language goals incorporate the development of intercultural competence (U1.D3, U2.D2, U5.D2), while the most common language policy intention encompasses the improvement of communicative competence (U1.D3, U2.D3, U4.D3, U6.D2). Only a few universities connect their language or internationalization policies to macro policy recommendations such as the OECD and the World Bank's (2012) or the MoE's (2010, 2006). Nevertheless, this does not mean that these recommendations are disregarded when outlining institutional documents or enacting practices.

The tension between multilingualism and English

All language policies of participating universities speak of several foreign languages (U1.D3, U2.D3, U3.D3, U4.D2, U5.D2, U6.D2), and at the same time, many set competence in English as a graduation requisite (U1.D3, U2.D3, U4.D4, U6.D2), mainly in a pre-intermediate B1 level for most undergraduate programmes, B2 for international business and C1 for foreign language teaching education programmes. EMI courses are a graduation requirement for all programmes in U1 (U1.D3) and mandatory for the international business programme in U3 (U3.D3), while U4 recommends them to improve language competence in order to impact internationalization (U4.D1).

By contrast, some universities alluded to a context-sensitive approach that considers the region's actual needs and takes a critical stance to globalization through a territorial approach (U2.D2, U4.D2), which seems to be at odds with the extended focus on English. This is the case of U2:

> Taking into account the particularity of the places, territories and networks of which it is a part, [the territorial approach] proposes concrete actions to improve the specific conditions of territories and ... incorporates the opportunities that each territory offers.
>
> [This understanding] leads to rethinking internationalization and regionalization strategies so as not to reproduce unequal globalization – or regionalization – schemes of intellectual work that contribute to the homogenization of knowledge. (U2.D2, p. 37–8)

In practical terms, regulations following a territorial approach translate into the acknowledgement of local languages, such as in one institution where Indigenous students enrolled in the pedagogy of mother earth programme can comply with the second-language requirement through their proficiency in Spanish (U2.D3). The territorial approach seems to attempt to harmonize with an ecological perspective to language policy with space for Spanish and Indigenous languages, as well as English and other foreign languages. In this sense, the inclusion of several foreign languages in institutional documents found in this study seems to be a necessary, yet insufficient step to lay the ground to a more inclusive multilingual university, a goal explicitly stated in different documents. In the next section of the chapter, we present findings from interviews with professors and administrators to analyse EMI in practice.

A look at EMI practice

Two salient trends related to EMI practices emerged in our research: the rationale for EMI initiatives and institutional support. Both top-down and bottom-up actions were identified, as the incorporation of EMI depends on the nature of each academic programme and the professors teaching the courses.

Rationale for EMI practices

All six participants mentioned that EMI practices in their institutions are linked to the academic disciplines in which they are implemented, the students' English proficiency levels and/or the university's internationalization initiatives.

According to our participants, EMI is seen as a chief component in academic programmes such as international business and business administration because these have 'an international profile' (P5) and English is 'the lingua franca' which makes professionals in these areas 'insert in their world' (P3). In the foreign language teacher education programmes, EMI has been used for more than two decades to strengthen students' language levels, something they need to become teachers. In U4, EMI has been initiated in this programme 'mostly ... by professors who already master the language and propose some courses along these lines' (P4). Something similar occurs in U6, where EMI courses 'are proposed by professors' who have just finished their studies in 'Germany, France, or England' (P6). In both language teacher education programmes, French is also used as a medium of instruction.

Regarding the students' English levels, P2 identified differences based on the students' backgrounds (private vs. public school and urban vs. rural areas); he stated that the students from the public university and rural areas often have a lower proficiency level, so he tends to be 'more lenient' in the classroom. By contrast, P3 in a private university mentioned that most students have a B2-C1 level; thus, when they are close to finishing their studies, they take 'project courses', small seminars in which they write a research proposal in English. Language proficiency seems to be an issue worth considering in public universities more than in private ones. Finally, P1 revealed that, despite their level, 'the students are much shier when they have to speak English'; so it makes sense to have a language expert who helps them to leave 'their comfort zone'.

Concerning EMI practices and internationalization, P1 expressed that EMI courses are important because 'part of what accreditation organizations evaluate is the degree of internationalization of the programmes in the school'. P5 explained that she and her team 'are part of an IaH Task Force' which attempts to 'determine all of the aspects that will be included in the IaH policy [and]; EMI courses are part of this discussion'. Last, P6 stated that, jointly with the internationalization office, 'we are trying to persuade professors who completed their studies in English-speaking and French-speaking countries to use of English and French as media of instruction in their courses'.

Institutional support for EMI emergent practices

Four participants mentioned support strategies for professors and students. In U1, collaboration between content and language experts has happened for some years now; P1 stated that, thanks to the support of the English teacher, she can concentrate on the communicative competence and added, "I feel lucky to be working with him." In U5, they had a learning community with professors and administrators who met for three years to discuss EMI and internationalization-related issues; P5 claimed that this experience 'is even serving as a basis for the IaH policy'.

U2 and U6 provide opportunities for students to be more exposed to English and strengthen their proficiency. In U2, they host an 'English Fair' in which the students from the international business programme present projects in English and take part in cultural activities twice a year (P2). In U6, students from the language teacher education programme are sent to the United States to study English and didactics in a university for eight weeks. Once they return, they teach English to students from different majors. This immersion programme is intended to enhance 'the development and strengthening of the English learning policy at the university' (P6).

Discussion, conclusions and implications

Overall, findings match those of previous studies that associate EMI with internationalization (e.g. Bowles and Murphy 2020; Tejada-Sánchez and Molina-Naar 2020). By and large, English is indexed as the lingua academica, 'an instrument for international collaboration in higher education' (Phillipson 2010: 338) and a means for students to access knowledge. Universities' policies and participants' answers indicate a beneficial relationship between internationalization and English if the two areas are addressed in tandem through planned efforts. While not necessarily in overt and explicit language policies, strategies for internationalization are often present in documents such as development plans (Bowles and Murphy 2020), which also include programmes for language acquisition and use. Thus, the increasing importance of English and internationalization is apparent as development plans constitute a roadmap for universities' future.

EMI initiatives have existed in universities' practices longer than in policy documents, and English has often been given a privileged role in comparison with other foreign languages. Evidence of the status of English is the growth of EMI and its recommendation and the establishment of English mastery as a graduation requisite for students. In addition, deeply attached to academic disciplines, EMI courses have been part of foreign language teacher education programmes as well as international business, which require high competencies in foreign languages, particularly in English, at the present time. Following Trowler's (2014) work, Dafouz and Smit (2020) suggest that the role of language, more specifically English, in certain disciplines is of prime importance, especially because knowledge building in education is bound to specific contexts, cultures and languages. This fact does not deny the efforts to promote the national and Indigenous languages in some of the participating universities.

The study confirmed that English and EMI continue to be seen as key for the internationalization of HEIs (Tejada-Sánchez and Molina-Naar 2020; Bowles and Murphy 2020). In agreement with other studies, the connection between achieving the internationalization and/or accreditation of the curricula (Montoya and Salamanca 2017) and English-language competencies (Escobar Urmeneta 2020) partly explain the initiatives intended to help students increase their language competencies. Similar to Sierra and Tamayo's (2016) and Escalona Sibaja's (2020) works, the initiatives included collaboration between language and context experts, and fostering exchange programmes and extracurricular activities.

Universities acknowledge the importance of English as the language that serves to perform competently in academic reading and writing, research and knowledge dissemination. At the same time, they are also starting to debate and embrace a broader and more critical view of internationalization that posits a relevant role to minoritized languages and to foreign languages other than English. Findings in this chapter confirm Araujo Quiroz's (2013) and Miranda et al.'s (2016) concern for the recognition of the multilingual nature of the country, as well as the recent decolonial perspective towards language teaching that Ortiz et al. (2020) advocate. In these multilingual and decolonial perspectives, English stands in an ecological relationship with other languages, and policy decisions are sensitive to 'the particularity of the places', as it was found in U2 when referring to the territorial approach. This approach is of special relevance in the Colombian context where speakers of multiple languages coexist and regional and socio-economic differences are marked.

Considering that EMI is likely to continue growing as the literature and this study predict, a word of caution needs to be mentioned. In countries like Colombia, where enrolment in higher education remains low, particularly for minority groups and for families of low socio-economic status, and where English proficiency of students belonging to such groups is not high or even intermediate, making EMI mandatory would lead to a new form of exclusion. Planning for EMI must consider these issues besides others involving the positioning of universities or accreditation plans if education is meant to contribute to social justice, thus, following the recommendation that a one-size-fits-all internationalization model is neither appropriate nor desirable in HEIs. By contrast, internationalization and language policies with a territorial and ecological approach to multilingualism seem to be adequate.

More research on current EMI practices from a bottom-up approach would be needed in order to nourish institutional policies and improve classroom practices at the micro level (see e.g. the micro-level chapters in this volume); this is because, above all, it is the responsibility of HEIs to guarantee the effective learning of local students. Also, while promoting international cooperation, partnerships and exchange, three of the original values associated with the internationalization of higher education is of great relevance, it would be equally important to foster knowledge and research from a national perspective, and thus, equip students with the adequate social and professional competencies that will help them to be better prepared to work for their own communities.

Notes

1 The National Council of Higher Education (CESU) is the organism of the national government linked to the Ministry of Education with functions of coordination, planning, recommendation and advice. It proposes policies and plans for higher education.
2 The conventions are used in order to avoid writing the complete name of the documents in every citation (see Table 9.1).

References

Alvaredo, F., Chancel, L., Piketty, T., Saez, E., and Zucman, G. (2017), *World Inequality Report 2018*, World Inequality Lab.

Araujo Quiroz, C. B. (2013), 'Bilingüismo: herramienta clave en el contexto universitario', *Revista Historia de la Educación Latinoamericana*, 15 (20): 189–204. ISSN: 0122-7238.

Benavides, J. E. (2021), 'Level of English in Colombian higher education: A decade of stagnation', *Profile: Issues in Teachers' Professional Development*, 23 (1): 57–73. Available online: https://doi.org/10.15446/profile.v23n1.83135.

Bowles, H. C., and Murphy, A. C. (2020), 'EMI and the internationalization of universities: An overview', in H. C. Bowles and A. C. Murphy (eds), *English-Medium Instruction and the Internationalization of Universities*, 1–26, Cham, Switzerland: Palgrave Macmillan.

Céspedes Gómez, D. P., and Laverde Montero, J. (2020), 'Factores Asociados en el Desempeño de Estudiantes de Enfermería – Pruebas Saber-Pro Inglés', MA diss., Universidad El Bosque, Bogotá.

Consejo Nacional de Educación (CESU) (2014), *Acuerdo por lo superior 2034*, Bogotá: CESU.

Corrales, K. A., Rey, L. A. P., & Escamilla, N. S. (2016). 'Is EMI enough? Perceptions from university professors and students.' *Latin American Journal of Content & Language Integrated Learning*, 9(2), 318–344. https://doi.org/10.5294/laclil.2016.9.2.4

Council of Europe (2002), *Common European Framework of Reference for Languages: Learning, Teaching, Assessment*, Strasbourg: Cambridge University Press.

Dafouz, E., and Smit, U. (2020), *ROAD-MAPPING English Medium Education in the Internationalised University*, Cham, Switzerland: Palgrave Macmillan.

Escalona Sibaja, M. (2020), *Professional Development for EMI Faculty in Mexico: The Case of Bilingual, International, and Sustainable Universities*, New York: Routledge.

Escobar Urmeneta, C. (2020), 'From EMI to ICLHE: Teacher development for L2-medium instruction in a teacher education institution', in N. Sánchez-Pérez (ed.), *Teacher Training for English-Medium Instruction in Higher Education*, 179–204, Hershey, PA: IGI Global.

Martínez, R. (2016), 'English as a medium of instruction (EMI) in Brazilian higher education: Challenges and opportunities', in K. Finardi (ed.), *English in Brazil: Views, Policies and Programs*, 191–228, Londrina: Eduel.

Miranda, N., Berdugo, M., and Tejada, H. (2016), 'Conflicting views on language policy and planning at a Colombian university', *Current Issues in Language Planning*, 17 (3-4): 422–40. DOI: 10.1080/14664208.2016.1204052.

MoE (2006), 'Estándares básicos de competencias en lenguas extranjeras: inglés' [Basic standards for foreign language competences]. National Ministry of Education.

MoE (2010), 'Decreto 1295 de 2010 [Decree 1295, 2010]. National Ministry of Education.

Montoya, S. I., and Salamanca, C. (2017), 'Uso del enfoque AICLE/CLIL como estrategia de internacionalización del currículo en una institución de educación superior colombiana', *Latin American Journal of Content and Language Integrated Learning*, 10 (1): 105–31. DOI: 10.5294/laclil.2017.10.1.5.OECD and the World Bank (2012), *Reviews of National Policies for Education: Tertiary Education in Colombia*, Paris: OECD & the World Bank.

Ortiz, J. M., Usma, J. A., and Gutiérrez, C. P. (2020), 'Critical intercultural dialogue opening new paths to internationalisation in higher education: Repositioning local languages and cultures in foreign language policies', in U. Lundgren, P. Castro and J. Woodin (eds), *Educational Approaches to Internationalization through Intercultural Dialogues: Reflections on Theory and Practice*, 71–85, London: Routledge.

Phillipson, R. (2010), 'English in globalisation, a lingua franca or a lingua Frankensteinia?' *TESOL Quarterly*, 43 (2): 335–9.

Rose, H., and McKinley, J. (2018). 'Japan's English-medium instruction initiatives and the globalization of higher education', *Higher Education*, 75 (1): 111–29.

Selvi, A. F. (2020). 'Qualitative content analysis', in J. McKinley and H. Rose (eds), *The Routledge Handbook of Research Methods in Applied Linguistics*, 440–52, London: Routledge.

Sierra, N., and Tamayo, L. (2016), 'La implementación del Modelo Adjunto de la Enseñanza Basada en Contenidos en un Laboratorio de Química Farmacéutica en una universidad pública colombiana', *Lenguaje*, 44 (2): 341–69.

Tejada-Sánchez, I., and Molina-Naar, M. (2020), 'English medium instruction and the internationalization of higher education in Latin America: A case study from a Colombian university', *Latin American Journal of Content and Language Integrated Learning*, 13(2): 339–67. https://doi.org/10.5294/laclil.2020.13.2.8.

Trowler, P. (2014), 'Depicting and researching disciplines: Strong and moderate essentialist approaches', *Studies in Higher Education*, 39 (10): 1720–31.

Valencia Giraldo, S., Miranda, N., and de Mejia, A. M. (2022), 'Multilingual Colombia: Dimensions of linguistic and cultural diversity', in N. Miranda, A. M. de Mejía and S. Valencia Giraldo (eds), *Language Education in Multilingual Colombia: Critical Perspectives and Voices from the Field*. New York: Routledge.

World Bank (2019), *Data for Colombia, Upper Middle Income*. Available online: https://data.worldbank.org/?locations=CO-XT.

10

A Longitudinal Perspective on Language Ideological Debates in Estonian Higher Education: Current Trends and Tensions

Josep Soler

Introduction

Even though the growth of English-medium instruction (EMI) in higher education has been well documented for some time, particularly in Europe (Wächter and Maiworm 2014), its exponential increase in university systems around the world, notably in Asia, 'has preceded and outpaced empirical research' (Galloway et al. 2017: 9). This is despite the significant amount of attention that applied linguists have devoted to investigating EMI and its implications both for individuals (e.g. students' and teachers' beliefs and practices about EMI) and for institutions alike (e.g. university and/or governmental language policymaking) (for an overview of recent work on these two scales, see Macaro et al. 2018). The implementation of EMI programmes, in addition, has consequences that go beyond issues of an applied nature. In fact, very often, the decision to establish EMI programmes responds rather to questions of economic and political order, linked to universities' internationalization efforts and to governments' political-economic goals (Piller and Cho 2013). As a result, researchers have also concerned themselves with the discursive dimension of EMI development, scrutinizing the tensions and ambiguities it generates for local language ecologies, where different actors may compete in agenda-setting struggles (Hultgren 2014).

In line with these critical discursive orientations to EMI, in this chapter I investigate the growth of EMI as a phenomenon in Estonia. In particular, I explore the linguistic representations emerging from two language ideological debates situated in two different time frames: the first in 2012, and the second in 2018–20. Both debates revolved around similar questions concerning the future of the Estonian language in the country's higher education system in the context of an increasing presence of English (particularly for teaching and learning purposes). The analysis focuses on the opinions offered in public media by key stakeholders from Estonian universities (mostly professors and administration officials), with a particular focus on members from the University of Tartu (UT), considered by law as Estonia's national university (University of Tartu Act 1995).

The central argument to be developed in the chapter is that, in the face of an increase and consolidation of EMI programmes in the country, linguistic polarization (i.e. the opposition between Estonian and English) has also grown in parallel, reaching new heat levels as in the neighbouring Nordic countries (Kuteeva et al. 2020). In fact, the contrast between the two debates (the 2012 vs. 2018–20) allows mapping of the consolidation of the two camps discursively confronted in language ideological debates around the internationalization of higher education: the 'internationalists' versus the 'culturalists' (Hultgren et al. 2014: 2). To substantiate the analysis presented below, I draw on previous work of mine on the topic of language policy and the internationalization of Estonian higher education (see Soler (2019) and Soler and Vihman (2018) for the 2012 debate; and Soler and Rozenvalde (2021) for the second debate). Before delving into the details of the debates and the main arguments aired in them, in the next section I first provide a brief contextualization of EMI development in the UT. I conclude the chapter by sketching the potential implications at a practical level of these language ideological debates, which, I argue, extend beyond a simple struggle for the discursive hegemony between key stakeholders in competition.

Overview of EMI development at the University of Tartu

EMI development at the UT can be divided into three periods: initial efforts (1993–2004), expansion (2005–14) and consolidation (2015–to present) (see both Soler and Vihman (2018) and Vihman and Tensing (2014) for lengthier overviews of the internationalization trends at UT). EMI courses and programmes were established only after 1991, following the collapse of the Soviet Union. UT acted fast in that regard, and after joining the International Student Exchange Programs (www.isep.org) in 1992, UT developed Estonia's first EMI programme, 'Semester in the Baltics', designed to attract international students on the basis of the English language. Those early efforts for EMI development in the 1990s may be considered to some extent symbolically and politically motivated, in line with what has been termed the country's return to the West (Kasekamp 2010).

Indeed, it was not until 2005 that the first fully fledged EMI programme would be in place at UT: a master's programme in the Baltic Sea Region Studies, run by the Faculty of Social Sciences. This first EMI MA programme emerged in the context of a more conscious and organized effort by the university to develop English-taught courses and programmes in order to enhance its international dimension. This was in line, at the time, with both state and institutional policy frameworks. In that context, the 2005–14 period saw a boom in EMI programmes at UT, with fourteen newly created MA and one BA programme. In fact, in just three years (from 2010 to 2013), the proportion of EMI programmes rose from 6 per cent to 10 per cent (Soler and Vihman 2018: 27). However, the significant increase in EMI programmes did not run in parallel with an equal growth in students registered in such programmes (Klaas-Lang and Metslang (2015: 168) report a total of 5 per cent of students were enrolled in EMI programmes throughout the country in 2014).

Currently, UT offers a total of twenty-four MA programmes taught in English. It seems fair to say that after the period of expansion (2005–14), since 2015 UT has aimed at consolidating its EMI offer, focusing on enhancing the quality, rather than the quantity, of programmes available. UT, however, is not against exploring new options for developing programmes in different languages. Indeed, starting in 2021, the university launched a Russian-medium programme: teaching Russian as a foreign language, run by its Narva College (situated at the north-eastern Estonia-Russia border city of Narva). While not in line with the general decline of Russian-medium instruction in Estonia (Klaas-Lang and Metslang 2015), this move indicates UT's desire to continue to innovate and explore different options to enhance its offer of MA programmes internationally.

Finally, it is important to bear in mind that the above changes have happened in a country with a solid history of language policy development, indeed, in a context where policies for the protection and promotion of the national language have been considered crucial for the sustainability of the very nation (Hogan-Brun et al. 2008). In the domain of higher education, this means that, much like Latvia (Rozenvalde 2018) and Lithuania (Bulajeva and Hogan-Brun 2014), Estonia has had to reconcile two seemingly opposed trends: the historically grounded ethnocentric policies for the protection, promotion and development of the national language, and the more recent Eurocentric trends associated with the universities' internationalization efforts, which entail the fostering of multilingualism and multiculturalism. This is a crucial aspect to remember as we move on to see the language ideological debates that have unfolded in the context of Estonian higher education, to which we turn in the next section.

Language ideological debates at the University of Tartu

In what follows, I summarize the key arguments that emerged during two language ideological debates in connection with the internationalization of Estonian higher education in 2012 and 2018–20. As with every language ideological debate, moments like this represent key instances in which language ideological constructs crystalize and become more readily observable (Blommaert 1999). In this case in particular, the two debates allow us to map the emergence, evolution and consolidation of the two discursively confronted sides, the 'internationalists' versus the 'culturalists' (Hultgren et al. 2014). On the one hand, those committed to an 'internationalist' stance emphasize the global dimension of higher education and the importance for universities to become or remain internationally competitive. On the other hand, those behind 'culturalist' discourses underscore the national side of universities and their key role as institutions spearheading the protection, promotion and development of the national language and culture. While presented here as 'black-or-white', these two discursive positions are never clearly separable but appear intertwined in complex ways, particularly so in language ideological debates held publicly. Table 10.1 provides the list of items referred to in the debates below.

The 2012 debate

In October 2012, the then rector of the UT, the late Professor Volli Kalm, was invited to speak at the Pärnu Leadership Conference, just shortly after he had been nominated rector. Kalm (2012) was quoted as pronouncing the following remarks, in connection to the future of Estonian higher education:

> The difficult questions regarding the future of Estonian higher education are tied to the competitiveness of Estonian HE compared to English HE. Master's and doctoral studies are inevitably becoming more English-based. Students will increasingly go abroad for niche disciplines ... We are often unaware of the price of preserving Estonian-language higher education.

Table 10.1 List of Items of the 2012 and the 2018–20 Language Ideological Debates at the University of Tartu

2012 Debate	
Almann, A. (2012)	EBSi rektor: äri õppimisel ainult eesti keeles puudub mõte [EBS's rector: Studying business only in Estonian makes no sense], juhtimine.ee, 15 October 2012
Kalm, V. (2012)	Ahistavad keelehirmud [Oppressive language fears], *Postimees, Arvamus*, 25 October 2012
Kull, K. (2012)	Eesti keel valitsegu eesti ülikooli [May the Estonian language govern the Estonian university], *Postimees, Arvamus*, 18 October 2012
Niit, J. (2012)	Estonglish kui uus sund Eesti kõrgharidusmaastikul? [Estonglish as a new direction in the Estonian higher education landscape?], *Postimees, Arvamus*, 8 October 2012
	Pärnu Leadership Conference, 12 October 2012, https://www.konverentsid.ee/blog/
Veldre, E. (2012)	Inglise keel pole võluvits [English is not a magic wand], *Postimees, Arvamus*, 19 October 2012
2018–20 Debate	
Berg, E. (2018)	Rahvusülikooli säilimine rahvusvahelistumise kaudu [Preservation of the national university through internationalization], *Postimees, Meie Eesti*, 10 December 2018
Berg, E. (2019)	Ingliskeelset õpet ei pea kartma [No need to fear English-medium instruction], *ERR Arvamus*, 22 February 2019
Ehala, M. (2018a)	Röövkapitalism kõrghariduses [Robbery capitalism in higher education], *Postimees, Arvamus*, 24 September 2018.
Ehala, M. (2018b)	Kuidas kõrgharidus ingliskeelseks muutub [How higher education is shifting to English], *Postimees, Meie Eesti*, 4 December 2018
Ehala, M. (2019)	Hääletu alistumine ideoloogilisel rindel [Silent surrender on the ideological front], *Postimees, Arvamus*, 1 February 2019
Valk, A. (2020)	Why on earth are they coming to study here? *ERR Arvamus*, 29 September 2020
Vilo, J. (2019)	Eesti tuleviku määravad teaduse ja kõrghariduse valikud [The future of Estonia will be determined by the choices in science and higher education], *Postimees, Arvamus*, 26 January 2019

This sparked a flurry of responses, both supportive and critical, many of which took the statement above out of context and continued a more general conversation about the perception of a changing balance of languages in higher education. Indeed, Kalm's remarks were seemingly taken as endorsing an internationalist discourse, and therefore, as posing a threat to the long-term sustainability of the presence of Estonian in the country's universities. Some contributors to the debate came out in support of Kalm's statement, for example, Arno Almann, the then rector of the Estonian Business School (EBS; the single private university in the country), who stated that by 2020, EBS would have moved towards 'entirely English-language education' (Almann 2012). Others, however, were more critical of Kalm's initial remarks, and confronted him publicly with 'culturalist' arguments. For example, UT professor of biosemiotics Kalevi Kull (2012: n.p.) called for Estonian universities to remember their duty to uphold teaching in Estonian:

> A culture is alive only if it teaches its young people in the language of that culture... The first duty of Estonian universities is to teach Estonian youth the values, customs and speech of Estonian high-culture. We can justify teaching the youth of other cultures in those fields in which we are the best.

As the debate developed and gained in intensity toward the end of 2012, Rector Kalm made two further public interventions with the goal of clarifying the comments that had sparked the controversy. In an opinion piece, he specified that his initial intention was to underline that 'delivering internationally competitive higher education in Estonian is expensive, but it is our nation's, universities' and especially the University of Tartu's responsibility' (Kalm 2012). Kalm also highlighted the conundrum facing Estonian universities then: a steady decline of the demographic basis of high-school graduates able to enter tertiary education, and the consequent need for universities to look for alternatives to expand their student intake.

In his subsequent interventions, Kalm very cleverly navigated the 'internationalist' versus 'culturalist' tensions. On the one hand, he flagged ideas that have later become part of the 'internationalist' discourse, as we shall see below in the 2018–20 debate, namely: (i) international students studying in English can in fact learn Estonian to continue their studies in this language or to establish themselves in the country (despite the obstacles posed by immigration laws); and (ii) former international students who leave after their studies are among Estonia's best ambassadors for promoting and introducing the language and culture they were immersed in during their studies. On the other hand, Kalm was very careful to emphasize that Estonian must not be allowed to decline excessively and that the main motivation for the development of EMI programmes was not economic.

Nevertheless, it is fair to say that the debate was dominated by 'culturalist' arguments, as subsequent statements by other contributors illustrate (e.g. Veldre 2012; Niit 2012). Veldre (2012: n.p.) warned that 'widespread adoption of English-language teaching does not guarantee world-class education', particularly if lecturers fall short in their language skills, citing a survey in which international students in Estonia judged their lecturers' English language skills very critically. In a similar vein, Niit voiced concern about how the increasing use of English was affecting her generation's ability to express themselves and even think in Estonian. 'Estonian and English are structurally so different,' she claimed, 'that these two languages cannot be fruitfully used together – they will begin to disturb each other, and to degrade the grammatical quality of written texts and speakers' language intuitions' (Niit 2012: n.p.).

The 2018–20 debate

As opposed to the 2012 debate, the 2018–20 one was more polyphonic, with more contributors involved in it (up to eighteen participants); it stretched for a longer period of time and included a larger number of contributions (up to twenty-one items, in the analysis provided by Soler and Rozenvalde (2021)). If in the 2012 debate, the 'internationalist' position only began to emerge, in 2018–20 it had consolidated itself, and while the 'culturalists' still seem to dominate the discussion (perhaps due to their over-representation in public media), the two sides are now clearly observable and identifiable. Amongst the culturalist side of the debate, key contributions are provided by Ehala (e.g. Ehala, 2018a,b and 2019), while on the internationalists' camp, relevant contributions come from Berg (2018 and 2019), Vilo (2019) and Valk (2020). Ehala hails from the faculty of humanities, Berg from social sciences, Vilo from technology and engineering and Valk from the rector's office, all of them at UT.

Culturalists' key concern is that universities have all too uncritically assumed the race towards internationalization at all costs, including at the expense of the Estonian language and culture. They see a combination of both demographic and economic factors as contributing to this trend (in particular, the funding system of universities, restructured in the 2013 higher education reform). Indeed, culturalists consider taxpayers' money being misused if they are employed to fund study places in EMI programmes, as is sometimes the case. So, in order to address the current Englishization of the country's higher education system, culturalists suggest the following: (i) turning EMI programmes into bilingual ones, in which Estonian becomes an obligatory part of the studies (Ehala 2018b); (ii) teaching Estonian effectively to international students, so that they can better integrate into Estonian society upon completing their studies, if they wish to stay in the country; and (iii) teaching Estonian effectively to international staff, especially to those in tenure track positions, so that once they apply for tenure, they can demonstrate a good command of Estonian and, in this way, ensure they do not shift the balance of the working language of the institution towards English. To ensure that these goals are achieved (and, hence, that Englishization can be redressed), culturalists appeal to strengthening legislative action, so that the government can more closely monitor developments at universities (Ehala 2018a).

In sum, for culturalists, developing EMI programmes comes with the danger of sidelining Estonian too heavily from higher education. In addition, they do not believe that EMI is a prerequisite for universities (and particularly UT) to maintain their top-level, international profile. In fact, as Martin Ehala puts it (2019: n.p.): 'If the University of Tartu has reached the absolute top of the world without English-medium instruction, then EMI is not a prerequisite to be at the top.' On the contrary, Ehala contrasts Estonia with Finland, where the proportion of EMI programmes is lower, but the number of top 100 universities is, indeed, larger.

Naturally, internationalists disagree on that point with culturalists. For them, the only way for Estonian universities to maintain their level of competitiveness is to continue being internationally visible and offer attractive programmes, which inevitably means engaging with English substantially, both for teaching and research purposes. Internationalists share the concern about university funding with culturalists, but rather than seeing it as an issue of the system in which universities receive public funds, they consider more problematic the fact that the general state-level expenditure on higher education has decreased substantially over the past few years (Vilo 2019). In this context, internationalists argue that universities run the risk of stagnation, without the possibility of growing at the speed that they should.

Internationalists' arguments resonate with those presented by Kalm in 2012. In the 2018–20 debate, these arguments are taken up and developed further. For internationalists, foreign students and staff are important because they enrich the university system in many ways. In addition, if international students establish themselves in Estonia upon graduation, they not only return Estonian taxpayers' contribution in a short period of time, but they can also be considered qualified workers imported at a low cost for the country (Valk 2020). However, if international students end up returning to their home countries, they become important critical friends of Estonia, a means of soft power that any small nation needs to value positively (Berg 2018; see also Li and McKinley (forthcoming) on soft power EMI in China). Foreign lecturers are also an important asset for universities. Many of them are in the top ranks of their fields of specialization; students being trained under their guidance can take this as a significant opportunity to learn first-hand from the best in their fields (Vilo 2019). Therefore, English-medium programmes are important to continue attracting excellent students and lecturers from abroad; without such programmes, in the internationalists' view, universities in Estonia would find themselves in a more difficult position to offer something attractive to these two important collectives. As Berg (2019: n.p.) explains: 'English-language teaching creates the conditions to ensure a decent quality of education that retains our best student candidates and internationally renowned researchers.'

Discussion, implications and conclusion

In this chapter, I have explored the discursive dimension of EMI by focusing on two recent language ideological debates amongst key stakeholders at the UT, Estonia's national university. As is the case with all language ideological debates (Blommaert 1999), the two debates analysed here emerged at points in time where important societal changes were unfolding. In 2012, economic and demographic factors may have helped spark and fuel the debate. By then, the decline in number of students eligible to enter university was already clearly felt by university officials, who also worried about the changes in the universities' funding scheme that the 2013 higher education reform would bring. At that time, the growing number of EMI programmes was also a reality, and it may have prompted many of the reactions expressing concern over the influence of English. In 2018–20, by contrast, changes in the political context may have influenced the debate even more than economic matters. Indeed, the rhetoric on the misuse of taxpayers' money, or the need to ensure that international students and staff learn Estonian beyond a conversational level, seems likely to have been shaped by the growing populist and neo-nationalist discourses in Estonia (following the parliamentary elections in April 2019, a coalition government was formed which would include EKRE, the Estonian People's Conservative Party, a far-right, populist party). As such, Estonia has not been immune to populist discourses that have mushroomed throughout Europe, discourses that have also been felt at higher education systems in, for example, Finland, with a more consolidated trajectory of internationalization (Saarinen 2020).

In closing, I believe it is important to underscore the implications deriving from language ideological debates like these. Indeed, it seems to me that these debates are not simply about key stakeholders struggling for hegemony in given discursive confrontations. Each side's arguments may entail practical consequences that can be very vividly felt by other university members, particularly those whose voices are not well represented (if not virtually absent) from the debates themselves. For example, if a legislative reform imposes the need for foreign staff to know Estonian at an intermediate level by the time they apply for tenure, this will mean that they will need to invest a number of resources to reach that level; and if the university cannot adequately cover that need (which will certainly entail something beyond general language courses for international students and staff), then it will be down to the individual to carve time out of their busy schedules to learn the language well. A similar hypothetical scenario could be imagined for a senior lecturer who is asked to develop English-taught courses without proper institutional support. My point is clear: language ideological debates are important because of the (unintended) consequences they may entail. So, research on the discursive dimension of EMI is central in order to shed light on this side of this rapidly growing phenomenon.

References

Blommaert, J., ed. (1999), *Language Ideological Debates*, Berlin: Walter de Gruyter.

Bulajeva, T., and Hogan-Brun, G. (2014), 'Internationalisation of higher education and nation building: Resolving language policy dilemmas in Lithuania', *Journal of Multilingual and Multicultural Development*, 35 (4): 318–31.

Galloway, N., Kriukow, J., and Numajiri, T. (2017), 'Internationalisation, higher education and the growing demand for English: An investigation into the English medium of instruction (EMI) movement in China and Japan', *ELT Research Papers* 17 (2), British Council. Available online: https://www.teachingenglish.org.uk/sites/teacheng/files/H035%20ELTRA%20 Internationalisation_HE_and%20the%20 growing%20 demand%20for%20English%20A4_FINAL_WEB.pdf.

Hogan-Brun, G., Ozolins, U., Ramonienė, M., and Rannut, M. (2008), 'Language politics and practices in the Baltic States', *Current Issues in Language Planning*, 8 (4): 469–631.

Hultgren, A. K. (2014), 'Whose parallellingualism? Over and covert ideologies in Danish university language policies', *Multilingua: Journal of Cross-Cultural and Interlanguage Communication*, 33 (1–2): 61–87.

Hultgren, A. K., Gregersen, F., and Thøgersen, J. (2014), 'Introduction. English at Nordic universities: Ideologies and practices', in A. K. Hultgren, F. Gregersen and J. Thøgersen (eds), *English in Nordic Universities: Ideologies and Practices*, 1–25, Amsterdam: John Benjamins.

Kasekamp, A. (2010), *A History of the Baltic States*, Basingstoke: Palgrave Macmillan.

Klaas-Lang, B., and Metslang, H. (2015), 'Language policy and sustainability of Estonian in higher education', in G. Stickel and C. Robustelli (eds), *Language Use in University Teaching and Research*, 161–77, Frankfurt: Peter Lang.

Kuteeva, M., Kaufhold, K., and Hynninen, N., eds (2020), *Language Perceptions and Practices in Multilingual Universities*, Basingstoke: Palgrave Macmillan.

Li, W. X., and McKinley, J. (Forthcoming), 'International EMI programs in China: Mapping the territory for international students'.

Macaro, E., Curle, S., Pun, J., An, J., and Dearden, J. (2018), 'A systematic review of English medium instruction in higher education', *Language Teaching*, 51 (1): 36–76.

Piller, I., and Cho, J. (2013), 'Neoliberalism as language policy', *Language in Society*, 42 (1): 23–44.

Rozenvalde, K. (2018), 'Multi-layered language policy in higher education in Estonia and Latvia: Case of national universities', doctoral thesis, Riga: University of Latvia Press.

Saarinen, T. (2020), *Higher Education, Language and New Nationalism in Finland. Recycled Histories*, Basingstoke: Palgrave Macmillan.

Soler, J. (2019), *Language Policy and the Internationalisation of Universities: A Focus on Estonian Higher Education*, Berlin: Mouton de Gruyter.

Soler, J., and Rozenvalde, K. (2021), 'The Englishization of higher education in Estonia and Latvia: Actors, positionings and linguistic tensions', in B. Wilkinson and R. Gabriëls (eds), *Englishisation of European Higher Education*, 57–75, Amsterdam: Amsterdam University Press.

Soler, J., and Vihman, V. A. (2018), 'Language ideology and language planning in Estonian higher education: Nationalising and globalising discourses', *Current Issues in Language Planning*, 19 (1): 22–41.

University of Tartu Act (1995), available online: https://www.riigiteataja.ee/en/eli/527122019004/consolide.

Vihman, V. A., and Tensing, Ü. (2014), 'English-medium studies in the Estonian national university: Globalisation and organic change', in L. Lepik (ed.), *Keelevahetus ülikoolis – probleem või võimalus?* [Language shift in the university: problem or opportunity?] T*artu Ülikooli ajaloo küsimusi*, XLII: 12–34, Tartu: Tartu Ülikooli Ajaloo Muuseum.

Wächter, B., and Maiworm, F. (2014), *English-Taught Programmes in European Higher Education: The State of Play in 2014*, Bonn: Lemmens.

11

Perceived Needs of English-Medium Instruction Lecturers in an Italian University: Before and after Training

Francesca Costa and Roberta Grassi

Introduction

English-medium instruction (EMI) in Italy has grown considerably at the university level (Ackerley et al. 2017; Broggini and Costa 2017; Campagna and Pulcini 2014; Costa 2017; Molino and Campagna 2014). Initially, this use of English for university courses in Italy was implemented with little pedagogical vision by recruiting available professors (usually non-English speakers) on a voluntary, and at times even non-voluntary, basis. However, nearly fifteen years after the first EMI courses burst onto the scene, there is an increasing need at both the bottom-up and the institutional level for training for EMI professors throughout Europe (Ball and Lindsay 2013; Doiz et al. 2019; Sánchez-Pérez 2020a; Long 2017). As Sánchez-Pérez (2020b: xviii) notes:

> The rapid spread of such programmes has resulted in a rising concern among teaching staff, who feels pushed towards teaching their subject content through a non-native language, with little or no previous training. As a result, many recent studies have highlighted the importance of and urgency to train university faculty, not only in terms of language proficiency, but on the appropriate teaching methodologies.

Before Sánchez-Pérez (2020a), there were not many references that provided an overview of EMI training courses and the need to implement them in Europe. Among these are the articles by Costa (2015) and O'Dowd (2018), both of which highlight the need for training, with the latter noting that: 'Many teachers are confronting these issues without a great deal of training and preparation and are therefore forced to come to terms with the challenges as they teach through English on a daily basis' (O'Dowd 2018: 554).

One of the latest studies (Sánchez-Pérez 2020a) testifies to the fact that many new examples exist of EMI training organized by the various European universities for their lecturers. Each of these training programmes is tailored to the university in question, among which is the Italian university mentioned in this study.

The present chapter provides an overview of some EMI training courses in Italy, describing one such course at a university in Northern Italy and illustrating the investigation carried out during this course concerning the evolution in the lecturers' perception of their EMI training-related needs before and after the training itself.

Overview of EMI training in Italy

The first general consideration is that training courses in different European countries are designed both to improve English-language skills and to train teachers in new methodologies. By referring to Kurtán's (2003) work, Fortanet-Gómez (2020) identifies three components for EMI teacher training: language proficiency, appropriate pedagogy and multicultural/multilingual aspects. There are two main aspects to the various training courses in Italian universities: first, they are organized by the university language centres; and second, they tend to focus on both linguistic and methodological aspects, which in some ways overlap (Costa 2015). Three such courses in Italy are illustrated below. Examples were chosen where at the time of writing, alongside the training, a research group existed that had worked on and investigated the issue of training programmes.

In 2013, the University of Padua launched a project called Learning English for Academic Purposes (LEAP) based on a top-down approach starting with the university administration.

The project allowed interested teachers to undertake training on four fronts: by attending a two-week course at a Dublin summer school; by attending a nine-day summer school near Venice; by attending a 100-hour five-month blended course; and by receiving personalized individual support (Language Advising Service).

An integral part of the LEAP project involved research on the needs of EMI teachers. The survey uncovered many problems perceived by lecturers (Ackerley et al. 2017; Guarda and Helm 2017; Helm and Guarda 2015). One salient aspect in this regard is the methodology of teaching. Several lecturers noted their own uneasiness in improvising during the EMI lesson as well as the feeling of not being in control of their teaching. Another thorny issue noted by many lecturers was their own oral competence in English, as well as weakness in the use of English during informal conversation.

Since 2017, the CHEI (Centre for Higher Education Internationalisation)[1] has organized professional development courses in support of EMI and for the management of international classes. Two course modules are offered: a basic nine-hour course on teaching international classes and EMI (Costa and Mair, forthcoming) and a three-hour course on assessment. At the end of the basic course, lecturers must prepare a mini-lecture for which they receive feedback from both trainees and fellow lecturers.

The Academic Lecturing course at Ca' Foscari began in 2016 as both a traditional course and a linguistic advice course in response to the need for training advocated by this university. The aim of the course is to raise awareness of internationalization processes; to promote innovation in academic teaching in multilingual contexts; to increase student involvement and support (see also Galloway and Ruegg 2020); to identify the language characteristics of the discipline in question; to improve the evaluation phase; and to work on language weaknesses (Bier and Borsetto 2020). A questionnaire was administered after the course at Ca' Foscari (see also Martinez and Fernandes (2020) for similar studies) which led in part to a revision of the contents so as to include more blended learning.

Case study overview

The context

The present study is based on a recently founded, midsize university in Northern Italy (twenty thousand students) offering fourteen bachelor's degree courses, eighteen master's degree courses and three five-year courses, with a faculty of 93 full professors and 134 associate professors. The following full courses are taught through English: clinical psychology, engineering and management for health, management engineering, planning and management of tourism systems, business administration, professional and managerial accounting, economics and data analysis, and international management entrepreneurship and finance.

Description of the EMI training course

The course provided twenty-two hours of training and was divided into: (1) introduction to EMI (two hours); (ii) B2-/C1-level language drills based on oral interaction and miscellaneous topic presentation strategies (fourteen hours); (3) micro-teaching (six hours) to develop presentation skills. The first part included an overview of the terms linked to EMI issues from the point of view of the various stakeholders (institutions/lecturers/students) in Italy. It also illustrated several input presentation strategies and practical tools to better address lessons by providing real-world examples of EMI lectures. The more strictly linguistic part involved the following topics: differences between spoken and written English, the importance of phonological elements (volume of voice, pacing, intonation, correcting the pronunciation of key words), extralinguistic strategies (ways of engaging your audience, body language, eye contact), useful classroom language (introducing the topic, getting the audience interested, giving the structure of the presentation/lecture, introducing a new section, conclusions) and avoiding/solving linguistic problems (paraphrasing, speculating, asking for more information). The final part of the course included the presentation of mini-lectures by lecturers with peer feedback and feedback from the teacher trainers.

Methodology

The fundamental research approach of the present study is qualitative. As mentioned above, the study is linked to the training course and involves two phases of research methodology: an initial survey of all the faculty at the university before the course began and a much narrower second phase (also given the sample numbers) in which the faculty was asked in a short questionnaire at the end of the course about the critical and the positive aspects of the training course. Therefore, the analysis follows a QUAL→qual sequence.

Data collection instruments

The tools used for the analysis were studied ad hoc and involve an initial questionnaire sent by the Language Competence Centre to all the university teachers by email and a short follow-up questionnaire (Iwaniec 2020) administered only to the course participants.

Initial questionnaire

The questionnaire was prepared by the university language centre to gauge the interest in participating in a future training course for EMI lecturers and to better tailor the content of that course to the needs of the lecturers. The questionnaire was in part taken from an already-existing one (Broggini and Costa 2017) and was sent to all the teachers representing all the departments.

The five-page questionnaire (twenty-two questions) had a title, which clearly identified the subject of the research, followed by an introduction describing its purpose. The questions were divided into sections: the first consisting of multiple-choice factual questions investigating the mother tongue, the academic role and the department the respondents belonged to; the second presenting a multiple-choice question regarding the experiences of the teachers with EMI. The next part sought to ascertain interest in a possible training course in English for university teachers by means of open-ended aptitude questions. Open-ended questions (n=3) were included in this part in the form of aptitude questions examining the interests and opinions of teachers regarding the proposed training courses. The last part dealt with the organization of the training courses: through multiple-choice questions, the preferences of teachers were gauged regarding the type of organization, the hourly schedule, the location and the intensity of commitment to a possible ad hoc training course.

To administer the questionnaire Google Forms was used, an easy and functional online application which allows data to be collected without having to install particular software on the computer. Once the questionnaire was entered, it was sent by e-mail to the sample of respondents. Google Forms also allowed us to receive results accurately as it can be linked to spreadsheets in Google Sheets, which allows the responses to automatically be sent to the spreadsheet. The Microsoft Excel programme was used for the spreadsheets.

Follow-up questionnaire

The qualitative part of the study involved a follow-up individualized questionnaire only for the course participants, which compared the questions in the first questionnaire to the perceptions of the same topics at the end of the course. The topics of discussion were: interest in EMI training at t1–t2, the impact of EMI training on EMI lectures – L1 lectures, EMI training course feedback/appreciation, and perceived needs at t1–t2.

Sample

Regarding the sampling, the initial questionnaire was sent to the entire population (census) of 440 lecturers at the university in question. The follow-up questionnaire was sent only to the lecturers (n=13) who had completed the training course, thereby representing purposeful sampling (Duff 2008).

Questionnaire sample

Access to the questionnaire was given to 440 teachers as follows: 69 from the Department of Foreign Languages, 62 from the Department of Social Sciences (SUS), 46 from the Department of Law, 70 from the Department of Humanities, 115 from the Engineering Departments and 78 from the Department of Economics. Of the 440 lecturers, 98 responded, representing 22.3 per cent of the sample, divided as follows: 24 from Foreign Languages, 10 from the Department of Social Sciences, 10 from the Department of Law, 14 from Humanities, 24 from the Engineering departments (13 of whom are professors of Engineering and Applied Sciences and 11 teachers of Management, Information and Production Engineering) and 16 from the Department of Economics.

Of the 98 respondents, 41 reported not being involved in EMI at present and not likely to be involved in the future. Those were henceforth excluded from the rest of the questionnaire analysis leaving a sample of 57 subjects whose answers are analysed in § 5.1. These respondents were distributed across the six departments as follows: 12 (21 per cent) from Foreign Languages, 4 (7 per cent) from the Department of Social Sciences, 5 (9 per cent) from the Department of Law, 6 (10.5 per cent) from Humanities, 16 (28 per cent) from the Engineering departments and 14 (24.5 per cent) from the Department of Economics.

Follow-up questionnaire sample

The follow-up questionnaire was submitted to all the participants in the training programme (n=13), but answers were received by just half of them (n=7): 4 from Economics, 2 from Engineering and 1 from the Social Sciences.

Results

Initial questionnaire

The first topic considered was 'experience'. Lecturers with EMI experience were concentrated in Economics (31 per cent), Engineering (30 per cent) and Foreign Languages (29 per cent).

The percentage of respondents interested in EMI training was 89 per cent overall, with 46 per cent being 'very interested'. Those expressing no interest in EMI training belonged to different schools and academic ranks, but all reported previous solid experience in EMI, with 'more than one EMI course' taught. Engineering and Economics again had the highest percentage of interested respondents (with 64 per cent and 43 per cent, respectively, 'very interested'), whereas areas like the Social Sciences showed less interest in EMI training (25 per cent).

The questionnaire then went on to ask what sort of training was desired. The choices were 'language', 'methodology' or 'both'. Overall, interest was shown mainly for both aspects of the recommended EMI training according to the literature: namely, language and methodology together (scoring up to 65 per cent of the sample). For the other respondents, interest was equally divided between Language only (17 per cent) or Methodology only (18 per cent). The results in the different schools showed general interest in both aspects across the board, especially in Law, the Humanities (80 per cent) and Economics (79 per cent). Purely methodological concerns account for a significant share of interest particularly for Foreign Languages (40 per cent) and the Social Sciences (33 per cent). On the contrary, Language was preferred to Methodology only in Engineering (where it was almost double: 29 per cent compared to 14 per cent). Purely methodological concerns do not appear in Law and the Humanities.

Moving on to the qualitative part of the data: after choosing among Methodology, Language or both, open answers were made relevant, of which a structural or conventional qualitative content analysis was conducted, aimed at determining data-driven categories (Mayring 2000; Hsieh and Shannon 2005). The raw data was decontextualized and then recontextualized in order to code relevant categories. A synthesis of the main results is presented here as a suggestion for further investigation.

Those who chose Language only as their main training expectation were mostly inexperienced in EMI teaching (78 per cent), and their concerns mainly refer to fluency, conversation and discourse, not grammar (never mentioned).

Those who expressed a need for methodology training were, on the contrary, mainly experienced lecturers concerned about the multicultural aspects of EMI. Interest was also shown in having the opportunity to differentiate teaching from the traditional courses. Individual comments referred to adapting to students' low language proficiency, on the one hand, and to the impact of EMI on students' language improvement, on the other.

Where both methodological and linguistic concerns were expressed, no answers or vague statements like 'improve/training' were expressed on the linguistic side. Where more specific concerns are indicated, an interesting dualism emerges between two conflicting areas of proficiency: accuracy and fluency. The aim for accuracy is mentioned both in general and with particular reference to either vocabulary or pronunciation (never both), more so than to grammar, which is a topic that is almost unmentioned. Reference to fluency is to be interpreted as oral fluency, given the specific interest in speaking/communication that is mentioned. The methodological needs of those interested in both language and methodological training show the main cluster of answers revolve around vagueness.

Another recurrent concern is with involvement/attention/interaction/effectiveness. The topic of differentiation with L1 courses was brought up, alongside the question of how to relate to a multicultural audience and how to help students with low language proficiency.

Qualitative content analysis on the main objectives of further training revealed a concern with fluency, conversation, interaction and discourse, as well as accuracy and pronunciation; techniques and strategies alternative to monologue to produce more 'effectiveness' and 'involvement'; multicultural relativism; the differentiation of EMI teaching from teaching in the L1; and concerns with students' language proficiency and/or the effects of EMI on students' language improvement.

Follow-up questionnaire

The follow-up questionnaire was customized, since the questions referred specifically to the answers each subject had provided in the first questionnaire, both in close-ended questions (e.g. 'You expressed interest in a *Language Course*. Would you express the same interest now?') and in open-ended ones ('You expressed specific interest for *Methodology: ad hoc suggestions on how to overcome Italian students' specific difficulties with English. Language: improve my pronunciation*'. What specific interests would you express now?').[2] This feature was implemented in an attempt to stimulate recall and thus encourage the respondents to overtly compare their perceptions and opinions before and after the training. As stated above, seven participants (out of thirteen) returned the questionnaire.

All experienced EMI teachers (six) reported an impact on their EMI course management. Four out of seven reported 'some impact' on L1 courses as well: 'more structured lectures', 'better classroom management', 'better lecture organization', 'control over gestures' and 'better speech rate control'. All seven showed great appreciation for the course and significant interest in further training. Requests for further training point to both aspects (language and methodology), with some more detailed language foci (specific grammatical structures). Positive references to the creation of a teaching/learning community with colleagues also emerged, although with some criticism of the 'softness' of the peer evaluation. One participant found the microteaching sessions 'rather useless and long', expressing a preference for practising specific classroom language (e.g. opening and closing a lesson; Q&A sessions management).

Implications for researchers and practitioners

EMI teacher training is changing because EMI is changing (Helm and Guarda 2015): Experience and training have produced further, more articulated and differentiated, partly discipline-related needs in both methodology and language issues, which research on training is tracking down. Nonetheless, disciplinary differences are visible in our corpus: the highest response rate to Q1 was from Foreign Languages, but the greatest interest in EMI training came from Engineering and Economics (the lowest, from the Social Sciences). This partially reflects the actual degree of 'internationalization' within the departments, since Economics has three EMI master's degrees out of five, Engineering has two out of six, the Social Sciences has one out of three and SUS has one mixed degree out of three.

Current or foreseeable involvement in actual EMI courses, and so the actual proportion of EMI courses within each school, play a role in the degree of interest. Specifically, training interest was mainly for both Language and Methodology, even though Methodology overruled Language at FL (maybe linked to a higher EFL proficiency in the teaching staff there), and Language overcame Methodology at Engineering (possibly denoting a lower stigma in expressing language needs). The absence of purely methodological concerns at Humanities and Law can be related to the unquestioning of canonical, transmissive teaching approaches in those areas on the one side, and to the fact that current reference literature in those disciplines in a romance area is more likely linked to Italian and classical languages, so that a lower proficiency in English is in general more to be expected, thus, making Language needs perceived as more cogent.

As for the impact of training on lecturer persona, a shift in pedagogy (Pagèze and Lasagabaster 2017) appears in both EMI and L1 lectures: interestingly, both the need for some sort of differentiation of EMI teaching from teaching in L1 on one side and some impact of EMI-induced pedagogical shifts into the traditional, transmissive pedagogy in L1 on the other appear in the data. This comes alongside the perception of further needs. Among those are fluency- and conversation-management-related abilities on one side and accuracy-related proficiency on the other; 'effectiveness' and 'involvement' are seen as major goals, but multicultural relativism and, finally, concerns with the effects of EMI on students' language improvement are also mentioned. Yet, those concerns are not detailed and so our interpretation shifts from hope in L2 proficiency improvement to preoccupations as to the quality of the language model provided, or even to worries about loss in academic proficiency in L1.[3]

Notes

1 CHEI was founded in 2012 with the aim of promoting research and training on the internationalization of higher education globally (https://centridiricerca.unicatt.it/chei-home).
2 The personalized references to the respondent's answers in the initial questionnaire in italics.
3 This chapter was developed by both authors. Specifically, Costa's sections are from 'Introduction' to 'Sample' under the heading 'Methodology', and Grassi's sections extend from 'Questionnaire sample' under the heading 'Methodology' to the end of the chapter

References

Ackerley, K., Guarda, M., and Helm, F. (2017), *Sharing Perspectives on English-Medium Instruction*, Berlin: Peter Lang.
Ball, P., and Lindsay, D. (2013), 'Language demands and support for English-medium instruction in tertiary education: Learning from a specific context', in A. Doiz,

D. Lasagabaster and J. M. Sierra (eds), *English-Medium Instruction at Universities*, 44–61, Bristol: Multilingual Matters.

Bier, A., and Borsetto, E. (2020), 'Una buona pratica di supporto all'insegnamento accademico: l'esperienza di Academic Lecturing a Ca' Foscari', *Expressio*, 4: 31–53.

Broggini, S., and Costa, F. (2017), 'A survey of English-medium instruction in Italian higher education: An updated perspective from 2012 to 2015', *Journal of Immersion and Content-Based Language Education*, 5 (2): 240–66.

Campagna, S., and Pulcini, V. (2014), 'English as a medium of instruction in Italian universities: Linguistic policies, pedagogical implications', in M. G. Guido and B. Seidlhofer (eds), *Textus. English Studies in Italy: Perspectives on English as a Lingua Franca*, XXVII (1): 173–90.

Costa, F. (2015), 'EMI teacher-training courses in Europe', *RiCOGNIZIONI*, 2 (4): 119–27.

Costa, F. (2017), 'If we're gonna do it do it right, right? English-medium instruction in Italian universities', in F. Helm, K. Ackerley and M. Guarda (eds), *Sharing Perspectives on English-Medium Instruction*, 77–93, Bern: Peter Lang.

Costa, F., and Mair, O.(2022), 'Multimodality and pronunciation in ICLHE (integrating content and language in higher education) training', *Innovation in Language Learning and Teaching*.accepted..

Sánchez-Pérez, M., ed. (2020a), *Teacher Training for English-Medium Instruction in Higher Education*, Hershey: IGI Global.

Sánchez-Pérez, M. (2020b), 'Preface', in M. M. Sánchez-Pérez (ed.), *Teacher Training for English-Medium Instruction in Higher Education*, XVIII–XXIV, Hershey: IGI Global.

Doiz, A., Costa, F., Lasagabaster, D., and Mariotti, C. (2019), 'Linguistic demands and language assistance in EMI courses: What is the stance of Italian and Spanish undergraduates?', *Lingue e Linguaggi*, 33: 69–85.

Duff, P. (2008), *Case Study Research in Applied Linguistics*, London: Routledge.

Fortanet-Gómez, I. (2020), 'The dimensions of EMI in the international classroom: Training teachers for the future university', in M. M. Sánchez-Pérez (ed.), *Teacher Training for English-Medium Instruction in Higher Education*, 1–20, Hershey: IGI Global.

Galloway, N., and Ruegg, R. (2020), 'The provision of student support on English medium instruction programmes in Japan and China', *Journal of English for Academic Purposes* [100846]. https://doi.org/10.1016/j.jeap.2020.100846.

Guarda, M., and Helm, F. (2017), 'A survey of lecturers' needs and feedback on EMI training', in K. Ackerley, M. Guarda and F. Helm (eds), *Sharing Perspectives on English-Medium Instruction*, 167–94, Bern: Peter Lang.

Helm, F., and Guarda, M. (2015), ' "Improvisation is not allowed in a second language": A survey of Italian lecturers' concerns about teaching their subjects through English', *Language Learning in Higher Education*, 5 (2), 353–73. DOI: https://doi.org/10.1515/cercles-2015-0017.

Hsieh, H. F., and Shannon, S. E. (2005), 'Three approaches to qualitative content analysis'. *Qualitative Health Research*, 15: 1277–88.

Iwaniec, J. (2020), 'Questionnaires: Implications for effective implementation', in J. McKinley and H. Rose (eds), *The Routledge Handbook of Research Methods in Applied Linguistics*, 324–35, New York: Routledge.

Kurtán, Z. (2003), 'Teacher training for English-medium instruction', in C. van Leeuwen and R. Wilkinson (eds), *Multilingual Approaches in University Education: Challenges and Practices*, 145–62, Maastricht: Maastricht University Press.

Long, L. (2017), 'Have we got the lecturing lingo?', *L'analisi linguistica letteraria*, supplemento 2: 311–24.

Martinez, R., and Fernandes, K. (2020), 'Development of a teacher training course for English medium instruction for higher education professors in Brazil', in M. M. Sánchez-Pérez (ed.), *Teacher Training for English-Medium Instruction in Higher Education*, 125–52, Hershey: IGI Global.

Mayring, P. (2000), *Qualitative Inhaltsanalyse*, Weinreim: Beltz.

Molino, A., and Campagna, S. (2014), 'English-mediated instruction in Italian universities: Conflicting views', *Sociolinguistica – International Yearbook of European Sociolinguistics/Internationales Jahrbuch für europäische Soziolinguistik*, November: 155–71.

O'Dowd, R. (2018), 'The training and accreditation of teachers for English medium instruction: An overview of practice in European universities', *International Journal of Bilingual Education and Bilingualism*, 21 (5): 553–63, DOI: 10.1080/13670050.2018.1491945.

Pagèze, J., and Lasagabaster, D. (2017), 'Teacher development for teaching and learning in English in a French higher education context', *L'analisi linguistica letteraria*, supplemento 2: 289–310.

12

English-Medium Instruction in Polish Higher Education: Insights Provided by Classroom-Level Analysis

Agata Mikołajewska and Izabela Mikołajewska

Introduction

Poland has seen a rapid expansion and development of higher education since the fall of the Soviet Union in 1989. Although it has been an independent country since 1918, until the fall of the Soviet Union, it was under the *influence* of Russia. Thus, in 1989, Poland became to truly function as a fully independent country and a series of reforms were introduced across all sectors, including higher education (HE).

Between 1989 and 2008 there was an exponential increase of educational provisions across the country. This resulted in an enormous expansion of the HE sector (for instance, the number of students grew from about 0.38 million in 1989 to over 1.9 million in 2008 (MNiSW 2013)), and creation of a governmental unit responsible for regulating tertiary education, the Ministry of Science and Higher Education (pl. Ministerstwo Nauki i Szkolnictwa Wyższego, henceforth called 'MNiSW'), created in 2006.

The initial reorganization of higher education in the 1990s was based around two pillars. Firstly, increasing the provision of HE. Secondly, opening up the HE sector to international collaboration. Regarding the second pillar, Chojnacka and Macukow (1995: 46) argued that teaching in languages other than Polish was 'of highest importance for the reason that they can bring foreign students from all over the world', thereby lifting the language barrier for non-Polish-speaking students. Therefore, the trend to increase the provision of English-medium instruction (EMI) started when the first EMI degrees opened at universities in main Polish cities, such as Warsaw, Poznań and Łódź, between 1992 and 1995 (Chojnacka and Macukow 1995).

The second wave of exponential growth of Polish HE commenced after it joined the European Union in 2004. Thanks to the European exchange programmes and freedom of movement between European countries, Poland managed to attract more and more foreign students. Starting with only 8,800 in 2004/5 (GUS 2010), the number of foreign students doubled in just four years; and at the start of 2019, there were about 82,200 international students studying in Poland (GUS 2020).

Concurrent with the expansion of HE was the increase in EMI provision. However, this lasted only until 2010. Over the past decade, the HE sector has been decreasing in size due to several reasons: declining birth rate, an aging population and a student population choosing to go abroad to study thanks to freedom of movement within Europe since joining the EU in 2004. As a result of these factors, the university student population dropped from 1.95 million at its peak point, to 1.2 million at present. It was also predicted that the student population will decline to 1.25 million by 2024 (OECD 2017), although the number already surpassed this in 2018 (GUS 2019). Furthermore, the number of HE institutions (HEIs) functioning in Poland was 460 in 2010 and is now down to 373 (Pol-on.pl 2021). Despite (or perhaps due to) the shrinking HE sector, there continues to be a significant increase in provision of EMI, as well as increase in the number of international students. It seems that the move towards EMI and the need of universities to attract more foreign students is a response to the declining number of students studying at Polish HEIs. It may be that the international students are to fill the seats that would normally have been taken by Polish students.

Overview of EMI in Poland

Provision of EMI in Poland is a fairly recent phenomenon. Starting with a handful of degree programmes in the early 1990s (Chojnacka and Macukow 1995), Polish HEIs were recently reported to offer around 750 EMI degrees across the country (Ready, Study, Go! Poland 2021). At the time of finalizing this chapter, there is still no EMI policy established at the macro (national) level.

In terms of research, there is an undeniable gap in the literature on teaching in English in the Polish context. It was recently reported in a systematic review of EMI research that there are only four empirical studies that discuss teaching in

English in Poland at any level of education, and in the case of this review the four studies highlighted considered secondary schooling only (Macaro 2018). The recognition of EMI at university level is less visible, which is especially surprising considering the widespread provision of EMI across Polish universities.

Nevertheless, there are studies that explore certain aspects of EMI in Poland at the tertiary level of education, when looking at Poland and other countries. For example, the study conducted by Briggs et al. (2018) compared secondary and tertiary teachers' beliefs about EMI in three countries: Austria, Italy and Poland. It did not pull out any context-specific characteristics of EMI in Poland. However, it was reported that, according to the university lecturers, the goal of EMI is to 'improve the financial situation of my institution', which appears to be true in the case of Poland. There are a number of factors contributing to this. What seems to be currently taking place in Poland is a 'commodification of the English language' – a phrase used by Li Wei in a roundtable discussion on EMI (Coleman et al. 2018: 707). That is, universities seem to be using the money from fee-paying students to subsidize their budgets. In Poland, a majority of public universities' income comes from teaching (GUS 2020). The amount of money which the MNiSW allocates to each university is dependent on the number of students studying at each university. Thus, more students equals more funding. As noted earlier, the HE sector has been shrinking in size and the number of students decreased by 0.75 million between the years 2005 and 2019. This means that universities need to offer more paid courses to help keep the institutions afloat. Considering that the MNiSW allowed for teaching in foreign languages and to charge fees for such courses, this opened a new opportunity for universities to subsidize their budget. They can now charge more for courses taught in English, and they can open up to an international HE market by offering EMI degrees.

Another study looked at university lecturers in three countries – Poland, Italy and Austria – to explore lecturers' attitudes towards EMI (Dearden and Macaro 2016). A few features specific to Poland were identified. In Poland, there was a recognition that preparing to teach in English takes more time in terms of preparation for classes, and thus, lecturers teaching classes in English are entitled to extra financial rewards. It was also reported that in the interviews, Polish lecturers' main focus was to discuss the type of international students received by the universities. This may stem from the fact that the Polish MNiSW defines internationalization in terms of increasing the number of international students studying at Polish Universities (see, for instance, MNiSW 2015). One way to do this, as recommended in the Higher Education Internationalisation

Program (pl. Program Umiędzynarodowienia Szkolnictwa Wyższego), is to offer more EMI programmes (MNiSW 2015). Therefore, commonly when talking about issues of studies in English or internationalization, the lecturers elaborate on the international student body at their university (see discussion of implicit policies in Chapter 16 of this volume).

In addition to empirical studies, Golenko's (2014) paper documents his own experience of teaching in English at a Polish university for over a decade. He highlighted some of the main challenges of EMI, including scarce access to literature in English and the fact that the curriculum and syllabus are designed to be taught in Polish, not English. Oftentimes, other teaching aids, such as coursebooks prepared by the module teachers, already available in Polish, need to be translated into English, so the students have the essential material to learn from.

Access to data and information on EMI in Poland is restricted and problematic. Sandström and Neghina (2017) reported on difficulties comparing data received from the national resources in Poland with those on Studyportal, which is an online resource comprising information on degrees and various educational courses. In Poland, there are no national statistics gathered by the National Centre of Statistics on the exact number of EMI programmes that are currently on offer by Polish universities, and how many students study on these programmes. Thus, the only way to determine the student population enrolled on EMI programmes across Poland would be to contact each individual university.

As mentioned earlier, there is no explicit EMI policy in Poland. There are only general calls for the need to increase EMI provision in non-binding documents such as the Higher Education Internationalisation Program. In this way, the requirements – which would normally form a part of national policies – are implicitly imposed on universities. As a result of these top-down implicit pressures from the MNiSW, and the financial struggles that Polish universities have been going through, the universities adapt their development and internationalization plans accordingly. To illustrate this, a report prepared by Domański et al. (2017) includes information on the internationalization experiences of Political Science Departments across Polish universities. According to the document, the Political Science Department of University of Wrocław's intention is to 'widen the educational offer in English language' (Sula 2017: 188) in efforts to internationalize the university. The University of Łódź's department aims to provide a financially competitive educational offer for both home and international students by introducing attractive fees for EMI courses – 600 euros for Polish and EU students and 2,500 euros for non-EU students (Machnikowski and Włodarska-Frykowska 2017). Other important internationalization efforts include international exchanges for staff and students, which is also associated with the need for at least some subjects to be taught in English. Therefore, we can see that the MNiSW 'suggestions' and 'recommendations' together with financial drivers have an impact on the universities in Poland, leading them to widening the provision of EMI.

Defining EMI

Quite a distinct characteristic for the context is the fact that the term 'EMI' or 'English-medium instruction' is not used in Poland. Despite the fact that conducting studies in English in Poland meets the hallmarks of the EMI definition presented by Macaro (2018: 1), 'where the first language of the majority of the population is not English', the term is very rarely used in the Polish context. The use of English as the language of instruction is most commonly referred to as 'studies in English', 'degrees in English' or 'English-taught programmes'. The nuances in the terminology most likely stem from the fact that the term 'EMI' is not being used in the MNiSW ordinances, normative acts or university policies. Further, the EMI phenomenon has not yet attracted interest from Polish researchers, and thus, all issues surrounding EMI are being discussed to a very limited extent. There is only one normative act issued by the MNiSW (Act of 20 July 2018, the Law on Higher Education and Science) that states the government allows for introduction of degrees and courses taught in languages other than Polish at Polish HEIs and that universities can charge fees for those degrees and courses. As a result, all programmes taught in a foreign language are referred to as 'studies in German' or 'studies in Russian'. However, it is undeniable that EMI programmes make up the vast majority of the foreign-taught programmes. According to a website established in 2017 by the National Agency for Academic Exchange (pl. Narodowa Agencja Wymiany Narodowej, NAWA) there are only about 10 programmes taught in German and around 5 in Russian, while there is about 750 programmes taught in English (Ready, Study, Go! Poland 2021). Thus, 'studies taught in a foreign language' in Poland clearly refer to 'EMI' programmes.

The non-existence of the term 'EMI' is reflected in the fact that there are so few discussions on teaching in English in the Polish literature. There are neither guidelines as to what the policy implementation process ought to look like nor recommended standards for such programmes. It would appear that EMI is not considered to exist as a phenomenon that requires consideration and attention. Teaching in English is being discussed at the secondary level of education, however, and the term 'EMI' is being used by a very small number of academics (see e.g. Król and Romanowski (2020) for discussion of EMI at the level of secondary schooling). Yet, at the higher education level, EMI is referred to as 'studies/programmes in English' or simply 'teaching in English' (e.g. Golenko 2014).

Challenges of EMI in Poland

Since there is very limited research on EMI in Polish HE, we report on a recent study conducted by one of the authors. The project investigated challenges encountered by the key stakeholders of EMI – students and lecturers. Data collected included (i) quantitative data from questionnaire surveys with students (n=395) and lecturers (n=322) who teach in English at Polish HEIs; and (ii) qualitative data from interviews (n=28) and focus groups (n=2) conducted with students and lecturers who took part in the survey (see Table 12.1).

Due to space constraints, we only present a 'sneak peak' into some of the most commonly reported linguistic challenges experienced by EMI students and content teachers.

According to Bradford (2016), 'linguistic challenges' refer to problems experienced by students, lecturers and other university staff who work in English and it is not their first language. In the questionnaire, lecturers reported on the difficulty of everyday tasks conducted in EMI classrooms on a scale from 0, 'very easy', to 6, 'very difficult'. From responses of 322 lecturers we learned that the most difficult tasks were, from across all dimensions of using English (i.e. speaking, reading, writing and listening):

1. Using appropriate academic style when writing in English ($M=3.10$, SD=1.69)
2. Paraphrasing ideas in English ($M=2.98$, SD=1.63)
3. Understanding students' accents ($M=2.90$, SD=1.60)

All in all, these numbers are not overly worrying because they oscillate around the central value of the response scale (i.e. three), indicating that these tasks are neither very easy nor very difficult. However, these three items are concerned with conveying knowledge *during* classes with students, not preparation for

Table 12.1 Number of EMI Students and Lecturers in Poland by Mode of Data Collection

	Interview	Focus Group
Students	8	16
Lecturers	20	–

teaching or assessment. In the follow-up interviews, lecturers shared that understanding students' accents may impede comprehending a question asked:

> It is often the case that they [students] speak English very well, however, their accent is so thick, that understanding them is often a problem. (Lecturer 13)

In such case, lecturers need to give themselves time to familiarize with the new accent encountered. As one lecturer said, it took her three to five classes to start grasping a Hindi accent. Students' have also reported a problem when asking the lecturer a question:

> And teacher don't get it and he answered a completely different question, in a way he understands it. (Student 24)

Reportedly, the miscommunication can be caused by the fact the lecturer was not familiarized with student's accent, that the question asked was poorly constructed or misunderstanding of the question by the lecturer (due to lack of vocabulary in English). Regardless of the reason, usually students do not repeat the question, as they are afraid of being misunderstood again, which in turn, may have serious, negative implications on the content learning. Additionally, students would like to see lecturers being able to express the same idea or argument in different ways:

> Maybe they should know five ways to describe a word, maybe paraphrase or something. (Student 17)

Students report that hearing the exact same response twice does not always allow them to grasp what the teacher is conveying. Hence, the need to take time to paraphrase and attempt to explain the idea in a slightly different, hopefully easier to understand, way.

Students have also highlighted a problem of literal translations of slides from Polish to English. During classes, the students were shown a task to 'Exchange the places …' instead of 'Name the places …' (pl. 'Wymień miejsca …'), and they had no idea what the exercise was about. In such a situation, students need to collaboratively work out what the lecturer is trying to say in Polish and translate it into English or their own language to be able to do the task. It takes more time than it would in one's first language, but it also requires developing additional learning strategies on the part of the students.

For the 395 students that took part in the questionnaire survey, the biggest challenges in EMI were:

1. Using appropriate academic style when writing in English ($M=2.30$, $SD=1.55$)
2. Proofreading written work ($M=2.04$, $SD=1.42$)
3. Understanding specific vocabulary [when reading] ($M=2.04$, $SD=1.46$)

All three areas connect with skills needed for written examinations. Thus, student's main challenges were associated with knowledge assessment. One of the main concerns was that, for example, in an exam, students want to make sure they are understood by the examiner. They write longer essays and take more space to express the ideas and arguments, just so they can be certain the message they are sending across is the message they intended to convey. Additionally, sometimes, they lack or simply forget vocabulary in English and need to describe a word in a rather lengthy way:

> Sometimes I have this word in my native language … I can't memorise it [in English] and I just finish it with huge sentence of explanation of this word that I wanted to say. (Student 24)

Lecturers understand this, and they see the difference between native and non-native students in the classroom; that non-native students write longer, more elaborate, not concise essays. However, what is most important for the lecturers is that the students demonstrate the knowledge of the content material well. The grammatical structures used are not being assessed. Nevertheless, students worry because, as they say, the more concise and to the point one's writing is, the more confident and knowledgeable the person comes across as.

It seems that the common problem for both, students and lecturers, is the fact that EMI is almost set to 'needing more time' than studying in one's native language. As one student phrased it:

> I really don't care if he [the lecturer] is a native speaker or fat or small. As long as I can understand what he's saying and he takes his time, maybe the classes will

be slower, it can ... but if it's clear for everybody, like it's not too rushed because sometimes teachers they need to teach this in one hour. (Student 17)

Students need more time to understand what the lecturers teach, lecturers need more time to comprehend and respond to students' questions and students need more time to sit an exam. However, how are they supposed to manage these problems in a tight schedule that follows the exact same structure as programmes taught in Polish? How can a class be 'slower' if certain material has to be covered in sixty minutes, regardless of it being taught in English or Polish? These are the questions that need to be addressed after letting the unheard voices be heard.

Implications for researchers and practitioners

Despite the fact that research into EMI has increased exponentially in recent years (for an overview, see Curle et al. 2020), there is still a disproportion between EMI provision worldwide and EMI research. The rapid growth of EMI is faster than the progress we see in research policy and planning (Galloway et al. 2020). This is true in the case of Poland. There is no EMI policy and, as mentioned earlier, the scarcity of research is undeniable. The development of EMI in Poland can be informed and supported by the results of research conducted in different contexts across the globe. Nevertheless, further research in Poland is needed to unpack the specificities of the issues and complexities of EMI in the context in order to be able to appropriately respond to the problems encountered in EMI. As Lin emphasizes in Chapter 16 of this volume, students' and lecturers' voices need to be heard. Until we seek to identify and address problems encountered by the key players in EMI, we will not be able to see any positive changes taking place.

Additionally, since the term 'EMI' is almost non-existent in Poland and the phenomenon undefined, it translates into the kind of information that can be gathered related to the organization of studies conducted in English in Poland at the meso (legislative), macro (university) and micro (individual) levels. Without filling the gap between theory (terminology used) and practice (implementing programmes conducted in English in Poland), it will still be difficult to recognize EMI as a phenomenon and monitor the development of EMI. This proves not only the poverty of recognizing the EMI topic in Poland but above all indicates the need to standardize the EMI development nomenclature.

References

Briggs, J., Dearden, J., and Macaro, E. (2018), 'English medium instruction: Comparing teacher beliefs in secondary and tertiary education', *Studies in Second Language Learning and Teaching*, 8 (3): 673–96. DOI: http://dx.doi.org/10.14746/ssllt.2018.8.3.7.

Bradford, A. (2016), 'Toward a Typology of Implementation Challenges Facing English-Medium Instruction in Higher Education: Evidence From Japan', *Journal of Studies in International Education*, 20 (4): 339–56. DOI: 10.1177/1028315316647165.

Chojnacka, E., and Macukow, B. (1995), 'Engineering education taught in foreign languages in Poland', *European Journal of Engineering Education*, 20 (1): 45–52. DOI: 10.1080/0304379950200108.

Coleman, J., Hultgren, K., LiWei, Cheng-Fang Tsui, C., and Shaw, P. (2018), 'Forum on English-medium instruction', *TESOL Quarterly*, 52 (3): 701–20.

Curle, S, Jablonkai, Mittelmeier, Sahan, & Veitch, (2020), 'English Medium Part 1: Literature review', in Galloway (ed.), *English in Higher Education (Report No. 978-0-86355-977-8)*, London, UK: British Council.

Dearden, J., and Macaro, E. (2016), 'Higher education teachers' attitudes towards English medium instruction: A three-country comparison', *Studies in Second Language Learning and Teaching*, 6 (3): 455–86.

Domański, T., Stępień-Kuczyńska, A., and Włodarska-Frykowska, A. (2017), 'Internacjonalizacja: Zdoświadczeń polskich ośrodków politologicznych', in T. Domański, A. Stępień-Kuczyńska and A. Włodarska-Frykowska (eds), *Internacjonalizacja polskich ośrodków politologicznych*, 111–92, Łódź: Wydawnictwo Uniwersytetu Łódzkiego. DOI: 10.18778/8088-741-1.08.

Galloway, N., Numajiri, T., and Rees, N. (2020), 'The "internationalisation", or "Englishisation", of higher education in East Asia', *Higher Education*, 80: 395–414.

Golenko, A. (2014), 'Teaching fundamentals of machine design in English', *Zeszyty Naukowe Politechniki Śląskiej: Transport*, 83 (1904): 91–7.

GUS (2010), *Szkoły Wyższe i ich Finanse w 2009 r.*, Warsaw: Główny Urząd Statystyczny.

GUS (2019), *Szkolnictwo Wyższe w roku akademickim 2018/2019*, Warsaw: Główny Urząd Statystyczny.

GUS (2020), *Szkoły Wyższe i ich Finance w 2019 r.*, Warsaw: Główny Urząd Statystyczny.

Król, A., and Romanowski, P. (2020), 'Internationalizing secondary education in Poland through English as a medium of instruction', *Baltic Journal of English Language, Literature and Culture*, 10: 100–15. ps://doi.org/10.22364/BJELLC.10.2020.07.

Macaro, E. (2018), *English Medium Instruction: Content and Language in Policy and Practice*, Oxford: Oxford University Press.

Machnikowski, R., and Włodarska-Frykowska, A. (2017). 'Uniwersytet Łódzki', in T. Domański, A. Stępień-Kuczyńska and A. Włodarska-Frykowska (eds), *Internacjonalizacja polskich ośrodków politologicznych*, 144–7, Łódź: Wydawnictwo Uniwersytetu Łódzkiego. DOI: 10.18778/8088-741-1.08.

MNiSW (2013), *Szkolnictwo Wyższe w Polsce*, Warsaw: MNiSW.
MNiSW (2015), *Program Umiędzynarodowienia Szkolnictwa Wyższego*, Warsaw: Public Information Bulletin. Available online: https://www.bip.nauka.gov.pl/komunikaty-rzecznika-prasowego-mnisw/program-umiedzynarodowienia-szkolnictwa-wyszego.html.
OECD (2017), *Supporting Entrepreneurship and Innovation in Higher Education in Poland*, Paris: OECD Skills Studies, OECD Publishing. Available online: https://doi.org/10.1787/9789264270923-en.
Pol-on.pl, (2021), *Instytucje Szkolnictwa Wyższego*. Available online: https://polon.nauka.gov.pl/opi/aa/rejestry/szkolnictwo?execution=e1s1.
Ready, Study, Go! Poland (2021), Studyfinder. Study in Poland – Go Poland! Available online: https://study.gov.pl/studyfinder?field_area_tid=All&field_level_tid=All&field_language_tid=18.
Romanowski, P. (2019), 'Translanguaging as a norm in multilingual education: An example from Poland', *Foreign Language Teaching*, 46 (6): 590–9.
Romanowski, P. (2020), 'Perceptions of translanguaging among the students and teachers of EMI classrooms in Poland', *Lenguas Modernas*, 55: 151–65.
Sandström, A., and Neghina, (2017), *English-taught bachelor's programmes: Internationalising European higher education. European Association for International Education*. Amsterdam, NL: EAIE.
Sula, P. (2017), 'Uniwersytet Wrocławski', in T. Domański, A. Stępień-Kuczyńska and A. Włodarska-Frykowska (eds), *Internacjonalizacja polskich ośrodków politologicznych*, 188–92, Łódź: Wydawnictwo Uniwersytetu Łódzkiego. DOI: 10.18778/8088-741-1.08.
Ustawa z dnia 7 lipca 2017 r. o Narodowej Agencji Wymiany Akademickiej, DZ.U (2017), poz. 1582 D20191582L.pdf (nawa.gov.pl).

13

Finding Space for Languages of Instruction alongside English: Language Management in South African Higher Education

Christa van der Walt

Introduction

The headline of the Western Cape Afrikaans newspaper *Die Burger* has yet another headline about the new language policy of the University of Stellenbosch as one of the top articles in its online feed: 'Departement sê Afrikaans is níe inheems' (Department says Afrikaans is *not* indigenous). Articles like these have been the staple of this newspaper since the university published a new draft version of its language policy for public comment[1] on 8 March. The previous version led to a number of costly challenges in court from a collection of people who call themselves 'Gelyke Kanse' (equal opportunity). They objected to the 2016 version of the university's language policy because it weakened the position of Afrikaans and gave English a more prominent position in teaching and learning and official status as the de facto medium of instruction. In other words, Afrikaans and English did not have equal status (hence the name of the group). After two years of court cases, the Constitutional Court found on 10 October 2019 that the language policy was justified in constitutional terms.

These types of court cases have become a feature of language policy revisions at historically Afrikaans universities from 2016 onwards. See, for example, the protests at the University of Pretoria (Politicsweb 2015) and at the University of the Free State (eNCA 2016). These protests occurred in the wake of the Fallist movements (#Rhodesmustfall, #Feesmustfall and others) which focused attention on access to higher education, colonial symbols and decolonizing the curriculum. Language use in education, with a specific focus on the use of

Afrikaans, formed part of this debate. Since the majority of South Africans who may qualify for access to higher education receive their schooling in English, it was argued that Afrikaans, in addition to its historical burden as *the* language of apartheid, is not useful in higher education and constitutes a barrier to understanding lectures and discussions.

As an academic who is interested in multilingual education, for me the debate and protests about Afrikaans were not as interesting as the lack of debate about the widespread use of a colonial language (English) and the absence of African languages not only at the higher education level but at all levels of education. Despite a variety of policies and initiatives, South African higher education and historically Afrikaans universities, in particular, are following global trends by increasingly offering programmes in English, with some support in other languages, as will be discussed next.

Setting the scene: English and other languages

Language policy in higher education is regulated by the national Department of Higher Education and Training (DHET). In the final phase of the court battle about Stellenbosch University's language policy and its use of English as the default language of instruction, the national department published a draft language policy to address the shortcomings of the previous policy (2002). After taking feedback from universities and other higher education institutions into account, the final policy was published on 30 October 2020. Since the draft version of the policy was criticized for its lack of even mention of English, the final policy explicitly refers to its status at higher education level and demonstrates an awareness of translanguaging practices, even though the word is not used. Under the heading 'Domains of Language Use', the policy notes (Language Policy Framework 2020: 15):

> Recognising the de facto status of English as the language of learning and teaching across South African higher education institutions, this policy calls upon universities to adopt a flexible approach in the implementation of English as the language of learning and teaching.

The role of other languages is acknowledged, with a proviso:

> Where demonstrable competencies have been established in one or more languages other than English, such competencies and initiatives should not be

impeded, but rather, nurtured and encouraged *as long as they do not serve as barriers of access to speakers of other languages*. (15; emphasis added)

To somebody who is familiar with language policy debates in South Africa, the italicized words can refer only to Afrikaans.

The main purpose of the Language Policy Framework (2020) seems to be the fostering of African languages, particularly since the 2002 version of the policy is acknowledged to have been unsuccessful in raising the status and use of African languages in higher education (10). A particular strength of the 2020 Language Policy Framework is that it puts higher education in the context of education in general, with a clear directive for teacher training and the development of African languages at school level. This means that developing competence in African languages is a requirement for student teachers, which in turn means that the offering of African languages is extended beyond traditional language departments in faculties or schools of arts, social sciences and humanities.

The 2020 Language Policy Framework for higher education requires that universities re-evaluate their policies and revise them if necessary. The DHET introduces a number of monitoring strategies to ensure policy implementation, including the requirement that universities submit their policies and implementation plans to the department and report annually on progress with their implementation plans.

This is the backdrop against which English-medium instruction (EMI) is supposed to take place in higher education classrooms in South Africa. The debate about Afrikaans at Stellenbosch University has been repeated at other historically Afrikaans universities, although most of them have now moved to teaching and learning mainly in English. The arguments raised in this debate come from different perspectives, some of which are more than a century old.

Language as an object in policies and policy discussions

In his much-quoted argument about orientations to language management, Ruiz (1994) points to the different ways in which policymakers look at language. He distinguishes the 'language as a problem' orientation as opposed to the 'language as a resource' orientation. The latter is mentioned explicitly in the Language Policy Framework (2020: 14) as one of its principles: 'A recognition that languages are critical resources in the transmission of knowledge, cognitive development and effective participation in the knowledge economy'. For academics who argue for the value of using the full repertoire of one's language resources to make meaning in academia (see discussions of translanguaging in Siu and Lin's chapter on EMI in Hong Kong in this volume), the 'language as a resource' orientation is important not only to support learning and teaching but also to validate minoritized languages in high-status domains such as higher education. The misconception that a language or variety of a language needs to be 'fully developed' as an academic language (whatever that may mean) is avoided here since translanguaging strategies can be acknowledged and encouraged in classrooms and other teaching and learning contexts. In accordance with the idea of creating space for other languages, Li Wei (2011: 1223) points out that 'the notion of translanguaging space is particularly relevant to multilinguals not only because of their capacity to use multiple linguistic resources to form and transform their own lives, but also because the space they create through their multilingual practices, or translanguaging, has its own transformative power'.

However, the 'language as a problem' orientation seems to be deeply ingrained and the way in which it manifests in discussions about which language to use when and how can be seen in conceptualizations of language as a physical entity that takes up space. In a physical world (and in a very basic sense), an object takes up space that is therefore not available to another object, unless they merge in some way or the one consumes the other. This limited and limiting view of language use constructs English as taking up space, with the result that there is less space for other languages. Of course, the more extreme version of this view can be seen in discussions around 'Killer English', where the language is seen as 'consuming' other language(s) because it is used exclusively in particular domains. This view is not limited to South Africa. Worldwide there seems to be resurgence in discussions about linguistic imperialism, specifically regarding the role of English. In the case of academic articles, they also seem to appear often in languages other than English (see e.g. Popova and Beavitt (2017); or in relation to sign languages e.g. Rose and Conoma (2018); or in the context of so-called developing countries e.g. Mackenzie (2021)).

The construction of languages taking up space is at the heart of the debate that pits languages against each other; in the case of Stellenbosch University, Afrikaans against English. The university started as an English-speaking institution (the Victoria College) but as the result of the bequest of a wealthy farmer, it had the money to further Afrikaans. In his will, the farmer J. H. Marais made money available to the then Victoria College in 1915 on condition that it be used 'specifically for education in and through the Dutch language in both its forms (that is, Afrikaans and Dutch)' (as translated by Brink 2006: 20).[2] The corporeality of these two languages is striking in the formulation of their relation to English: 'the Dutch language in both its forms as mentioned will occupy *no lesser place* than the other official language' (20). It is the same idea that underpins the court case and arguments brought by the Gelyke Kanse pressure group when they link languages with their home language speakers. On their Facebook page they compare the sizes of population groups and their representation in higher education. They declare that 'the White English-speaking component of the SU student corps is the largest English-speaking component by a significant margin' compared to 'Brown people' who form the largest 'population group'[3] of which the majority speaks Afrikaans. They, according to the website, 'are by far the most under-represented group at tertiary education institutions' (see https://www.facebook.com/gelykekanse/). The link with physical size is again indicative of the argument that languages take up space and can edge out other languages, even when the population is in the majority.

The Language Policy Framework (2020) is guilty of constructing language as a physical entity in similar ways. In the introduction it is said that indigenous languages have '*structurally* not been afforded the official *space* to function as academic and scientific languages' (9; emphases added). The use of languages other than English should not 'serve as *barriers* of access to speakers of other languages' (15; emphasis added).

It may appear trivial to pick on the use of metaphors, but the problem is that this construction of language hides the way in which language is used by multilingual students, who would hardly experience the languages in their heads as physically distinct or actively pushing each other out. In studies of how students use languages in academic environments, they often describe how they move between the languages, thinking in one and writing in another (Pfeiffer and Van der Walt 2019: 66). Despite having their schooling in Swedish, Airey (2009: 89 and 110) found that most of the Swedish students in his study may have struggled in their first year, but by their second year they seemed to have developed bilingual scientific literacy. It is necessary to see language less as an object (that can be compartmentalized, moved around or tucked away) and more as a pervasive presence that can be directed, either by the users themselves or by fellow students, lecturers or tutors.

Seeing languages as objects that occupy particular, separate spaces is a view of multilingualism that has been criticized extensively, notably by Makoni and Pennycook (2007: 31), who argue against separating and enumerating languages, particularly in Africa. Similarly, García (2009: 141) objects to the view of languages as 'bounded autonomous systems', which is particularly problematic in multilingual contexts (see Simie's chapter on EMI in Ethiopia in this volume). However, this is exactly the view of the Language Policy Framework (2020) when it lists and enumerates the various languages. This is the view of any language policy that prescribes the use of a particular language in a particular space, like most language policies do. As Shohamy (2006: xvi) explains, the fluid nature of language use transcends the boundaries of Language X and Language Y.

The Language Policy Framework (2020) and its previous version, the Language Policy for Higher Education (2002), are not the only policies that prescribe language use and language learning in higher education. In 2015, the Department of Basic Education published its *Minimum Requirements for Teacher Education Qualifications* (hereafter MRTEQ, 2015). Just like the higher education policies of 2002 and the 2020, it is required that student teachers who are Afrikaans-English bilinguals, learn an African language for conversational purposes. When the Language Policy for Higher Education was first promulgated (in 2002), an increased focus was placed on African languages which led to all higher education institutions adopting an African language or languages of the region where the institution is located. When the MRTEQ policy was published in 2025, it was the easiest route for institutions to simply use the African language that had already been chosen to comply with the national policy for higher education. The practice of choosing a regional language seems logical, specifically since the Language Policy Framework (2020) builds on its 2002 version, but of course neither universities nor groups of speakers are spread evenly throughout the country. Moreover, higher education students do not necessarily study in the region where they grew up. If they want to enrol for programmes like veterinary sciences, dentistry or oenology – which are costly and not offered at all universities – they will move to an institution that may not offer support in the language(s) with which they are familiar. This means that the student body on most South African campuses would include speakers of all official South African languages.

In the absence of consultation with universities, the national education departments were not able to steer the so-called development of African languages as academic languages in a coordinated way. In a survey of African languages offered by student teachers (according to the requirements of the Language Policy Framework), done by me and Xeketwana (forthcoming), there is an overemphasis on some languages (isiXhosa, Afrikaans), with one of the official languages (Siswati) not appearing on any university website and with only two institutions offering South African Sign Language. Student mobility means that it is difficult to adhere to the ideal of the Language Policy Framework (2020: 14) that requires of institutions to develop language implementation plans that need to 'indicate at least two official languages, other than the medium of instruction or language of teaching and learning [which is predominantly English], for development for scholarly discourse as well as official communication'. If the idea is to create 'a receptive institutional culture' (Language Policy Framework 2020: 13), then universities are set to fail because of unrealistic expectations and a lack of coordination in terms of language offerings.

It seems, therefore, that the national policies favour a top-down process that has led to higher education institutions inserting particular languages into particular spaces (and these words are used very deliberately). This means that there is no awareness of the language resources in the institutions and in classrooms particularly, with the result that the unique contributions that these languages can make in each classroom are not acknowledged.

Moving the pieces on the chessboard

In terms of the view that languages take up space in particular domains, language policies are expected to be developed in tandem with implementation plans to show the way in which broad policy guidelines should be implemented. The Language Policy Framework (2020: 14) states in section 24 that 'all institutions must develop strategies, policies and *implementation plans* [emphasis added] for promoting multilingualism as defined by this policy framework'. At historically Afrikaans universities, a variety of language arrangements have been used, as described in Van der Walt (2013). They include splitting big classrooms into Afrikaans and English groups (so-called parallel-medium classrooms) using translanguaging strategies such as code-switching when lecturing and co-languaging on PowerPoint presentations and in study materials (so-called dual-medium classrooms) and, finally, using a simultaneous (or whispering) interpretation service during monolingual lectures.[4] The university's 2016 language policy[5] makes some provision for different contexts by requiring in Section 7.4.2 that 'each faculty and support services division describes its implementation of this Policy in its Language Implementation Plan' (Stellenbosch University 2016: 8). However, the faculties are still bound by the language arrangements that prescribe spaces and limits for different languages.

In the case of isiXhosa at Stellenbosch University, there does not seem to be the same intense debate as the one around Afrikaans, mainly because speakers of isiXhosa are in the minority and the university does not have a history of using the language to the extent that it has used and promoted Afrikaans. IsiXhosa is supposed to be 'developed' by means of special projects (see e.g. Van der Merwe 2020). Its position can be seen as peripheral because in the Language Policy (Stellenbosch University 2016: 9) it is stated:

> SU is committed to increasing the use of isiXhosa, to the extent that this is *reasonably practicable*, for example through basic communication skills short courses for staff and students, career-specific communication, discipline-specific terminology guides (printed and mobile applications) and phrase books. (Section 7.5.4; emphasis added)

In fairness, it must be mentioned that the university has implemented all of these measures.

In 2016, as mentioned previously, Fallist movements such as #Rhodesmustfall and #Feesmustfall demonstrated the widespread student dissatisfaction with the higher education section in general. These debates included discussions about the use of particular language arrangements, specifically simultaneous interpretation and the so-called dual-medium arrangement. Kannemeyer (2017) reports on the role of Afrikaans, where it is said that simultaneous interpretation is not always done equally well at all institutions. In personal communication, colleagues at other historically Afrikaans institutions mention that attendance at Afrikaans classes in the parallel-medium arrangements often decrease rapidly so that the English class becomes bigger than the Afrikaans class. Since universities invest much money in buying in additional help for parallel-medium classes, the 'migration' of students can render this language arrangement ineffective and even wasteful. Students often argue that they prefer their lectures to be in the same language as the textbook (see e.g. Van der Walt 2008). Perceptions like these lead to a decline in the demand for Afrikaans textbooks which in turn influences the medium of instruction.

Conclusion: Implications for EMI researchers and practitioners

This chapter started with what is euphemistically called the 'language debate' at Stellenbosch University. The language debate is a proxy for what scholars, students and alumni see as a fight to give Afrikaans space and to maintain its status as a scholarly language. In the context of the recent Language Policy Framework (2020), such a debate must be relativized in view of the responsibility to also develop an African language as a scholarly language.

One of the biggest dangers of this debate is the assumption that nobody has a problem using English in everyday life and in academic contexts. The assumption that there will be enough material available in English and that all lecturers can use English as a language of learning and teaching is never discussed. If there is a gap in study material, it is assumed that academics will write a document (study notes, an academic article, a monograph). Since students exit school with English as one of their subjects, and since most programmes require a particular level of English-language proficiency, the assumption is that students are more or less prepared for university study in English. If students struggle, there is a language centre where they can get help. However, there is no proficiency test for lecturers – it is simply accepted that Afrikaans and international lecturers can use English. Academics from other countries are mostly appointed for their scientific standing rather than their ability to use English for teaching. It is only when students complain that a problem with language proficiency may be addressed, usually by sending an interpreter to the classroom (if the lecturer is Afrikaans-speaking) or by allocating smaller groups of postgraduate students to lecturers from other countries.

Using EMI in higher education implies financial stability. It implies that institutions are able to buy academic materials (books, articles and other resources) in English or that they have the resources to develop such materials themselves. It also implies that institutions can support students who struggle with academic English (or Afrikaans in the case of historically Afrikaans institutions). We can argue that such money is well spent when students graduate successfully, but of course the completion rate at South African universities is unimpressive, to say the least. According to a 2021 report by the Centre for Risk Analysis (CRA), 'the proportion of students who graduated in each degree category as a share of all those who were enrolled in that field three or four years earlier' was 16.6 per cent in 2019 (Ndebele 2021: 72).

Rather than look at languages as if they can be 'managed' like pieces on a chessboard, we need to acknowledge the languages, particularly the African languages, that are there and develop strategies and materials that will build on the rich potential of such languages.

Notes

1 The university has to revise its language policy every five years. In addition, a new national policy was published in October 2020, which added impetus to the current policy revision.
2 The original document is available in Dutch at the university.
3 This view of people as a 'population group' is highly problematic, particularly in the case of so-called Brown people. It harks back to the Apartheid Population Registration Act whereby people were classified according to their ethnicity, a concept that is similarly problematic.
4 For a description of whispering interpretation, see Van der Walt (2013).
5 This policy is currently being revised.

References

Airey, J. (2009), *Science, Language and Literacy: Case Studies of Learning in Swedish University Physics*, Uppsala: Uppsala University.

Brink, C. (2006), *No Lesser Place: The 'Taaldebat' at Stellenbosch University*, Stellenbosch: African Sun Media.

eNCA. (2016, 18 November), 'UFS wins language policy case against Afriforum'. Available online: https://www.enca.com/south-africa/ufs-wins-language-case-against-afriforum (accessed 21 March 2021).

García, O. (2009), *Bilingual Education in the 21st Century: A Global Perspective*, Chichester: Wiley-Blackwell.

Kannemeyer, M. (2017), 'Die stand van Afrikaans aan universiteite' [The status of Afrikaans at universities], debate series presented on the Afrikaans website *Litnet* as part of a series *University Seminar 2017*. Available online: https://www.litnet.co.za/die-stand-van-afrikaans-aan-universiteite/ (accessed 18 April 2021).

Language Policy Framework for Public Higher Education Institutions, Determined in Terms of Section 27(2) of the Higher Education Act 101 of 1997 (as amended) (2020). Pretoria: Department of Higher Education and Training. Available online: https://www.gov.za/sites/default/files/gcis_document/202011/43860gon1160.pdf (accessed 21 March 2021).

Li, W. (2011), 'Moment analysis and translanguaging space: Discursive construction of identities by multilingual Chinese youth in Britain', *Journal of Pragmatics*, 43: 1222–35.

Mackenzie, L. (2021), 'Linguistic imperialism, English, and development: Implications for Colombia', *Current Issues in Language Planning*. DOI: 10.1080/14664208.2021.1939977.

Makoni, S. B., and Pennycook, A. (2007), 'Introduction', in S. B. Makoni and A. Pennycook (eds), *Disi and Reconstituting Languages*, Clevedon: Multilingual Matters.

Marang, O. (2016), 'University of Pretoria "like Alcatraz" – EFF students'. *Politicsweb*, 18 April. Available online: https://www.politicsweb.co.za/opinion/university-of-pretoria-like-alcatraz--eff-students (accessed 18 April 2021).

Ndebele, T. (2021), *Education June 2021*, Johannesburg: Centre for Risk Analysis.

Pfeiffer, V. F., and Van der Walt, C. (2019), 'Ethno-linguistically diverse South African students' writing', *Per Linguam*, 35 (3): 58–73 (special edition).

Policy on the Minimum Requirements for Teacher Education (2015), Government Gazette no. 34467, Department of Education, Pretoria: South Africa. Available online: https://saide.org.za/resources/Library/Policy%20on%20Min%20Requirements%20for%20Teacher%20Ed%20Qualifications.pdf#:~:text=The%20Minimum%20Requirements%20for%20Teacher%20Education%20Qualifications%20replaces,should%20be%20read%20in%20conjunction%20with%20the%20HEQF (accessed on 21 March 2021).

Politicsweb (2015, 8 June), 'University of Pretoria "like Alcatraz" – EFF students'. Available online: https://www.politicsweb.co.za/opinion/university-of-pretoria-like-alcatraz--eff-students.

Popova, N. G., and Beavitt, T. A. (2017), 'English as a means of scientific communication: Linguistic imperialism or interlingua?', *Integration of Education*, 21 (1): 54–70.

Rose, H., and Conoma, J. B. (2018), 'Linguistic imperialism: Still a valid construct in relation to language policy for Irish sign language', *Language Policy*, 17: 385–404.

Ruiz, R. (1994), 'Language policy and planning in the United States', *Annual Review of Applied Linguistics*, 14: 111–25. Available online: https://doi.org/10.1017/S0267190500002841.

Shohamy, E. (2006), *Language Policy: Hidden Agendas and New Approaches*, London: Routledge.

Stellenbosch University (2016), *Language Policy of Stellenbosch University*.

Van der Merwe, M. (2020), 'Scaffolding for content knowledge of home language learning by collaborative online dictionaries', *Per Linguam*, 36 (1): 1–14.

Van der Walt, C. (2008), 'University students' attitudes towards and experiences of bilingual classrooms', in Anthony J. Liddicoat and Richard B. Baldauf Jr. (eds), *Language Planning and Policy: Language Planning in Local Contexts*, Clevedon: Multilingual Matters..

Van der Walt, C. (2013), *Multilingual Higher Education: Beyond English-Medium Orientations*, Clevedon: Multilingual Matters.

English-Medium Instruction in Vietnamese Higher Education: From Government Policies to Institutional Practices

Huong Thu Nguyen

Introduction

English-medium instruction (EMI) programmes were introduced in Vietnam in the 1990s at the postgraduate level in partnership with overseas higher education institutions (HEIs) mostly from the West (e.g. France, the UK, United States, etc.). They were first offered at the undergraduate level in the early 2000s to cater to the unmet demands and domestic thirst for foreign qualifications (Nhan and Le 2019). With the government's policies in (i) reforming the HE system to be on par with the global trends of internationalization and world universities benchmarking and (ii) improving Vietnamese youth's English proficiency to contribute to national development and international competitiveness, EMI programmes have gained new momentum (Tran and Nguyen 2018).

EMI is now offered extensively in Vietnam from kindergarten to tertiary education in partial or full EMI modes (Nguyen and Komarnisky 2020). Approaches vary, some programmes being offered by Vietnamese providers, joint ventures between domestic and foreign partners or wholly international branch campuses (Vietnamese Government 2012). Such developments regarding EMI reflect a quest for quality education, the demand for internationalization and the pursuit of human capital development and economic progress on governmental, institutional and individual levels (similar to other East and Southeast Asian contexts; see e.g. Aizawa et al. in this volume). Research on the EMI development in Vietnamese higher education (VHE) reveals challenges in implementation and outcomes (Pham and Doan

2020). Over the years, however, some benefits of EMI have been perceived by lecturers, students and local HEIs such as the improvement in lecturers' and students' English proficiency and the access to high-quality textbooks (Le 2020; Phuong and Nguyen 2019). This chapter focuses on the deployment of EMI policies at the tertiary level through a systematic review of the research on EMI in VHE.

Overview of EMI policy in the Vietnamese higher education context

In this section, I provide a brief overview of VHE EMI policy as it concerns EMI provision. Before 1986, VHE was a backward and inefficient system, incapable of supporting the government's development and globalization policies due to the country's long history of foreign colonialism, invasion and war. Since the introduction of the Đổi Mới (economic and social reform) policy in 1986, Vietnam has pursued an open-door policy and intensified its global participation, creating an urgent demand for VHE reform to educate a population of graduates with 'academic, technical, thinking, and behavioural skills' (World Bank 2012: 1) and with capacities to effectively engage and perform in a globalized context. In response, since 1986, Vietnam has opened 202 new universities and colleges, totalling 297 universities and colleges as of April 2020 (MOET 2020). However, VHE quality has yet to meet the country's economic development needs (Nhan and Le 2019).

Against this background, the government has promulgated a number of important policies in a bid to transform its HE, which also serves as the driving force for EMI growth. These include the HE reform agenda, or HERA 2006–20, to introduce measures to renovate the HE system for national economic development (Vietnamese Government 2005), which led to institutional autonomy for an increasing number of universities and a surge in partnerships between domestic and overseas HEIs. The internationalization amendment of the education law in 2005 has allowed other languages of instruction in addition to Vietnamese (Vietnamese National Assembly 2005: Article 7), with English being the most popular (Duong and Chua 2016; Tran and Nguyen 2018). Third, the National Foreign Language 2008–20 project (now extended to 2025) was approved to improve the foreign-language (mainly English) proficiency of Vietnamese students and school teachers (Vietnamese Government 2008).

EMI programmes in Vietnamese higher education

Different EMI programmes are offered in VHE (Table 14.1), including foreign and domestic programmes (MOET 2014).

In operating foreign EMI programmes, or *Chương trình Đào tạo Nước ngoài*, Vietnamese HEIs have input from partner HEIs in terms of curriculum, materials and assessment. There are two subtypes of foreign programmes: advanced programmes (APs) or *Chương trình Tiên tiến*, and joint programmes (JPs) or *Chương trình Liên kết*. The main approach of APs is to 'import' the curriculum of partner HEIs overseas (mostly from the West) into the Vietnamese university (MOET 2016). JPs mainly aim to develop transnational education programmes (Nhan and Nguyen 2018) that use the imported curricula from partner HEIs overseas where delivery can be completely local or in articulation arrangements in which the first phase is in Vietnam and the second phase overseas (Nguyen and Shillabeer 2013). The attraction of such programmes is the foreign degree awarded to enrolees upon graduation.

Domestic EMI programmes are local institutions' initiatives to develop their own version of EMI programmes. There are two subtypes of domestic programmes: high-quality programmes (HQPs) or *Chương trình Đào tạo*

Table 14.1 Types of EMI Programmes in Vietnam

Types of EMI Programmes	Programme Nature	Degree Conferred	Teaching Staff	Program Nomenclature in VHE
Foreign programmes	In corporation with foreign partner HEIs – 'imported curriculum'	Local degree	Local and foreign lecturers	Advanced programmes
		Foreign degree	Local lecturers	Joint programmes
Domestic programmes	Locally developed with reference to foreign programme	Local degree	Local lecturers	High-quality programmes
		Local degree	Local lecturers	Profession-oriented higher education programmes (selected programmes are EMI, others are in Vietnamese-medium)

Source: Adapted from Nguyen et al. (2017).

Chất lượng cao, and profession-oriented higher education programmes (POHEs) or *Chương trình Đào tạo Định hướng Nghề nghiệp - Ứng dụng*. HQPs are EMI programmes developed with reference from the curriculum, materials and assessment of foreign partner HEIs, being offered at a relatively lower tuition fee than foreign-type EMI (MOET 2014). POHEs are the outcome of the Vietnamese-Netherlands international cooperation project to ensure graduate employment (POHE 2016). However, to date, only two universities offer POHEs in EMI with the other institutions offering POHEs in Vietnamese-medium.

At the time of writing, 70 Vietnamese HEIs are coordinating 352 JPs, 37 APs and 53 POHEs (Giao duc 2020; MOET 2016; POHE 2016). There are no official statistics available on the rapid growth of HQPs on offer; however, the 24 autonomous HEIs have been recruiting 25–50 per cent of the new enrolees to their HQPs (Nghiem 2020).

EMI implementation in Vietnamese universities

Focus on the meso (implementation) level of EMI

Research on EMI implementation in VHE has been undertaken from a number of theoretical perspectives. The first is language policy and planning to examine how EMI policy is translated from the macro level of policy provision (e.g. Nguyen et al. 2018) to the meso level of EMI institutionalization (e.g. Duong and Chua 2016; Nguyen et al. 2016; Pham and Doan 2020; Tri and Moskovsky 2019) to the micro challenges in teaching and learning through English (e.g. Le 2020; Nguyen 2018; Nguyen et al. 2017; Phuong and Nguyen 2019).

These studies have revealed that even though EMI in Vietnam has been regulated by quite a number of government legislative documents, as introduced in the previous sections, the interpretation from macro to meso to micro level is far from seamless. The first reason is these policies tend to be too general to lead to informed practice and tend to follow rather than precede new developments in the system (Nguyen et al. 2017; Tri and Moskovsky 2019). For example, MOET's brief correspondence approving autonomous HEIs to develop HQPs with higher tuition fee was hastily disseminated in 2011 (MOET 2011) amid its boom in the system since HERA came into effect in 2006 (Nguyen et al. 2016). Not until 2014 was the circular with more detailed regulations on HPQs issued (MOET 2014). Similarly, the foreign EMI JPs were largely unregulated until 2012 when the decree on foreign cooperation and investment in education was issued (Nguyen and Shillabeer 2013; Vietnamese Government 2012).

Secondly, EMI is implemented in a top-down manner. This 'policy dumping' approach (Hamid and Nguyen 2016: 35) has not involved much consultation with the micro implementers in the classroom. Indeed, studies on lecturers' perspectives on EMI implementation unveil that they were required to start teaching in English without knowing the objectives of the policy or being trained for the new task (Hamid et al. 2019; Le 2020), leading to the 'pedagogies of assumption' (Pham and Doan 2020: 262). That means the task of coordinating EMI courses and delivering EMI lectures is often left to the individual lecturers' capacity and resourcefulness. Further, institutional support for lecturers is not common as it was reported in only one study by Duong and Chua (2016). Teacher training for EMI is not yet available in VHE, apart from one course 'EMI teaching methodology' in the mater's applied linguistics or teaching English for students of other languages in one university (Vu 2020). Therefore, it is not unexpected to discern that Vietnamese lecturers are not yet confident or efficient in different educational aspects in EMI teaching, such as assessment practice (Truong et al. 2020).

In addition, a myriad of issues has been documented on how EMI is practiced in classrooms. These include a lack of necessary proficiency on the part of lecturers and students to teach and learn disciplinary content through English, the dearth of relevant teaching materials and others. Local HEIs are in shortage of the resources needed for developing EMI programmes, thereby exercising 'policies of encouragement' (Pham and Doan 2020: 262). Lecturers are 'encouraged', for example, to try their best to teach through English (269–70), to be self-responsible for the textbooks by utilizing the materials from their previous postgraduate studies overseas (Nguyen et al. 2016: 678) or download online (Le 2020: 124). Fly-in foreign lecturers teach their courses in compressed time (two to three weeks) because local HEIs cannot afford for their longer stay (MOET 2016). In that context, the efforts of local lecturers and students in EMI programmes have been conceptualized as agency or the active implementers of EMI policy, who have adapted their teaching and learning practices and exerted extra effort to meet the policy demand imposed upon them (Hamid et al. 2019; Nguyen et al. 2021; Phan et al. 2019; Trinh and Conner 2019). This is also the main reason for local HEIs operating different EMI modes: very few local HEIs can offer 100 per cent EMI courses (e.g. in Nguyen et al. 2016) while most institutions offer partial – bilingual – EMI programmes (e.g. in Le 2020; Pham and Doan 2020), depending on the readiness of the lecturers and the available materials and resources.

Another reason for the bumpy macro-micro policy conversion is the institutions' overuse of their newly granted autonomy to establish linkages with overseas partners and to develop foreign and domestic EMI programmes without due diligence in quality assurance (Nguyen et al. 2016). Many HEIs have joined in offering the domestic EMI HQPs (developed by local HEIs) in various shapes and sizes to generate higher tuition fees without paying sufficient attention to quality of provision (Le 2014). In particular, during the initial years of operating, local HEIs were found to be lowering the entry requirements to increase student intake by accepting students without sufficient English proficiency and with low academic achievements from high school (Le 2014). Research on EMI implementation during this period revealed classroom challenges due to such recruitment practices (Nguyen 2018; Nguyen et al. 2016, 2017; Phuong and Nguyen 2019). At present, the labour market and the public at large are still very much suspicious of the proliferation of those domestic EMI HQPs (Nghiem 2020). Similarly, the foreign EMI JPs also face criticism for unqualified intake and teaching, leading to 'degree mills' and the massive enforced close-down of approximately 250 JPs since the first JP was approved in 1994 (Giao duc 2020).

EMI and the internationalization of higher education in Vietnam

Increasingly, research also looks more broadly at the interplay between EMI stipulation and the internationalization of VHE (Dang et al. 2013; Tran and Nguyen 2018) with focus on the internationalization of the EMI curriculum (Nguyen 2016; Nguyen et al. 2021; Tran et al. 2020) and employability in the foreign EMI APs (Tran et al. 2019). These studies reveal some perceived benefits of EMI, although these have yet to be empirically investigated. Students have reported enjoying the range of English materials from well-known publishers, the more modern teaching methods (e.g. workshop style, case study, etc.), assessment (e.g. quizzes, presentation, assignment, etc.) and the opportunity to learn with foreign lecturers in APs. The frequent exposure to English has also been attributed to students' improvement in language proficiency, a more open mindset, creativity and readiness for future jobs (Dang et al. 2013; Tran et al. 2019). Further, some local HEIs have re-examined their student enrolment processes. From rather low English requirements, such as IELTS 4.5 in 2006, many HEIs have now raised the bar to the international standard of IELTS 6.5 for the 2019–20 enrolments (e.g. FTU 2018) which will expectantly create a positive impact on teaching and learning in EMI environment. Local lecturers consider using Western reference materials as a convenience because this is the source of knowledge without having to translate it to the local language (Le 2020; Pham and Doan 2020). For some of them, working with partner lecturers and/or visiting overseas HEIs is a great opportunity to improve their language proficiency and EMI teaching skills (Nguyen 2018).

However, caution has been recommended on the conflict between local and Western knowledge, values and ideologies in the internationalized curriculum (Nguyen 2016; Nguyen et al. 2021; Tran et al. 2020). In particular, the 'imported curriculum' in foreign EMI AP programmes contains jurisdiction-specific knowledge (Leask and Bridge 2013), and foreign lecturers are not always prepared to integrate relevant local examples in lectures to sufficiently illustrate the theory in the local context (Nguyen et al. 2021). In addition, all EMI programmes require students to complete a political module on socialism, political economy and communism (Phan and Dang 2020), which has reduced the academic autonomy of local HEIs (Nguyen et al. 2016) and which can be of potential conflict with the Western curriculum content in the foreign EMI programmes (Nguyen et al. 2021). Therefore, calls have been made to localize the foreign EMI curriculum in APs and JPs and to strengthen the role of the local lecturers as the intermediaries between the Western and the local knowledge and values to cater to the demand of the local students and context (Nguyen et al. 2021).

Implications for higher education institutions and practitioners

EMI is perceived as having brought about benefits to the reform of VHE and plays an imperative role in internationalization. Local HEIs have extended their connection with more advanced HE systems in the world for capacity building and increased mobility (academics, students and programmes), which has contributed to a more international ethos for local campuses. Internationalization at home through different EMI programmes – APs, JPs, HQPs and POHEs – has responded to the domestic demand for foreign-style education and English proficiency improvement. In the face of Covid-19 and border closure, local HEIs have enrolled a large number of Vietnamese students, who cannot travel back to their institutions overseas, to complete their studies in foreign EMI JPs at both undergraduate and postgraduate levels or to receive credits to continue their study overseas once the situation improves (Phan and

Phung 2020). Such arrangements between local and overseas HEIs demonstrate that internationalization at home is not just a convenience but a viable HE alternative in Vietnam.

However, in order to reap the benefits of EMI and internationalization, there is much to be done. At the meso level, it is the improvement of teaching skills for lecturers and English proficiency for students. Training should be provided for lecturers on teaching in English through seminars, peer observations and collaboration with foreign lecturers to share experiences. Lecturers can also benefit from participating in online courses on EMI teaching, which is readily available through a Google search. English education for students should gear towards English for academic purposes from senior high school onwards and continue through the first year of university study. Explicit training focuses on academic genres of textbooks, articles, presentations and assignments. To afford these improvements in an institutionalized supporting scheme for lecturers and students, HEIs need long-term strategies and securing of sufficient resources and facilities.

References

Dang, T. K. A., Nguyen, T. M. H., and Le, T. T. T. (2013), 'The impacts of globalisation on EFL teacher education through English as a medium of instruction: An example from Vietnam', *Current Issues in Language Planning*, 14 (1): 52–72. DOI:10.1080/14664208.2013.780321.

Duong, V. A., and Chua, C. S. (2016), 'English as a symbol of internationalization in higher education: A case study of Vietnam', *Higher Education Research & Development*, 35 (4): 669–83. DOI:10.1080/07294360.2015.1137876.

FTU (2018), 'Five admission schemes to Foreign Trade University'. Available online: http://qtkd.ftu.edu.vn/truong-dai-hoc-ngoai-thuong-cong-bo-5-phuong-thuc-xet-tuyen-dai-hoc-nam-2020/.

Giao duc (2020), 'MOET ceases more than 200 international joint education programmes', *Tuoi Tre*. Available online: https://tuoitre.vn/bo-gd-dt-dung-hon-200-chuong-trinh-lien-ket-dao-tao-quoc-te-20200721151713185.htm.

Hamid, M. O., and Nguyen, T. M. H. (2016), 'Globalization, English language policy and teacher agency: Focus on Asia', *International Education Journal: Comparative Perspectives*, 16 (1): 26–44.

Hamid, M. O., Nguyen, H. T., Nguyen, H. V., and Phan, T. T. H. (2019), 'Agency and language-in-education policy in Vietnamese higher education', in G. P. Glasgow and J. Bouchard (eds), *Researching Agency in Language Policy and Planning*, 102–24, New York: Routledge.

Le, T. K. H. (2014), 'Vietnamese higher education in the context of globalization: Qualitative or quantitative targets?', *The International Education Journal: Comparative Perspectives*, 13 (1): 17–29.

Le, T. T. N. (2020), 'University lecturers' perceived challenges in EMI: Implications for teacher professional development', in V. C. Le, H. T. M. Nguyen, T. T. M. Nguyen and R. Barnard (eds), *Building Teacher Capacity in English Language Teaching in Vietnam: Research, Policy and Practice*, 115–32, London: Routledge.

Leask, B., and Bridge, C. (2013), 'Comparing internationalisation of the curriculum in action across disciplines: Theoretical and practical perspectives', *Compare: A Journal of Comparative and International Education*, 43 (1): 79–101. DOI:10.1080/03057925. 2013.746566.

MOET (2011), *Correspondence No. 5746/2011/BGDĐT-GDĐH on 'Recruitment of High-Quality Programmes in Universities'*, Hanoi: Ministry of Education and Training.

MOET (2014), *Circular No. 23/2014/TT-BGDĐT on 'Regulations on High-Quality Programmes in Universities'*, Hanoi: Ministry of Education and Training.

MOET (2016), *Report on the 10-Year Implementation of Advanced Program Project*, Hanoi: Ministry of Education and Training.

MOET (2020), *Statistical Report on Tertiary Education 2018–2019*. Available online: https://moet.gov.vn/thong-ke/Pages/thong-ko-giao-duc-dai-hoc.aspx?ItemID=6636.

Nghiem, H. (2020), 'High quality programmes in universities – much to be desired', *TienPhong*, 18 May. Available online: https://tienphong.vn/chuong-trinh-chat-luong-cao-trong-cac-dh-nhieu-dieu-dang-noi-post1240885.tpo.

Nguyen, G., and Shillabeer, A. (2013), 'Issues in transnational higher education regulation in Vietnam', in P. Mandal (ed.), *Proceedings of the International Conference on Managing the Asian Century*, 637–44, Singapore: Springer.

Nguyen, H. T. (2018), 'English-medium-instruction management: The missing piece in the internationalisation puzzle of Vietnamese higher education', in T. L. Tran and S.Marginson (eds), *Internationalisation in Vietnamese Higher Education*, 119–37, Switzerland: Springer.

Nguyen, H. T., Hamid, M. O., and Moni, K. (2016), 'English-medium instruction and self-governance in higher education: The journey of a Vietnamese university through the institutional autonomy regime', *Higher Education*, 72 (5): 669–83. DOI:10.1007/s10734-015-9970-y.

Nguyen, H. T., Phan, H. L. T., and Tran, L. T. (2021), 'Internationalisation of the curriculum in Vietnamese higher education: mediating between 'Western' and local imaginaries', *Compare: A Journal of Comparative and International Education*, https://doi.org/10.1080/03057925.2021.1995699

Nguyen, H. T., Walkinshaw, I., and Pham, H. H. (2017), 'EMI programmes in a Vietnamese university: Language, pedagogy and policy issues', in B. Fenton-Smith, P. Humphreys and I. Walkinshaw (eds), *English Medium of Instruction in Higher Education in Asia-Pacific: From Policy to Pedagogy*, 37–52, Switzerland: Springer.

Nguyen, H. T. M., Nguyen, H. T., Nguyen, H. V., and Nguyen, T. T. T. (2018), 'Local challenges to global needs in English language education in Vietnam: The perspective of language policy and planning', in C. C. S. Kheng (ed.), *Un(intended) Language Planning in a Globalising World: Multiple Levels of Players at Work*, 213–32, Berlin: De Gruyter.

Nguyen, L. P., and Komarnisky, R. (2020), *New Requirements for International Schools to Provide Compulsory Vietnamese Language and Culture Studies to Enrolled Vietnamese Students*. Available online: https://f.datasrvr.com/fr1/420/46228/Client_alert_-_Education_-_Circular_No__4.pdf.

Nguyen, T. K. Q. (2016), 'The profession-oriented higher education project in Vietnam: When curricular knowledge is at stake', in S. Bohlinger, T. K. A. Dang and M. Klatt (eds), *Education Policy: Mapping the Landscape and Scope*, 97–121, Frankfurt: Peter Lang.

Nhan, T. T., and Le, K. A. T. (2019), 'Internationalisation of higher education in Vietnam', in C. H. Nguyen M. Shah (eds), *Quality Assurance in Vietnamese Higher Education: Policy and Practice in the 21st Century*, 25–58. Cham: Springer International.

Nhan, T. T., and Nguyen, H. C. (2018), 'Quality challenges in transnational higher education under profit-driven motives: The Vietnamese experience', *Issues in Educational Research*, 28 (1): 138–52. Available online: https://search.informit.com.au/fullText;dn=437886215574421;res=IELHSS.

Pham, M., and Doan, B. N. (2020), 'English as a medium of instruction (EMI) in Vietnamese universities: Policies of encouragement and pedagogies of assumption', in P. Le Ha and D. Ba Ngoc (eds), *Higher Education in Market-Oriented Socialist Vietnam: New Players, Discourses, and Practices*, 261–82, Cham, Switzerland: Springer International.

Phan, H. L., and Dang, V. H. (2020), 'Engaging (with) new insights: Where to start to move scholarship and the current debate forward', in P. Le Ha and D. Ba Ngoc (eds), *Higher Education in Market-Oriented Socialist Vietnam: New Players, Discourses, and Practices*, 363–78, Cham, Switzerland: Springer International.

Phan, H. L., and Phung, T. (2020), 'COVID-19 opportunities for internationalisation at home', *University World News*, 28 August. Available online: https://www.universityworldnews.com/post.php?story=20200828113510793.

Phuong, Y. H., and Nguyen, T. T. (2019), 'Students' perceptions towards the benefits and drawbacks of EMI classes', *English Language Teaching*, 12 (5): 88.

POHE (2016), 'Profession-oriented higher education: The Vietnamese-Netherlands international cooperation project'. Available online: http://giaoducdaihoc.moet.edu.vn/vi/.

Tran, L. H. N., Hoang, T. G., and Vo, P. Q. (2019), 'At-home international education in Vietnamese universities: Impact on graduates' employability and career prospects', *Higher Education*, 78 (5): 817–34. DOI:10.1007/s10734-019-00372-w.

Tran, L. T., and Nguyen, H. T. (2018), 'Internationalisation of higher education in Vietnam through English medium instruction (EMI): Practices, tensions and implications for local language policies', in I. Liyanage (ed.), *Multilingual Education Yearbook 2017: Internationalization, Stakeholders and Multilingual Education Contexts*, 91–106, Cham: Springer.

Tran, L. T., Tran, L. H. N., Nguyen, M. N., and Ngo, M. (2020), '"Let go of out-of-date values holding us back": Foreign influences on teaching-learning, research and community engagement in Vietnamese universities', *Cambridge Journal of Education*, 50 (3): 281–301. DOI:10.1080/0305764X.2019.1693504.

Tri, D. H., and Moskovsky, C. (2019), 'English-medium instruction in Vietnamese higher education: A "ROAD-MAPPING" perspective', *Issues in Educational Research*, 29 (4): 1330–47.

Trinh, A. N., and Conner, L. (2019), 'Student engagement in internationalization of the curriculum: Vietnamese domestic students' perspectives', *Journal of Studies in International Education*, 23 (1): 154–70. DOI:10.1177/1028315318814065.

Truong, L. T. T., Ngo, P. L. H., and Nguyen, M. X. N. C. (2020), 'Assessment practices in local and international EMI programmes: Perspectives of Vietnamese students', in P. Le Ha and D. Ba Ngoc (eds), *Higher Education in Market-Oriented Socialist Vietnam: New Players, Discourses, and Practices*, 307–29. Cham, Switzerland: Springer International.

Vietnamese Government (2005), *Resolution No. 14/2005/NQ-CP on 'Substantial and Comprehensive Reform of Vietnam's Higher Education in 2006–2020 Period'*, Hanoi: The Government.

Vietnamese Government (2008), *Decision No. 1505/QD-TTg on 'The Introduction of Advanced Programmes in Some Vietnamese Universities in the Period of 2008–2015'*, Hanoi: The Government.

Vietnamese Government (2012), *Decree No. 73/2012/ND-CP on 'Foreign Cooperation and Investment in Education'*, Hanoi: The Government.

Vietnamese National Assembly (2005), *Education Law No. 38/2005/QH11*, Hanoi: The Government.

Vu, T. T. N. (2020), 'Training English-medium teachers: Theoretical and implementational issues', in P. Le Ha and D. Ba Ngoc (eds), *Higher Education in Market-Oriented Socialist Vietnam: New Players, Discourses, and Practices*, 283–306, Cham, Switzerland: Springer International.

World Bank (2012), *Putting Higher Education to Work: Skills and Research for Growth in East Asia*, Washington, DC. Available online: https://openknowledge.worldbank.org/handle/10986/2364.

Part III
Micro-analysis

15

English-Medium Instruction in the South Caucasus: Listening to the Positive Voice

Andrew Linn

Introduction

This chapter draws on research carried out in late 2019 and early 2020 for the British Council (Linn and Radjabzade 2021), investigating the experience of English-medium instruction (EMI) in the three countries of the South Caucasus: the Republic of Armenia, the Republic of Azerbaijan and Georgia. The ministries responsible for education in all three countries are committed to growing foreign-language-medium courses in higher education (HE) as part of their broader education strategy and want to take stock of existing provision before implementing further programmes.

The research involved brief visits to the three capital cities (Baku, Tbilisi and Yerevan) providing the opportunity to observe teaching, meet students and teaching and administrative staff at a number of state and private institutions and talk to colleagues from the relevant ministries. The visits were followed up by an online survey at further institutions (eighteen in Armenia, twelve in Azerbaijan and six in Georgia, with 383, 263 and 240 respondents, respectively). We had used an earlier version of the survey to explore the experience of EMI in universities across Central Asia (Kyrgyzstan, Tajikistan, Uzbekistan; see Bezborodova and Radjabzade 2021), and the South Caucasus version was refined in consultation with the regional South Caucasus British Council offices. It began with ten questions on the respondents' national and linguistic background, followed by a further eighteen questions designed to elicit more details about their experience of using English at and outside university and their attitudes towards EMI.

In the following two sections, I provide an overview of the relevant context in the three countries in focus before moving on briefly to set out the 'voice from above' (i.e. top-down national and institutional policies), followed by the 'voice from below', in this case how students respond to their experience, the day-to-day reality of EMI. I draw in particular on the free-text comments included in the online survey as well as some of the comments made during the focus group sessions to listen to the student voice from below in EMI policy (in the next section), building on earlier work on *voices* in language planning (Linn 2010). Due to limitations of space, I will focus on Armenia and Georgia, the countries I visited.

The countries of the South Caucasus

The South Caucasus is the region, as the name indicates, to the south of the Greater Caucasus mountains. It is further geographically bound by the Black Sea to the west and the Caspian Sea to the east, with Russia to the north, Turkey to the south-west and Iran to the south. The region may be geographically contained and may have experienced a common political fate as part of the Soviet Union before the three countries gained independence in 1991, but divisions prevail across it.

As Thomas De Waal (2019: 1) writes, 'The countries of the South Caucasus have always been the "lands in-between"', such that 'Armenia, Azerbaijan, and Georgia, and the territories around them have the mixed blessing of being at the crossing-place of different cultures and political systems. These fault lines have made their region a geopolitical seismic zone'. The region is home to three politically contested areas – Abkhazia, South Ossetia and Nagorno-Karabakh – and between September and November 2020 (the time of writing) the Republics of Armenia and Azerbaijan were at war (the Second Nagorno-Karabakh War) over the latter territory. The geopolitical history of the South Caucasus has left it linguistically diverse, but the countries are unified in their commitment to the learning of English and the provision of EM programmes at tertiary level, both to attract international students and faculty to their universities and to prepare students for a job market in which English is seen to be a valuable commodity.

Higher education in the South Caucasus

Investment of GDP in education across the region varies against a 2016 world average of 4.46 per cent (World Bank 2020), ranging from 6.95 per cent of GDP in 2017 in Azerbaijan to 2.71 per cent in Armenia, and the level of investment has been rising in Azerbaijan while it has fallen in Armenia from 3.84 per cent over the past decade. All three countries have been members of the European Higher Education Area (Bologna Process) since 2005 and have a mix of private and state HE institutions as well as specialist research institutions and branch campuses.

There are currently fifty-nine HE institutions (HEIs) in Armenia, of which twenty-six are public universities, alongside thirty-three private for-profit institutions and branch campuses (Ministry of Foreign Affairs 2021). The existence of five transnational universities (institutions established in partnership with other countries) further signals the strong ambition to internationalize the HE landscape. Major reforms are currently underway with a new draft Law on Higher Education and Science debated by the National Assembly in 2020. The majority of international students are from the Armenian diaspora (3,395 in 2017–18) in addition to 2,708 from other countries (3 per cent of the total enrolment), and nearly half of the latter are from India (Strategy 2019: 3–4).

Azerbaijan has also committed to significant internationalization of HE with a little under 7,000 international students registered in the academic year 2019–20, the largest country cohort (1,927) coming from Turkey. Around half of that number were enrolled in programmes in general medicine, and indeed it is medical training which attracts the largest numbers of EM students to the region. HE has been undergoing marked expansion in the Republic of Azerbaijan with a 17 per cent increase in enrolments between 2013 and 2018, affecting both state (n=40) and private (n=12) institutions.

Georgia has seventy-five authorized HEIs (2017 Ministry figures), of which a full 73 per cent are private, although thirty-five of those 55 are teaching-only. The implementation plan for the various laws affecting HE in Georgia is set out in the *Unified Strategy for Education and Science for 2017–2021* (Ministry 2017: 29–31), published in both English and Georgian, and this presents one key goal for the HE sector:

> The specific goal of higher education is internationalization of higher education and ensuring access to quality higher education for the individual and professional development of the individual and the improvement of employment.

Thus, internationalization is quite literally at the top of the agenda, and the word 'international' appears eighty-seven times in this forty-page strategy document. Despite the very clear strategic commitment, while numbers on medical and veterinary programmes have skyrocketed from 2,805 in 2015–16 to 10,382 in 2019–20, other undergraduate and doctoral numbers have been steadily decreasing.

In all three countries, then, increasing the number of international students via the provision of EM programmes (although there are other foreign-language-taught programmes emerging too) is front and centre in HE policy.

Status of English and EMI in policy and practice

All three countries have moved away from the historic language of wider communication of the region, but Russian remains in use to varying extents, reflecting differing ongoing political allegiances. Russian is still widely known in the Republic of Armenia, and 'most of the adult population in Armenia is bilingual, or has some proficiency of Russian (in the broadest sense of bilingualism)' (Country Report 2008), which reflects the fact that it is still the first foreign language in schools. By contrast, in Azerbaijan the policy at the level of general education is clearly to embrace English, and teaching hours for English have doubled vis-à-vis Russian.

Despite the ongoing support for Russian in Armenian schools, once students are free to pursue their language-learning preferences, those preferences emerge clearly. Even ten years ago the number of students applying to study English at Yerevan State Languages University and Yerevan State University outstripped applications to study Russian by a factor of 5.75:1 (Country Report 2008).

English is by a considerable margin the most widely studied foreign language in Georgia, and this hunger for the language continues into HE. University applicants in Georgia are required to take a language exam, and, although this may be in English, Russian, French or German, 80 per cent of school leavers choose English, and 90 per cent of students on Georgian-medium programmes who choose to pursue a foreign language select English.

English is clearly riding high for reasons that are well understood and related to employability and international opportunities. Whatever the drivers at government or university level, the stock of English is high in the minds of students, and this is the key point of this chapter. As one Georgian university student responding to our survey wrote:

English is vital as it is a known world-wide language. An excellent knowledge & fluency provides a pathway for more success career-wise.

An Armenian student went further:

English is the key to knowledge. We have to know more.

None of the countries in focus has an explicit policy on EMI, but internationalization has become something of a mantra at ministry level. The Republic of Armenia has been developing a *Strategy for Internationalization of Higher Education and Research in the Republic of Armenia* (Strategy 2019) (the English version of which I am fortunate to have had shared with me). This is a thoughtful, wide-ranging and data-informed document which links 'the fact that international students are not very interested in studying in Armenia (6.8% of the total student population)' (8) to the fact that 'the proportion of courses offered in foreign languages in the total number of courses offered at HEIs is very low' (9). It is implicit policy that improvement in the latter will lead to improvement in the former:

The development and implementation of educational programs in foreign languages will make HE accessible to international students and will enhance the attractiveness of education for local students. Moreover, it will enable the integration of international students in the educational process and will improve the intercultural communication skills of Armenian students. (9)

Notably, 'English-medium' is nowhere specified in this document. Reference is made throughout to the study of 'foreign languages' and to 'courses offered in English, French and Russian'. This may speak to the political position of the country, but for me it comes across as a welcome recognition of the need for education via the medium of a number of strategically important languages in order to feed a diverse and internationally nimble workforce.

As I noted above, the *Unified Strategy for Education and Science 2017–2021* for Georgia is focused on more generic internationalization of HE, but the *Midterm Evaluation of the Strategy* (Ministry 2019) reports that 'there were 168 foreign-language accredited programs in 2016 and 182 in 2017' and, 'despite the increase in the number, significant efforts are required to further internationalise and improve the quality of higher education' (n.p.). Once again there is care not to refer only to English provision in an internationally diverse and politically sensitive HE landscape.

So while there is no explicit policy on EMI in HE in either Armenia or Georgia (see also Mikołajewska and Mikołajewska, in this volume, for a similar case in Poland), both countries are fundamentally committed to a broad vision of internationalized HE for the perceived benefit of home students as much as to attract overseas students, and it is politically expedient (in terms of maintaining a wide range of international partners) to refer only to 'foreign-medium' programmes in general. For the majority of students, however, as testified by the growth in English study noted above, 'foreign language' means English.

In two of the three countries the overwhelming response to the question 'What was the main reason for you to choose an English medium programme?' was: It helps me improve my English skills. Of the local students in Azerbaijan, 42 per cent selected this answer from a list of nine possible answers (including 'Other') with 44.4 per cent of students in Armenia also doing so. Responses from Georgian respondents were more variable, not least as 77 per cent of the respondents self-identified as international students, but nonetheless only 18.2 per cent of local students stated that an EM programme helps them improve their English skills. All in all, however, there is a strong indication that in the South Caucasus region a majority of local students view an EM university course above all as a means to improving their language skills, for reasons that will be obvious in the next section.

Listening to students

It is fair to say that much of the research literature on EMI or English-medium education (EME) is at best sceptical and at worst critical of the enterprise. Concluding their recent overview of research on EMI and the internationalization of universities, Bowles and Murphy (2020: 21) determine at the macro and meso levels not only that 'a convincing case for internationalization through EMI has still not been made' but also that 'the ideological assumption that internationalization through EMI improves societies is still questionable'. So the jury is out on whether EM is good for universities or for the societies they serve and feed. Summing up research at the micro level on the experience of teachers and students in another recent book on EMI, Henriksen et al. (2019: 3) further conclude from the point of view of individual stakeholders:

> Researchers from around the world have focused on a range of the varied and complex issues and challenges related to EMI for all stakeholders (i.e., students,

teaching staff, and administration), e.g., language proficiency, confidence in foreign language skills, lack of interest and/or motivation, increased workloads, quality of teaching and learning, willingness to study/teach in English, possible threat to cultural identity and L1, program organization and infrastructure, increased costs, availability of teaching materials, and equitable assessment of all students.

The authors here focus on listening to the voices of EMI teachers in the Nordic countries 'in order to convey clearly how strongly the lecturers react to and are emotionally affected by the shift to English' (5). They draw a rather grim, albeit not uniform, picture of creeping damage to the experience of teachers and learners and their institutions and societies. Any reader of these assessments of the 'frustration, anxiety, and lack of self-confidence' (157) experienced by teachers would question why ministries and universities are so committed to EMI when the outcomes and impacts appear to be so negative! Perspectives from South-east Asian universities are similarly cautionary (e.g. Barnard and Hasim 2018), and, listening to students from the South Caucasus speak of their experiences, there are causes for concern here, too.

Students commented on their lack of preparedness for English-medium study at university and on the perceived lack of language skills amongst both staff and fellow students. When we compare the fact that the overriding motivation in taking an English-medium course is to improve English-language competence, it is easy to understand the frustration inherent in comments like these from Armenian students:

> The lecturer doesn't know English so she can't teach us.
>
> Unfortunately, some professors don't know English very well, and use Eastern-Armenian to explain their subjects to the international students. I'm glad that I do know Western-Armenian, making me possible to translate the lesson into English for others to understand.

Students in Georgia were more critical still:

> My professors need improvements in English language mastery.
>
> Teachers are struggling to speak English so we need international teachers.
>
> The professors should be well versed in English language – there are many professors who barely speak English and teach native [Georgian] students which divides them from international students and it becomes difficult to have conversation with them because they are not very used to English. This leads to separate classes which creates a barrier between students which is not healthy.

In one group of students I met in Armenia, I heard that teachers have no choice but to translate into Armenian as, in the view of that informant, only two-thirds of students were sufficiently competent in English. This same group of students commented that they had little opportunity to use English in or out of class and that they have no (but would like to have) access to native English speakers. I also heard about the need for students to take private English tuition by way of a supplement to their high school studies, but it was recognized that this factor is divisive:

> As there are many humans who are fond of English training, but they can't to pay money for study.

The negative issues around EMI reported in the literature on other contexts internationally were to a greater or lesser extent articulated by staff and students on EMI programmes in the South Caucasus, but dwelling on the negatives as we have done to this point has the effect of drowning out the positive voice. In their study of the voices of lecturers, Henriksen et al.'s (2019: 157) statement that 'some concerns are expressed, often by as many as 25% of the lecturers' drowns out the other side of the equation, that 'positive attitudes are expressed by a majority of staff'.

In hindsight, I am aware that our survey focused on practical *challenges* but for good reason. Our task was to interrogate the lived reality for stakeholders in EMI to recommend ways of enhancing that experience rather than celebrating the positive; thus we concluded that

> (bottom up) the research tells us that there are non-trivial practical challenges for both students and teachers in engaging with the experience, and support for the enterprise [of EMI] tends to be limited in HE institutions, which introduce EMI without notable training and support for those involved. (Linn and Radjabzade 2021: 62)

Such a conclusion does a disservice to the positive voice heard from many students who were for the most part upbeat. The reality may be challenging, and I know from the research that it is challenging in a variety of ways, but any sense that EMI is a money-making project foisted on poorly prepared and poorly supported teachers and students is an interpretation which should be tensioned against the enthusiasm that emerges from the free-text sections of our survey:

> English is international language, we must learn it well, and also it can be so useful for career, for travel and for communication with abroad people.

Having good knowledge of the English language is necessary nowadays.

I am very glad and proud of my lectures and the knowledge that I am getting. Thank you!

Improving our English skills will help us use English more effectively and do well in our studies, get ahead at work and communicate in English in our free time.

I like studying English language so much

Hearing voices

The worldwide growth in EMI has been a top-down process. In a recent overview of research on EMI (Curle et al. 2020: 10) the principal drivers for its adoption are set out and include:

- specific inclusion of EMI in HE policies;
- desire to grow international reputation of HE system;
- pressure to increase institutional rankings;
- role of higher education in countries' knowledge diplomacy;
- bilingual education policies at primary and secondary level; and
- policies towards English in the workplace.

What this otherwise accurate picture fails to capture is that there is also a significant drive from below, and that means students themselves and their families. Whatever the downside of teaching and learning through the medium of a foreign language, and no matter how sociolinguists may view the fetishization of English as naïve or even damaging, the fact remains that there are significant market forces at play, and they must be recognized and understood if EMI is going to work for everyone. Many of the students we heard in the course of our project are excited about the prospect of enhancing their language skills via EMI programmes and also about the real or imagined opportunities that such study may provide. This view is not simply an endorsement of those top-down policies as it is not motivated by the same internationalization drivers.

Research on language policy tends to focus on policymakers and policymaking rather than the impact of those policies. Policymaking in practice tends to focus on planning rather than implementation. Where the voice from below is audible, the voices from above and below tend to talk differently and so talk past each other (Linn 2010). Successful language policy outcomes are more likely when these voices are combined and speak on terms each other can understand (cf.

Røyneland 2013). Considering perspectives on EMI from a number of Southeast Asian universities, Kirkpatrick (2018: 123) concludes:

> Staff and students are seldom consulted about the need for such courses. For the successful implementation of EMI ... it would appear that the development of coherent language policies in consultation with staff and students is essential. The people who will be working in EMI need to have a sense of ownership over the policy.

Such a holistic approach to language policy development is the one taken in the recent language policy proposals for an EMI HE institution in Uzbekistan, based on a survey of over one thousand students and teaching, administrative and support staff (Linn et al. 2020). The message from the South Caucasus countries includes a strong positive student voice which should not be shouted down by a loud critical research voice or a strident policy voice. *Voices* are explicitly being listened to in work on EMI (Henriksen et al. 2019; Ryan 2018; cf. earlier work e.g. Payne 2007). We need to be sure that EMI planning is listening to them all.

References

Barnard, R., and Hasim, Z.,eds (2018), *English Medium Instruction Programmes: Perspectives from South East Asian Universities*, Abingdon: Routledge.

Bezborodova, A., and Radjabzade, S. (2021), 'English in higher education in the Kyrgyz Republic, Tajikistan, and Uzbekistan', *World Englishes*, 1–20. DOI: 10.1111/weng.12556.

Bowles, H., and Murphy, A. C.,eds (2020), *English-Medium Instruction and the Internationalization of Universities*, Cham, Switzerland: Palgrave Macmillan.

Country Report (2008), *Language Education Policy Profile: Country Report Armenia*, Yerevan: RA Ministry of Education and Science/Yerevan State Linguistic University after V. Brusov.

Curle, S., Jablonkai, R., Mittelmeier, J., Sahan, K., and Veitch, A. (2020), 'English medium part 1: Literature review', in N. Galloway (ed.), *English in Higher Education* (Report No. 978-0-86355-977–8), British Council. Available online: https://www.teachingenglish.org.uk/article/english-higher-education-%E2%80%93-english-medium-part-1-literature-review (accessed 3 December 2020).

De Waal, T. (2019), *The Caucasus: An Introduction*, Oxford: Oxford University Press.

Henriksen, B., Holmen, A., and Kling, J. (2019), *English Medium Instruction in Multilingual and Multicultural Universities: Academics' Voices from the Northern European Context*, Abingdon: Routledge.

Kirkpatrick, A. (2018), 'Afterword', in R. Barnard and Z. Hasim (eds), *English Medium Instruction Programmes: Perspectives from South East Asian Universities*, 116–25, Abingdon: Routledge.

Linn, A. (2010), 'Voices from above – voices from below: Who is talking and who is listening in Norwegian language politics?', *Current Issues in Language Planning*, 11 (2): 114–29.

Linn, A. with Radjabzade, S. (2021), *English-Medium Instruction in the Countries of the South Caucasus*, London: British Council. Available online: https://www.teachingenglish.org.uk/sites/teacheng/files/EMI_Report_SouthCaucasus_v2.pdf (accessed 2 February 2022).

Linn, A., Bezborodova, A., and Radjabzade, S. (2020), 'Tolerance and control: Developing a language policy for an EMI university in Uzbekistan', *Sociolinguistica*, 34 (1): 217–37.

Ministry of Education, Science, Culture and Sport of Georgia (Ministry) (2017), *Unified Strategy for Education and Science for 2017–2021*. Available online: https://mes.gov.ge/content.php?id=7755&lang=eng (accessed 3 December 2020).

Ministry (2019), *Midterm Evaluation of the Implementation of Unified Strategy for Education and Science 2017–2021*. Available online: http://mes.gov.ge/uploads/files/Midterm%20evaluation_education%20strategy_ENG_final.pdf (accessed 27 November 2020).

Ministry of Foreign Affairs of the Republic of Armenia (2021), *Study in Armenia*. Available online: https://www.mfa.am/en/study-in-armenia (accessed 4 January 2021).

Payne, M. (2007), 'Foreign language planning: pupil choice and pupil voice', *Cambridge Journal of Education*, 37 (1): 89–109.

Røyneland, U. (2013), ' "The voice from below": Norwegian language reforms in the 21st century', in T. Lohndal (ed.), *In Search of Universal Grammar: From Old Norse to Zoque*, 53–76, Amsterdam: John Benjamins.

Ryan, J. (2018), 'Voices from the field: Email interviews with applied linguists in Asia', in R. Barnard and Z. Hasim (eds), *English Medium Instruction Programmes: Perspectives from South East Asian Universities*, 15–28, Abingdon: Routledge.

Strategy (2019), 'Strategy for internationalization of higher education and research in the Republic of Armenia', unpublished draft.

World Bank (2020), *Government Expenditure on Education*. Available online: https://data.worldbank.org/indicator/SE.XPD.TOTL.GD.ZS- (accessed 27 November 2020).

16

Translanguaging and Trans-semiotizing in English-Medium Instruction Tertiary Classrooms in Hong Kong: Creativity and Trans-semiotic Agency

Phoebe Siu and Angel M. Y. Lin

Introduction

Internationalization and globalization have driven the spread of English-medium instruction (EMI) in higher education in many Asian societies. Dearden (2014: para 4) defines 'EMI' as 'the use of the English language to teach academic subjects in countries or jurisdictions where the first language (L1) of the majority of the population is not English'. However, the monolingual perspective has aroused pressing concerns for investigating the limitations of English-only policies in EMI schools in a globalized and hybridized city like Hong Kong. For instance, curricular and pedagogical disconnects in EMI schools have been addressed in recent studies (Lin 2016; Tai and Li 2020). These studies focus on investigating how students' familiar linguistic and cultural resources (e.g. L1, pop culture) and multimodalities (e.g. gestures, facial expressions, visual images) can be leveraged to support content and language integrated learning (CLIL) in EMI contexts in Hong Kong (Wu and Lin 2019). Among the few studies on EMI in higher education in Hong Kong, the focus is on how teachers are determined to interact with their students in English (Evans 2017) and how students have overcome initial difficulties in EMI classes (Evans and Morrison 2018). Little research has been done on problematizing the monolingual perspective and on how alternative curricular and pedagogical practices can be possible in EMI classes in higher education in Hong Kong.

Literature review and key concepts

Translanguaging and trans-semiotizing in the EMI classroom

Theories of translanguaging (TL) and trans-semiotizing (TS) focus on the dynamic processes of meaning making as classroom participants mobilize all of the resources to communicate and co-create knowledge (Lin 2019).

TL and TS theories broaden the understanding of *languaging* as a complex entanglement with various semiotic resources (e.g. visuals, gestures, body movements) on top of written and spoken forms of named languages. In this study, we introduce the notion of trans-semiotizing agency to refer to the deliberate efforts of plurilingual teachers to push limits and break boundaries liberating themselves from the monolingual, discrete codes view (Li and Lin 2019) underlying the English-only policy. As a practical lesson planning tool to exercise trans-semiotic agency, the multimodalities-entextualization cycle (MEC) (Lin 2016, 2019) was used in this study by the teacher-researcher (first author of this chapter) to deliberately create spaces for students to translanguage and trans-semiotize, facilitating the free flow of creativity and ideas.

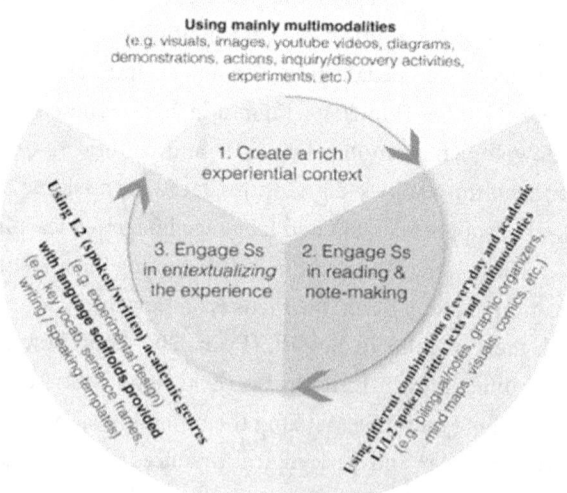

Figure 16.1 The multimodalities-entextualization cycle (MEC) (Lin 2016, 2019) as a socioculturally transformative pedagogical framework.

The multimodalities-entextualization cycle in EMI tertiary classrooms

The MEC is a curriculum planning framework consisting of three stages (Figure 16.1). It has been adapted to plan CLIL classes in different contexts; for example, in Hong Kong (Wu and Lin 2019), Mainland China (Liu et al. 2020) and Taiwan (Gupta 2020). Still, deploying the MEC to exercise trans-semiotic agency in not just lesson planning but also assessment design in EMI tertiary education will be groundbreaking as many TL studies typically end with monolingual assessment, still failing the transformative goal of breaking monolingual domination (Jaspers 2018).

The study

Research design

Renovating EMI assessment through the MEC

The first author of this chapter is the teacher-researcher in this study. She is interested in investigating the roles of TL/TS in developing dynamic flows of creativity, content knowledge and discipline-specific language skills when English (spoken/written) is not regarded as the only permissible meaning-making resource in EMI tertiary education. This study focused on transforming traditional EMI monolingual assessment tasks into a TL/TS space where students needed to compose multimodal design boards. Through the MEC-guided meaning-making stages, a series of teaching and learning activities was hosted in weeks 1–5 of the course, titled Design, as continuous assessment/learning cycles in the curriculum; it is an English for specific purposes (ESP) course that focuses on teaching English communication skills to design students. Two weeks of lecture (two hours per lecture) and tutorial classes (one hour per tutorial session) were allocated to complete the three stages of the MEC. Eighty-five students participated in the pilot study in the semester of January–June 2020 in a community college in Hong Kong. Ninety-one students participated in the main study of iterative cycles of teaching and research activities in the same course for another cohort of Design students in January–June 2021.

The individual assessment tasks invited students to create a multimodal design board for raising public awareness of a self-selected social issue. Students were encouraged to use a wide range of social semiotic resources, such as drawings, photos and words. The design of these tasks took into consideration a socioculturally transformative approach – to encourage and enable students to negotiate meanings and identities through reclaiming authorial voices creatively.

Research questions and methods

The research questions and methods adopted in this study include:

RQ1: What kinds of semiotic resources would be introduced into an EMI tertiary classroom with the curriculum genres guided by the MEC?

RQ2: What roles would TL/TS play in facilitating the flow of creative ideas in the processes of mastering content and language learning in an EMI tertiary classroom?

In the pilot study and the main study, the teacher-researcher conducted participatory action research (PAR) (Baum et al. 2006) with lessons observation (forty-eight hours of lesson video recording done via Microsoft TEAMS), two major assessment tasks (multimodal deign board and reflective writing) and relevant lesson materials reviews, four semi-structured interviews with students (phone interviews and follow-up emails), along with two sessions of focus group discussion (face-to-face focus group discussion) among students taking the same English for Academic Purposes (EAP)/English for Specific Purposes (ESP) course. All research informants were anonymized. Four sessions of semi-structured individual interviews with four in-depth case informants (15–20 minutes per session) and two sessions of focus group discussion (n=11) were done in English, supplemented with Cantonese (first language of the students). Audio recording and transcription were done in English, along with members checking through emails and follow-up phone calls to each research informant. Thematic coding of the interview data was done. Photos and digital copies of the multimodal design board drafts and submission copies were provided by research informants to the teacher-researcher through follow-up emails after completing the semi-structured interviews.

Research findings

Interviews and focus group discussion were analysed with qualitative content analysis, covering data processing steps such as data immersion, thematic coding and reporting. Both pre-categorized themes and new emerging themes were reported in the research findings in the following section. Four arching themes were addressed in the focus group discussion and in-depth interview questions: (i) the roles of L1/L2 in multimodal design board composition; (ii) the role of online multimodal resources in developing trans-semiotic agency and creativity; (iii) the roles of visual aids (e.g. mind-mapping) in multimodal design board composition; and (iv) the roles of teacher-to-student and/or student-to-student social interaction for multimodal design board composition.

Research Finding 1: The role of L1/L2 in multimodal design board composition. Research informants have shared the first-hand classroom experience in relation to watching YouTube videos to understand case housing issues in Hong Kong. For instance, in a focus group discussion conducted face-to-face in a school conference meeting room (22 January 2021, conducted with five informants in English), Student A commented that 'instead of just reading newspaper reporting cage home people's everyday lives, I think listening to the direct interview dialogues of a young mother telling her living stories with a cage home in Cantonese is useful. I understand her feelings and worries better'. Student B then elaborated her understanding of the YouTube video and other online website resources reporting local cage home residents' living conditions,

> Yes, I agree that we need to read more and watch more no matter in English or in Chinese to see how life is like in a cage home. Though some of my friends are living in public housing in Hong Kong, I never visit a real cage home in Shamshuipo. It must be dirty and smelly. Yet, we won't fully understand the conditions if we just read stories or newspaper reports in English. I prefer listening to their stories in person. Cantonese dialogues are helpful in the video shown in our EAS online class. Less sleepy to me when having online lessons only these days.

However, there are some student informants who show their uncertain perspective towards using Chinese or Cantonese in an ESP classroom. Student D questioned, 'Why do we have to watch the YouTube video during our 2-hour online lecture? You can give us the links to watch them personally after classes. No face-to-face discussion can be followed up in this semester during Microsoft TEAMS. If we need Chinese reading, we may search online flexibly on our own.'

Data Extract 1.1: YouTube video in L1/L2 live-streamed to Design students for visualizing living conditions in cage housing (RT Documentary 2020) (remarks: video interview dialogues were done in Cantonese; subtitles were broadcasted in English)

Data Extract 1.2: Multimodal design boards produced by a team of student informants after watching the YouTube videos about cage housing and conducting after-class teamwork discussion in L1/L2.

Figure 16.2 YouTube screenshot from 'Trapped inside Hong Kong's cage houses'.

Research Finding 2: The role of online multimodal resources in developing translanguaging and trans-semiotic agency and creativity.

During interviews and focus group discussion, another key theme is identified in students' experiences and perspectives towards using online multimodal resources to support their visualization of social issues in Hong Kong. They reported using and incorporating various visual images, facial expressions, gestures, objects observed from hybrid multimodal texts, such as Google images, YouTube videos, corporate websites and blog articles, when doing their multimodal composition of design board with written texts and visual images. For example, one interviewee (pseudo-named as Amy) reported her first-hand experience in creatively reflecting on a particular social issue through multimodal design board composition: 'I think I have used both online reading in Chinese and English. For example, to know more about light pollution, the social issue I used in my design board writing. I will go to some government and environmental protection groups' websites to browse the photos and descriptions.' Other three in-depth case informants interviewed reported similar TL/TS online engagement in the process of composing their design boards (see data extract 2).

Data Extract 2: A summary table is used to illustrate the roles of online multimodal resources adopted in each informant's multimodal composition of design boards.

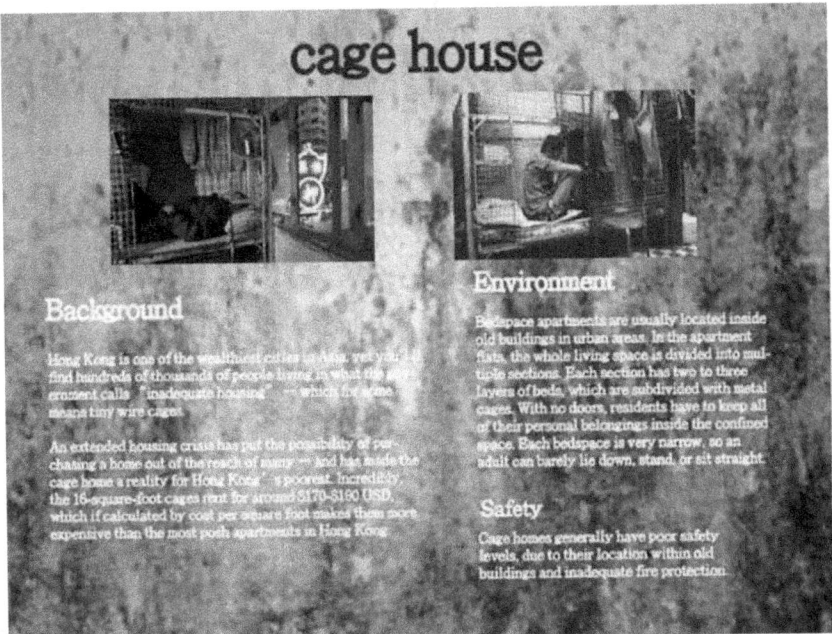

Figure 16.3 Hong Kong cage housing student design board.

Research Finding 3: The role of visual aids (e.g. mind-mapping) in multimodal design board composing.

To illustrate the process of creativity, another student informant pseudo-named as Amy provided her mind-map for composing a multimodal design board for addressing light pollution in Hong Kong through an e-mail with the first author. She explained rhetorically in her follow-up e-mail message:

> I use both visual and written resources at the same time (i.e., simultaneously, and alternatively with turn-taking flows). Sometimes, I search and create images with digital resources online and my personal sketching techniques in design. I can create visual graphics to match with my ideas and language expressions to deliver the content message. However, I don't just use images or written messages alone step-by-step. It is the 'togetherness' and mixing up that help my creativity. (Written in English, sent on 20 January 2021)

Data Extract 3: A process-map in L1/L2 provided by a student interviewee (pseudo-named as Amy) in the process of composing the assessment task of multimodal design board addressing light pollution.

Research Finding 4: The role of teacher-to-student and/or student-to-student social interaction for multimodal design board composition.

Table 16.1 Summary of Hong Kong Students' Online Multimodal Resources

Informant with Pseudo-names	Social Issue Addressed	Online Resources Used	Creative Ideas Illustrated with Fluid Flow of Semiotic Resources	Visual Images Adopted in the Design Board
Amy	Light pollution	Google images, environment protection websites in L1/L2, blog articles, YouTube videos	Amy's design board focuses on depicting a countless number of light window frames addressing light pollution as an overlooked social issue in Hong Kong	City landscapes, shadow of high-rise buildings, silhouettes of high-rise buildings, light bulbs, light window frames
David	Cage housing	Google images, YouTube videos, newspaper reports in L1/L2	David's design board focuses on illustrating how an elderly may be entrapped by the lonely and small space inside his cage home	Apple iPod cases, Apple product package box, stripes, cage patterns, elderly cartoon figures, plastic bags and wrapping rubber cloths
Kitty	Animals cruelty	Corporate websites in L1/L2, local newspaper in L1, non-profit making organizations' websites	Kitty's design board focuses on showing how lovely pets can be mistreated by pet keepers as if they were discarded toys of cats and dogs	Hand drawing of torn toy images of cats and dogs, bloodsheds, dark backdrops, human hands and ropes
Rose	Child abuse	Non-profit making organizations' websites, newspaper articles in L1/L2, YouTube videos	Rose's design board focuses on depicting how children may be potentially abused as acrobatic players when adults abuse their children physically and emotionally without noticing	Teardrops, the backs of some children, acrobatic postures, adult bodies a dark room

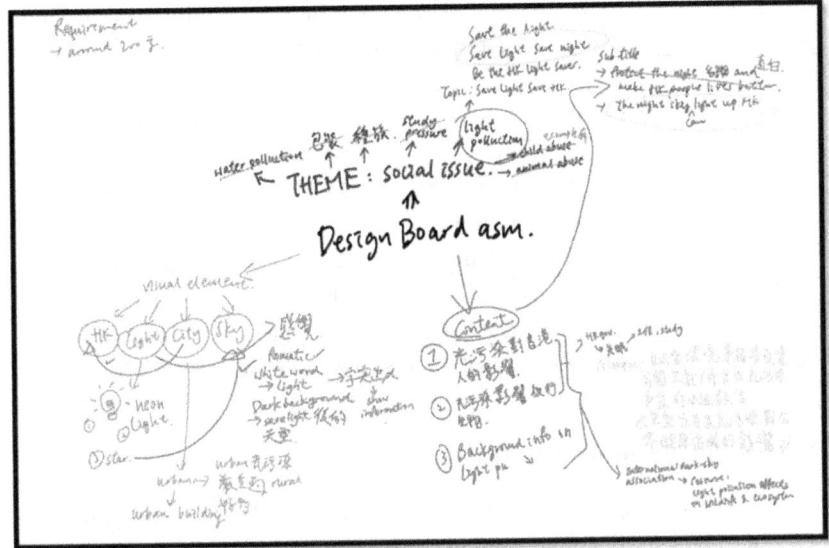

Figure 16.4 A student's L1/L2 process-map.

Three key research questions were addressed in the focus group discussion and semi-structured individual interviews with the in-depth case informants. The teacher-researcher focused on understanding Design students' perspectives in teacher-to-student and/or student-to-student social interactions. During the focus group discussion, the participants expressed positive views towards brainstorming design ideas with their peers in their preferred modes of communication. Some respondents used social networking tools, such as WhatsApp and Signal, to text with their study peers when they started composing their design boards. For instance, David, one of the student informants, explained why he preferred having 'at least two persons or above' when doing creative projects in L1/L2. He said, 'Sometimes, I think individual ideas may benefit me better for getting feedback or comments from my peers. To me, creativity is rather abstract. From my one-year experience in this community college, I think it is very important to get real-time feedback to evaluate my creative ideas.'

In addition, one unexpected new theme emerged when two in-depth case informants talked about their opinions regarding how they prevent peer-copying or plagiarism with TL and TS strategies. For instance, semi-structured interview informant Amy reflected on the ways she used the digital bilingual translation buttons when reading some social issue articles online,

> I can also avoid plagiarism if I don't just read the English written online information sources. You know, we need to submit to Turnitin for each English course assignment to avoid online copying and peer copying. I am aware of the temptations to copy the English words if I just read the English websites to get the ideas of light pollution problems in Hong Kong. When I read the Chinese articles, I can use my own words to translate the content into my choices of English expressions. Then, the Turnitin percentage won't be too high when I write explanation messages to go with the photos and image.

Discussion and implications

To sum up, based on the qualitative content analysis of data from the focus group discussion and semi-structured individual interviews, along with samples from students' multimodal design boards, the pilot study and the main study adopting the MEC in connecting TL/TS assessment and learning for Design students provided new opportunities for the teacher-researcher to reflect on the roles of TL/TS in facilitating the dynamic flow of creative ideas, especially with systematic and planned uses of multimodal plurilingual, pluricultural resources in curriculum genres (Christie 2002; Lin 2016).

In this concluding section, we will highlight three major roles of TL/TS in facilitating free flows of creativity in the classroom.

1. The MEC encourages fluid and creative use of multimodal meaning-making resources across plurilingual, pluricultural information sources shared among peer study groups.
2. The MEC provides emotional affordances for creative lesson activities among plurilingual students who feel more connected with L1/local sociocultural meaning-making resources.
3. Translanguaging provides boundary-crossing social interactions for plurilingual teachers and students to revisit their understanding of disciplinary creativity with multiple semiotic resources.

Conclusion

Throughout this chapter, we have emphasized the research and pedagogical value of promoting creativity and trans-semiotic agency in EMI higher education.

Redesigning MEC-guided assessment tasks in ESP tertiary classrooms may provide an example of bridging pedagogies (Lin 2016) amidst the uncertainties and challenges identified in breaking through the monolingual grip of TESOL traditions (Lin 2020a). Meanwhile, it is important to connect plurilingual researchers, teachers and students in Hong Kong through translanguaging and trans-semiotizing research and pedagogical co-designing and co-exploring. It is also important to raise social semiotic awareness among plurilingual university management, parents, teachers and students so that a wider range of ideological and implementational concerns may be addressed for promoting the 'translanguaging space' (Li 2016) in ESP assessments, especially when a multiple array of multimodal plurilingual, pluricultural meaning-making resources is adopted in physical/virtual/hybrid EMI tertiary classrooms during the global pandemic.[1]

Note

1 The first author wishes to express her gratitude to Pedro dos Santos (PhD candidate, Faculty of Education, Simon Fraser University) and to Dr. Jiajia Eve Liu (Postdoctoral fellow, Faculty of Education, The University of Hong Kong) for their unconditional critical support.

References

Baum, F., MacDougall, C., and Smith, D. (2006), 'Participatory action research', *Journal of Epidemiology and Community Health*, 60: 854–7.

Christie, F. (2002), *Classroom Discourse Analysis*, London: Continuum.

Dearden, J. (2014), *English as a Medium of Instruction – a Growing Global Phenomenon*, London: British Council.

Evans, S. (2017), 'English in Hong Kong higher education', *World Englishes*, 36 (4): 591–610.

Evans, S., and Morrison, B. (2018), 'Adjusting to higher education in Hong Kong: The influence of school medium of instruction', *International Journal of Bilingual Education and Bilingualism*, 21 (8): 1016–29.

García, O. (2009), *Bilingual Education in the 21st Century: A Global Perspective*, Malden, MA: Wiley/Blackwell.

García, O., and Li Wei (2014), *Translanguaging: Language, Bilingualism and Education*, London: Palgrave Macmillan.

García, O., Johnson, S., and Seltzer, K. (2017), *The Translanguaging Classroom: Leveraging Student Bilingualism for Learning*, Philadelphia, PA: Caslon.

Gibbons, P., and Cummins, J. (2002), *Scaffolding Language, Scaffolding Learning: Teaching Second Language Learners in the Mainstream Classroom*, Portsmouth: Heinemann.

Gupta, K. C.-L. (2020), 'Researcher-teacher collaboration in adopting critical content and language integrated learning (CLIL)', *Processes, Challenges and Outcomes. Trabalhos em Linguística Aplicada*, 59 (1): 42–77. DOI:10.1590/01031813601412591 2020.

Jaspers, J. (2018), 'The transformative limits of translanguaging', *Language and Communication*, 58: 1–10.

Li, W. (2016), 'Multi-competence and the translanguaging instinct', in V. Cook and W. Li (eds), *The Cambridge Handbook of Multi-Competence*, 533–43, Cambridge, NY: Cambridge University Press.

Li, W., and García, O. (2016), 'From researching translanguaging to translanguaging research', in K. King and Yi-Ju Lai (eds), *Research Methods: In Encyclopedia of Language and Education*, Switzerland: Springer.

Li, W., and Lin, A. M. Y. (2019), 'Translanguaging classroom discourse: Pushing limits, breaking boundaries', *Classroom Discourse*, 10 (3–4): 209–15.

Lin, A. M. Y. (2013), 'Towards paradigmatic change in TESOL methodologies: Building plurilingual pedagogies from the ground up', *TESOL Quarterly*, 47 (3), 521–45.

Lin, A. M. Y. (2016), *Language across the Curriculum and CLIL in English as an Additional Language (EAL) Contexts: Theory and Practice*. Singapore: Springer. Available online: https://doi.org/10.1007/978-981-10-1802-2.

Lin, A. M. Y. (2019), 'Theories of trans/languaging and trans-semiotizing: implications for content-based education classrooms', *International Journal of Bilingual Education and Bilingualism*, 22 (1): 5–16. DOI:10.1080/13670050.2018.1515175.

Lin, A. M. Y. (2020a), 'Cutting through the monolingual grip of TESOL traditions – the transformative power of the translanguaging lens', in Z. Tian, L. Aghai, P. Sayer and J. L. Schissel (eds), *Envisioning TESOL through a Translanguaging Lens*, 1–9, Switzerland: Springer.

Lin, A. M. Y. (2020b), 'From deficit-based teaching to asset-based teaching in higher education in BANA countries: Cutting through "either-or" binaries with a heteroglossic plurilingual lens', 1–10, *Culture and Curriculum: Language*, Taylor & Francis.

Lin, A. M. Y., and Man, E. Y. (2010), *Bilingual Education: Southeast Asian Perspectives*. Hong Kong: Hong Kong University Press.

Lin, A. M. Y., Y. Wu and J. L. Lemke (2020), '"It takes a village to research a village": Conversations with Jay Lemke on contemporary issues in translanguaging', in S. Lau and S. V. V. Stille (eds), *Critical Plurilingual Pedagogies: Struggling toward Equity Rather Than Equality*, 47–74, Switzerland: Springer.

Liu, J. E., Lo, Y.Y., and Lin, A. M. Y. (2020), 'Translanguaging pedagogy in teaching English for academic purposes: Researcher-teacher collaboration as a professional development model', *System*, 92: 102276. DOI: https://doi.org/10.1016/j.system.2020.102276.

Pun, J., and Macaro, E. (2019), 'The effect of first and second language use on question types in English medium instruction science classrooms in Hong Kong', *International Journal of Bilingual Education and Bilingualism*, 22 (1): 64–77.

RT Documentary (2020), *Trapped inside Hong Kong's Cage Houses* [online video]. Available online: https://www.youtube.com/watch?v=I2omC_s2odUandt=263s (accessed 30 April 2020).

Tai, K. W. H., and Li Wei (2020), 'Bringing the outside in: Connecting students' out-of-school knowledge and experience through translanguaging in Hong Kong English medium', *System*, 95: 102364. DOI:https://doi.org/10.1016/j.system.2020.102364.

Tian, Z., and Shepard-Carey, L. (2020), '(Re)imagining the future of translanguaging pedagogies in TESOL through researcher-teacher collaborations', *TESOL Quarterly*, 54 (4): 1131–43.

Tong, E., Pun, C., Siu, P., and Gube, J. (2017), 'Creating a transformed space for disciplinary discourse and knowledge creation through an adjunct instructional model', in P. Chappell and J. S. Knox (eds.), *Transforming Contexts: Papers from the 44th International Systemic Functional Congress*, 95–101, Wollongong: Organising Committee of the 44th International Systemic Functional Congress.

Wu, Y., and Lin, A. M. Y. (2019), 'Translanguaging and trans-semiotising in a CLIL biology class in Hong Kong: Whole-body sense-making in the flow of knowledge co-making', *Classroom Discourse*, 10 (3–4): 252–73. DOI: 10.1080/19463014.2019.1629322.

17

It's Worth the Extra Effort: Behind Student Perceptions of Success in the Study of Content via English-Medium Instruction in Japan

Gene Thompson, Samantha Curle and Ikuya Aizawa

Introduction

There is a scarcity of research on the effectiveness of gaining content knowledge through English-medium instruction (EMI) programmes in higher education (HE) contexts (Macaro et al. 2018). One theory driving the boom in EMI is that learners can develop their second language (L2) ability while acquiring content knowledge. However, Macaro (2018: 154) questions whether 'learning content through L2 English leads to at least as good learning of academic content as learning content through the students' L1' and urges that further empirical evidence on the cost-effectiveness of EMI is needed. While some research suggests that EMI does not adversely affect students' disciplinary learning in contrast to its first language (L1) instructed counterpart (e.g. Zaif et al. 2017), an overwhelming number of studies, especially very recently (e.g. Aizawa and Rose 2020; Doiz and Lasagabaster 2020; Macaro 2020), have identified various linguistic challenges faced by L2 English students (e.g. lacking the prerequisite academic and technical English vocabulary knowledge). Consequently, it seems inevitable that EMI students are considerably more disadvantaged in gaining content knowledge than their L1 instructed counterparts. Those with lower L2 English proficiency may struggle not only with the linguistic issues but also with difficulties associated with learning new academic disciplines. Nevertheless, more recently, researchers (e.g. Galloway et al. 2020; Thompson et al. 2019; Xie and Curle 2019) have also shed light on the positive aspects of acquiring content knowledge through EMI, highlighting some perceived benefits which are linked exclusively to EMI (e.g. access to a wider range of learning resources, simultaneous acquisition of content and language knowledge and improved self-efficacy and motivation).

Thus, key questions are whether these perceived benefits can outweigh the costs of seemingly lower disciplinary learning, and whether the EMI students are able to compensate against the costs by gaining these additional benefits. To examine these issues, this chapter draws on in-depth qualitative analyses of student interviews, exploring student perceptions of success at an undergraduate business programme in a Japanese HE EMI context.

Literature review

A vast majority of recent EMI literature has suggested that EMI students encounter language-related problems due to their insufficient L2 proficiency (for an overview, see Curle et al. 2020). For example, studies have highlighted challenges with understanding the grammar used in textbooks (Aizawa and Rose 2020), comprehending lectures (Hellekjær 2010) and insufficient vocabulary knowledge (Uchihara and Harada 2018).

Ignoring these challenges, an increasing number of Japanese universities have implemented EMI programmes as a means to internationalize their institutions. According to the most recent figures from the Japanese education ministry (MEXT 2018), thirty-seven universities have been funded as part of the Top Global University Project, or 'TGUP', since 2013. One of its main aims is to increase the number of EMI degree programmes from 19,533 to 55,928 (2.86 times) by the end of this ten-year initiative in 2023, indicating the centrality of EMI in its policy statement (Rose and McKinley 2018). Consistent with its rapid growth, scholarly attention has been placed mainly on challenges and difficulties in implementing EMI than on its successes and benefits.

Some studies have more recently observed successful student learning experiences via EMI (Rose et al. 2020). For example, McKinley (2018) conducted a case study at one of the TGUP participant universities to demonstrate a successful example of EMI provision, suggesting the role of effective preparatory language support schemes in improving student linguistic readiness for EMI. Similarly, Xie and Curle (2020) unpacked the multifaceted nature of success in EMI in China, revealing that their participants were successful in developing 'soft skills', such as knowing how to apply and transform knowledge and acquiring a new way of thinking through EMI. In Japan, Thompson et al. (2019) found that another TGUP university also demonstrated successful EMI provision which led to student perceptions of success in mastering content knowledge, as the greater effort required in preparation leads to perceptions of deeper understanding and success, strengthening motivation to learn via English.

Recognizing the scarcity of stories of student success from EMI programmes, the current chapter further explores the costs and benefits for EMI learners by examining student perceptions of success towards content learning in the Japanese EMI context. Further, Thompson et al. (2019) recognized one limitation of their study that concerned the interview participants, who were generally very successful (i.e. achieved high grades) and had achieved high L2 proficiency. They called for further studies with a greater range of participants. This chapter responds to that call. It focuses on the interplay between perceptions of success and the factors to which learners attribute their success in a group of learners.

The study

Utilizing qualitative content analysis of interview data with six students, this chapter addresses the following research questions:

1. How do students perceive their study of English management via English to be successful and beneficial?
2. What factors influence these perceptions?

Setting

This study was carried out with students majoring in international business at a business management school from a private university in Japan. After completing an eighteen-month academic foundation programme, students start EMI study during the second semester of their second year. Despite an entry requirement of CEFR B1 level at English, a small percentage of students regularly test at the upper A2 level after entering the programme. The test of English for International Communication (TOEIC) is used, and around 5 per cent of students score below 275 on each of the listening and reading subtests, placing them at the A2 level according to Tannenbaum and Wylie's (2019) CEFR mapping tool.

Students are required to take a certain number of their classes via English during their third and fourth years of study but have the option of choosing to take different classes (e.g. financial accounting) in English or Japanese. Data were collected from students starting their third year, who had completed the preparatory programme (including EAP and ESP classes) and their initial EMI lecture class named 'international business'.

Participants and procedures

A total of six students volunteered to participate in semi-structured interviews. To encourage participants to provide sufficient detail in their responses (McKinley and Rose 2020), interviews were carried out in Japanese and recorded, with permission, for translation and analysis. Utilizing a variation of Thompson and Dooley's (2020) Researcher as Translator Serial Approach (RTSA), interviews were translated by an independent translator with review by two bilingual members of the research team. Table 17.1 introduces the participants, including their L2 proficiency level and grade on the 'international business' class.

Data analyses and limitations

Interviews were analysed using qualitative content analysis (QCA), which involves preparation (immersion in the data), organization (coding, generation of categories), and reporting (see Selvi 2020). Codes were informed by theory and prior research (i.e. a 'directed' approach). Examples of perceived success and failure were identified in the transcripts, and these were coded using examples of (i) benefits (e.g. content understanding, L2 development), (ii) costs (e.g. efficiency) and (iii) perceived causes (e.g. effort, motivation). Categories in

Table 17.1 Interview Participants

Name	Gender	CEFR Level	International Business Grade
Student A	Female	B1	A
Student B	Female	B1	B
Student C	Female	B2	B
Student D	Male	B2	B
Student E	Female	B1	C
Student F	Male	A2	D

Notes: (1) CEFR levels were calculated using Tannenbaum and Wylie's (2019) CEFR mapping tool, using the highest TOEIC score that the participant had achieved during their studies; (2) at the institution, the highest passing grade is 'S', followed by A–C, while D represents a failing grade.

the data set were identified by grouping codes together when they represented patterns across the data set.

The findings presented in this chapter are potentially limited by the relatively small number of participants who agreed to participate in the interviews and their self-selection. However, as shown in Table 17.1, this participant pool represents a range of L2 proficiency levels and levels of achievement in their first EMI course named international business. Specifically, students from the A2 and B1 proficiency level are represented, and thus these participants provide a cross-section of the lower levels of student L2 proficiency from which to draw interpretations about perceptions of EMI success.

Results

Although some participants indicated that their perceptions of success in studying via EMI were limited to certain courses (e.g. marketing) and levels of difficulty (e.g. less advanced courses), each of the interview participants indicated success in their learning of business management content via EMI. This was somewhat surprising as one of the participants had failed their first EMI class, while another reported barely achieving a passing grade. Two key patterns emerged from our analysis of the interviews: (i) Studying via EMI leads to better understanding of content because of the *difficulty* of studying via English; and (ii) the extra effort is 'worth it' when it helps participants to achieve the dual purposes of attaining subject mastery and developing their English-language skills.

Pattern 1: It's less efficient but more valuable

All interview participants expressed positive affective responses towards EMI and perceptions of success about their past EMI experiences. Interestingly, each of the students suggested that studying business management via Japanese is easier; however, all the interview participants also suggested that the extra difficulty of studying via English made them attend more closely to the objectives and contents of classes, leading to perceptions of success in understanding the content more completely. In other words, this pattern represents a relationship between perceptions of positive understanding, negative efficiency and positive effort. For example, in response to the question 'Do you think that you can actually acquire business expertise through those English operated classes?'

Student C answered, 'Yes, I can,' explaining that learning via EMI made the content easier to remember and retain:

> It is harder to find the important part or takes time to understand ... [but] when I was taking the IB and ESP courses, I found out that I did not acquire the contents that I should have acquired in the Management class which was taught via Japanese.

Similarly, Student D indicated that they were successful in learning via EMI, although 'it is a bit inefficient' as they require greater preparation, need to use a dictionary for unknown words and take more time to understand the contents. Student D revealed that, as a result,

> I can understand the class more clearly ... I concentrate more in English than in Japanese. I think I can acquire the knowledge 'for real' in English operated courses.

When comparing the effort they expend when studying via Japanese versus English, students explained they can passively interact with Japanese lectures and content but need to regulate their behaviour more when studying via EMI. For example, Student F revealed that he carries out roughly thirty minutes of preparation before each EMI class (e.g. reviewing slides and content) but no preparation for classes carried out in Japanese, stating he does not feel it is necessary to help him pass the final exam.

Participants discussed various self-regulatory activities they carry out to manage the burden of studying via the L2, with dictionary usage and text review common to each participant. An interesting sub-theme revolved around their greater participation in class and reliance on collaboration with classmates. To illustrate, Student E indicated that in their preparation for class,

> I read the textbook in advance and try to understand the basic contents. When I have something I cannot understand, I ask my friends who are good at English.

Other participants were more explicit about the need for greater collaboration. Student B suggested that without the support of their classmates, she would not have been able to get through her early EMI classes:

Student B: I could not catch what the professor said and I kept asking my friends. I did not understand at all, so it was very hard.
Interviewer: I see. You and your friends helped each other.
Student B: Right. I could not get credit without my friends.

In summary, this theme centred around a perception amongst students that the greater time and effort of studying via EMI has benefits for their understanding of content. As a result, they expended more effort, carried out greater preparation and drew upon different sources of assistance to achieve subject mastery. This finding represents another view of success, as even students with relatively poor performance (e.g. Students E and F) noted that they had achieved success from this perspective.

Pattern 2: It's worth it because it serves two purposes

Five of the six participants expressed their willingness to carry out the extra preparation required of content study via future EMI study due to their perception that they are achieving subject mastery and developing their language skills. Thus, this pattern represents a relationship between perceptions of efficiency and motivation to carry out EMI study. Student F stated that study via EMI was beneficial as 'my English ability improves and I can acquire business expertise'. A second example comes from Student A, who explained that she had experienced success at learning via EMI despite it taking more time, stating,

> Speaking only about 'efficiency', I think studying in Japanese is better. However, from the language learning perspective, it is really good that we can improve our English while understanding the knowledge or concepts. Also, in the international business area of study, there is more information which we can get in English than in Japanese.

Student B provided a similar example:

Interviewer: Do you think there is a difference in how much you can learn between studying in English and studying via Japanese?

Student B: Not so much ... and I can improve my English at the same time. So in terms of efficiency, English operated courses are not so bad.

However, for one of the participants (Student E), the costs of carrying out future study via EMI was considered to exceed the benefit. She explained that she chooses Japanese classes as she no longer has any motivation to further improve her English skill:

Student E: Because preparation takes long and I cannot follow the class without that. I lower the priority of [EMI] classes.

Interviewer: So, the cost performance is bad for you?

Student E: Yes. I gave up on English and I decided to go to a long-term internship. I changed how I send my time and quit studying English.
Interviewer: So, you have your motivation to learn expertise but ...
Student E: But English is an obstacle.

It should also be noted that three of the six students also mentioned that their perceptions of past success studying via EMI did not necessarily lead them to always choose classes carried out in English. Participants suggested that their choice to study via EMI would be limited by the perceived difficulty of the content to be studied. For example, Student C explained,

> If there is no choice (of language) then I just take the English course. Otherwise, I think about whether I can manage it or not, and if it is not too difficult, I take the class in English.

Similarly, Student B revealed that the subject area of the class would influence her choice, stating,

> It depends on the level of the classes. For example, I could follow Financial Accounting class but International Human Resource is quite a high level class. I don't think I can understand the contents even in Japanese.

In other words, while our findings indicated student perceptions of success from their past studies, students still appeared to be carrying out a cost-benefit analysis when considering whether to carry out future classes via EMI. Further, language improvement and perceived language difficulty appeared an important factor influencing their cost-benefit analyses.

Discussion, implications and conclusion

A number of discussion points emerged from the findings of this study. Our first finding regarding student perceptions of the benefits and how successful they are when studying English management through English showed that all participants expressed positive affective responses towards EMI. Students noted that, like other studies, there was extra difficulty studying through EMI, but our findings revealed a new dimension: that expending this effort was 'worth it' as they had to pay closer attention in class and had to spend more time comprehending the content material. This in turn led to deeper understanding, mastery of content and therefore success. Our findings align with prior studies such as that of Thompson et al. (2019) who found that students felt that the greater the effort they expended in their EMI studies, the deeper their understanding of content, and therefore the more successful they were. This in turn strengthened their motivation to learn via the L2. One student in that study, for example, stated that EMI challenges could be overcome through increased motivation and effort in learning.

Our second finding concerning the factors that influence student perceptions illustrates that when students choose whether to continue with EMI or study via their L1, two key factors were at play: (i) whether they perceived their resources to be sufficient to interact with the content (i.e. whether the cost of carrying out the extra effort would be worth it in developing greater understanding of content); and (ii) whether they had achieved their language learning goals. For two of the students, despite perceiving success in studying via EMI, they indicated that they would choose classes carried out in Japanese due to a focus away from further developing their language ability. In other words, the cost of carrying out the extra effort to study content via English was reliant on students still having language learning goals. This finding also aligns with those of Galloway et al. (2020) who found that Japanese students studying via EMI were more likely to focus on the language benefits (and costs) in comparison to international students. This indicates that the factors underlying EMI cost-benefit analyses may be context bound and require further exploration. Results from Xie and Curle's (2020) study also reflected students' perceptions of the benefits of EMI outweighing the challenges experienced. Students reported that not only did they think their language proficiency would increase but also that the way they apply knowledge, and even their way of thinking, was transformed. These types of changes that students experience while studying through EMI require further research, and one challenge for EMI programmes is helping learners understand these potential additional benefits of EMI study.

While numerous studies have explored students' perceptions (see Macaro et al. 2018), most of these have done so on a superficial level. Further reflective data needs to be collected from students to delve deeper into what other 'soft skills' they might acquire during their EMI learning. This might be operationalized by asking students to write reflective journals. Once we better understand students' EMI experiences, practitioners can design programmes of support for students going beyond simply linguistic support. Galloway and Ruegg (2020) noted the differing needs of international and domestic EMI learners with respect to support systems; our study of domestic learners in similar contexts suggests that support systems – even within one programme – may need to be tailored to the various needs of learners with different L2 proficiency and support needs. In other words, greater personalization of support may be needed to help students realize their individual goals from EMI study.

Implications from the study

The findings of this study have several practical pedagogical implications. Our participants were at a lower English level in comparison to students in previous studies carried out in similar contexts. For example, compared with Thompson et al. (2019), this participant group had lower L2 proficiency and EMI success. These students were using EMI to achieve language learning goals, and it encompassed one aspect of their perception of their success in EMI. In other words, different groups of learners have different perceptions of success and different reasons for studying via EMI. Language improvement appears to be a key factor that could be further explored in future studies, for example, is it a factor for lower-level students but not higher-level students?

This finding has practical implications for the types of linguistic support programmes provided to students. Integrating language support may not only influence student success in studying via EMI (see Rose et al. 2020) but also influence student motivation towards EMI. It was found that students based their decision on continuing to study through EMI using a cost-benefit analysis (i.e. whether added effort brought additional benefits). Such costs-benefits could be made clearer to learners in EMI programmes by highlighting, based on empirical evidence, how their content knowledge and/or linguistic competence may improve as a result of studying through EMI.

This study has also shed light on students' perceptions of how successful they feel in their EMI studies. There needs to be a greater focus on understanding the motivations of different types of learners, that is, a greater focus on those with basic English ability – the stakeholders most likely to be negatively affected by EMI. This would shed further light on what drives different types of students to study through English, and how we might best support them to find success in their EMI studies.

References

Aizawa, I., and Rose, H. (2020), 'High school to university transitional challenges in English medium instruction in Japan', *System*, 95: 102390.

Curle, S., Jablonkai, R., Mittelmeier, J., Sahan, K., and Veitch, A. (2020), 'English medium part 1: Literature review', in N. Galloway (ed.), *English in Higher Education*

(Report No. 978-0-86355-977-8), London: British Council. Available online: https://www.teachingenglish.org.uk/article/english-higher-education-%E2%80%93-english-medium-part-1-literature-review.

Doiz, A., and Lasagabaster, D. (2020), 'Dealing with language issues in English-medium instruction at university: A comprehensive approach', *International Journal of Bilingual Education and Bilingualism*, 23 (3): 257–62.

Galloway, N., and Ruegg, R. (2020), 'The provision of student support on English medium instruction programmes in Japan and China', *Journal of English for Academic Purposes*, 45: 100846. Available online: https://doi.org/10.1016/j.jeap.2020.100846.

Galloway, N., Numajiri, T., and Rees, N. (2020), 'The "internationalization", or "Englishisation", of higher education in East Asia', *Higher Education*, 80 (3): 395–414.

Hellekjær, G. O. (2010), 'Lecture comprehension in English-medium higher education', *Hermes: Journal of Language and Communication Studies*, 45: 11–34.

Macaro, E. (2018), *English Medium Instruction*, Oxford: Oxford University Press.

Macaro, E. (2020), 'Exploring the role of language in English medium instruction', *International Journal of Bilingual Education and Bilingualism*, 23 (3): 263–76.

Macaro, E., Curle, S., Pun, J., An, J., and Dearden, J. (2018), 'A systematic review of English medium instruction in higher education', *Language Teaching*, 51 (1): 36–76.

McKinley, J. (2018). 'Making the EFL to ELF transition at a global traction university', in A. Bradford and H. Brown (eds), *English-Medium Instruction at Universities in Japan: Policy, Challenges and Outcomes*, 238–49, Bristol: Multilingual Matters.

MEXT (2018), 'Super Global Daigaku Sousei Shien Jigyo Chukan Hyoka Kekka No Soukatsu' [Summary of mid-term evaluation results of Super Global University Project], *Ministry of Education, Culture, Sports, Science and Technology*. Available online: https://www.jsps.go.jp/j-sgu/data/kekka/h29_sgu_chukan_kekkasoukatsu.pdf.

Rose, H., and McKinley, J. (2018), 'Japan's English-medium instruction initiatives and the globalization of higher education', *Higher Education*, 75 (1): 111–29.

Rose, H., Curle, S., Aizawa, I., and Thompson, G. (2020). 'What drives success in English medium taught courses? The interplay between language proficiency, academic skills, and motivation', *Studies in Higher Education*, 45 (11): 2149–61. https://www.tandfonline.com/doi/full/10.1080/03075079.2019.1590690

Selvi, A. F. (2020), 'Qualitative content analysis', in J. McKinley and H. Rose (eds), *The Routledge Handbook of Research Methods in Applied Linguistics*, 440–52, Abingdon: Routledge.

Tannenbaum, R. J., and Wylie, E. C. (2019), *Mapping the TOEIC®Tests on the CEFR*, Princeton, NJ: Educational Testing Service.

Thompson, G., and Dooley, K. (2020), 'Ensuring translation fidelity in multilingual research', in J. McKinley and H. Rose (eds), *The Routledge Handbook of Research Methods in Applied Linguistics*, 63–75, Abingdon: Routledge.

Thompson, G., Aizawa, I., Curle, S., and Rose, H. (2019), 'Exploring the role of self-efficacy beliefs and learner success in English medium instruction', *International*

Journal of Bilingual Education and Bilingualism, 25 (1): 196–209. Available online: https://doi.org/10.1080/13670050.2019.1651819.

Uchihara, T., and Harada, T. (2018), 'Roles of vocabulary knowledge for success in English-medium instruction: Self-perceptions and academic outcomes of Japanese undergraduates', *TESOL Quarterly*, 52 (3): 564–87.

Xie, W., and Curle, S. (2019), 'Success in English medium instruction in China: Significant indicators and implications', *International Journal of Bilingual Education and Bilingualism*, 1–13. Available online: https://doi.org/10.1080/13670050.2019.1703898.

Zaif, F., Karapınar, A., and Yangın Eksi, G. (2017), 'A comparative study on the effectiveness of English-medium and Turkish-medium accounting education: Gazi University case', *Journal of Education for Business*, 92 (2): 73–80.

18

Comprehension Issues in English-Medium Instruction Classrooms: Kuwait's Public Institutions

Abdullah Miteb Alazemi and Abdullah Ali Alenezi

Introduction

The spread of English throughout the world and its prominence as *the* world language has reinforced implementation of English-medium instruction (EMI) policies across many countries, including Kuwait. EMI policy in Kuwait necessitates that educational programmes be taught only in English and thus excludes the usage of national or regional languages. This situation is not unique to Kuwait, as observed in other chapters in this volume. With the continued rise of EMI programmes, critical applied linguistics (CALx) has contended that the arguments of mainstream applied linguistics have continually neutralized EMI policies and have overlooked essential educational and academic issues (Alazemi 2020; Canagarajah 1999; Pennycook 2001). One of these major issues is the comprehension of lectures, as practitioners and policymakers alike need to evaluate and explore how students work with EMI. Therefore, we argue there ought to be more empirical research on the cost-effectiveness of EMI and how it benefits or disadvantages those receiving such instruction.

Although research in EMI policies presents exclusive advantages to such programmes (Galloway et al. 2020) and offers a variety of options to students such as exposure to a vast quantity of learning resources (Sewell 2008), there are questions of cost and whether it puts students at a disadvantage. This chapter presents an exploration of comprehension issues arising in EMI classrooms.

EMI in Kuwait: Rationale and issues

EMI was introduced in teaching scientific courses in English at the tertiary level in Kuwait in the mid-1990s in a move towards following global educational trends. This move meant that lectures, exams and all aspects of teaching and learning in scientific colleges were to be conducted exclusively in English. Furthermore, the College of Business Administration in Kuwait University (KU), the site for our study, which is a non-scientific college, followed suit.

In addition to this global trend, English was considered a necessity in Kuwait because several sectors, especially oil and banking, needed their employees to have a good command of English due to increasing numbers of expatriates in the labour force, mainly from India, the Philippines and Sri Lanka. Thus, English exams were reinforced in Kuwaiti companies, and passing them became a decisive criterion for selecting candidates. Regardless of one's academic achievement, professional experiences or any other qualifications, it was difficult to obtain a job without a good command of English. These global and local trends have put major emphasis on the importance of English, and therefore shifting teaching and learning to EMI became a necessary step in catering to such job-related demands.

The shift from Arabic to EMI meant that other measures needed to be taken to properly implement the new policy. One such measure was the implementation of English placement tests for students applying to science colleges. These placement tests are also a pivotal criterion in admitting students to science majors; failure would mean they would not be accepted. In some cases, students who fail the placement tests would be given a chance to enrol in an English remedial course, and they would be admitted on the condition that they pass. In both cases, English is the main marker of acceptance in any of the science colleges (Kuwait University 2016).

Kuwait is a monocultural country in which the entire population shares the same language and similar traditions and culture; the Kuwaiti constitution establishes Arabic as the only official language. Furthermore, 70 per cent of school students attend public schools that offer Arabic as the only medium of instruction, even in science subjects such as physics, math, biology and chemistry. At this stage, English is regarded as a foreign language, as school students are only exposed to English for an hour each day. This has caused an evident gap between the level of English taught in school and that required at the tertiary level, which could affect students' smooth transition when they go to university, as the English ability required at the tertiary level is more advanced.

The new EMI policy has caused frustration amongst students (Al-Bustan and Al-Bustan 2009) as their academic eligibility relies heavily on their linguistic ability, thus disregarding how well they perform during school. Ultimately, students could be deprived of pursuing their preferred careers based on language barriers. Other academic issues such as comprehension of lectures continue even after being accepted by a science college, as students need to deal with a completely new environment. They will need to engage with textbooks written at an advanced level (CEFR C1–C2), comprehend lectures delivered in English and take their exams in English. Such comprehension issues are the focus of this chapter and will shed some light on what students have to deal with during their university/college experience.

A critical approach: Investigating from the bottom up

Several educational reforms were presented by the Kuwaiti government, and many studies were conducted in an attempt to improve students' English-language competence. However, these attempts have continuously failed to reach their intended outcome as they have been unsuccessful in grasping the essence of the issue, which is to improve students' English proficiency through EMI. The ample mainstream research in Kuwait has focused mainly on top-down approaches when evaluating, exploring and devising recommendations on how to improve students' English competence (Alazemi 2020). Previous research revisited language policies, teaching methods, textbooks and teachers' views while at the same time neglecting those at the centre of the educational system. Students' views and insights were overlooked, and they were thus constantly excluded from taking part in constructing better language policies.

CALx has drawn attention to the complexity of the issues regarding language policy and has called for more research to reflect views other than those of policymakers and those in authority (Ramanathan and Morgon 2007; Ricento 2010). As Canagarajah (2006) argued, it is important to assess the effects of language policies on those who work with them, namely students. Thus, policymakers need to evaluate the impact of EMI policy on students' progress and academic achievement, as they need to use a pragmatic lens when looking into English-language practices. It is hoped that critical approaches to EMI will stimulate academics, students and policymakers to debate possible consequences and possible solutions to create a more solid teaching/learning model. The first step to resolve such issues is to raise awareness in the academic and social fields, which could be achieved by calling for more critical research promoting the views of all stakeholders affected by EMI policies.

For several decades, research has investigated Kuwaiti students' low levels of English proficiency in general (Hajjaj 1997; Sawwan 1987) (similar to the situation in other national contexts such as Ethiopia – see Chapter 5 in this volume). However, these issues are still unresolved, which is now more important given the spread of EMI, and the same problems seem to exist, indicating that it is time to introduce a new line of research that brings in a new perspective and evaluation strategy.

Aims and methodology

The main aim of mixed-method research is to provide a thorough view of the topic, especially when embedded in a complex educational or/and social context. The purpose of this research is exploratory in nature, as it is a useful approach when the topic investigated has not been properly addressed (Shields and Rangarajan 2013). In line with its aim, this study implements a sequential mixed-method approach, beginning with a questionnaire and leading to semi-structured interviews, focused mainly on qualitative aspects. Thus, the issues of comprehensibility and what students face during EMI policies have not been properly discussed in Kuwait. For these reasons, this methodology seems aligned with the objectives of this research.

Data collection and participants

Participants of the study have been purposively chosen from KU and the Public Authority for Applied Education and Training PAAET, as they are the only two public institutions that align with the objectives of public secondary schools. Students were selected randomly from different study years, ages and genders. Their eligibility was determined using some general criteria: (i) public school graduate, and (2) enrolled in a college that implements EMI. The questionnaire items were translated into Arabic to ensure a better understanding of the items, and the Arabic translations were subsequently revised by two independent university professors. Furthermore, the interviews were also conducted in Arabic to allow students to express their ideas and views clearly, and the interview questions were translated and checked by the research team.

The sample of the study consisted of 237 Kuwaiti students attending KU (n=73) and PAAET (n=164), of which 63 attend the College of Nursing and 99 the College of Basic Education. Among the participants, 31.2 per cent (n=74) were working towards their bachelor's degrees, while 68.8 per cent (n=163) were enrolled in two-year diploma programmes. Of the respondents, 87.3 per cent (n=207) were female and 12.7 per cent (n=30) male.

Data analysis

The study was set to explore learners' perceptions of EMI in college courses by eliciting their responses regarding the effect of EMI on their academic comprehension and their overall attitudes during EMI classes. The study also considered learners' language challenges and ways to overcome them. For this purpose, the study employed two instruments: a questionnaire and interviews with random participants. Each label in the five-point Likert scale of the questionnaire was given a numerical value from 1 to 5, where 1 was 'strongly disagree' and 5 'strongly agree'. The mean and the standard deviation were calculated by SPSS software for each item in the questionnaire. For each table in the result, the total average of the table's items was calculated. As for the interviews, all participants were asked open-ended questions in Arabic, which were then translated into English.

Results

Based on the analysis of the qualitative data gathered from the questionnaire and the contents of the students' interviews, various themes emerged and were categorized in the tables below. Here we illustrate the results of our study.

Table 18.1 displays the learners' responses towards EMI in college classes and the effect of the language of instruction on their academic comprehension. The total average score for the items is 3.38, an average that exceeds the midpoint of the measurement scale. This indicates the respondents' attitude regarding the impact of EMI on academic comprehension is negative and slightly in agreement with the presented statements.

According to Table 18.1, most of the respondents found it 'difficult to understand the content' of EMI lectures. In the same vein, the majority of

Table 18.1 Students' Perceptions of the Impact of EMI on Academic Development in Kuwait (Values in %)

Item	5=SA	4=A	3=Not Sure	2=D	1=SD	Mean (SD)
It is difficult to understand some of the content of lectures when taught in English	25.3	34.2	12.2	22.8	5.5	3.51 (1.2)
Teachers' use of EMI in lectures hinders my academic development	16.5	11	27.4	30.4	14.8	2.84 (1.2)
Teachers' use of EMI in lectures does not help me much to understand the course	25.7	23.6	16.5	29.1	5.1	3.46 (1.3)
Teachers' dependency on EMI does not simplify the lessons of the lectures	30	24.1	15.6	25.3	5.1	3.57 (1.3)
I miss a lot of information when teachers rely on EMI	33.8	26.6	10.1	21.9	7.6	3.54 (1.2)
Total average score						3.38

students (30 per cent) strongly agreed and 24.1 per cent partially agreed that EMI does not contribute to simplifying the content of the lectures. Likewise, almost 50 per cent of the participants did not believe EMI helped them better understand the content of their courses. Notably, a significant percentage of students (60.4 per cent) expressed their strong and partial agreement in missing 'a lot of information' during EMI courses. However, in reacting to the statement 'teachers' use of EMI in lectures hinders my academic development', the mean value of the responses was the lowest in the table (2.84), in which more than 45.2 per cent of the respondents strongly and partially disagreed, while 27.4 per cent were unsure of their position.

The qualitative data from the interviews offered further details to the students' responses in the questionnaire. As for the challenge with comprehending academic content, interviewees emphasized the difficulty of understanding technical concepts and terms when presented in English.

> I skip many of the concepts in [EMI] lectures, because I don't understand what the lecturer meant, they are difficult to understand at first … I make sure to ask

a classmate after class for a translation of the concept, then I fully understand the meaning. (Student 1)

Another interviewee explained the challenges she faced in understanding the subject and feeling that she does not fully understands the content in an EMI course.

My English is good, yet I don't feel confident in grasping the content of lectures, sometimes I question myself if it is because of the content or the language of the lecture. (Student 2)

Similarly, another interviewee commented on the 'wasted' time and effort in lecturers explaining new concepts in an EMI course.

I feel we waste too much time in explaining some concepts that can be easily understood by many students if expressed in our first language. (Student 5)

Yet another student explained that he felt frustrated by missing some points on exams, not for lack of comprehending the concepts but due to the difficulty of properly explaining his exam answers in English.

Regarding students' attitudes during EMI lessons, Table 18.2 reflects the learners' overall impressions in such a learning environment. The average value of the three items in the table is 3.37, which shows that these attitudes are common among students in EMI classrooms.

Table 18.2 Students' Perceptions of the Impact of EMI on the Classroom Environment in Kuwait (Values in %)

Item	5=SA	4=A	3=Not Sure	2=D	1=SD	Mean (SD)
I feel apprehensive asking teachers about meanings of English words during lectures	31.6	24.1	7.2	26.2	11	3.39 (1.4)
I don't feel comfortable when my professor relies on using English to explain the lecture	29.1	26.2	11	29.1	4.6	3.23 (1.3)
I feel more anxious during EMI lectures	21.5	26.6	15.2	26.6	10.1	3.49 (1.2)
Total average score						3.37

As presented in Table 18.2, about 55 per cent of the participants expressed their strong agreement (31.6 per cent) and partial agreement (24.1 per cent) to feeling apprehensive asking about the meanings of English words during EMI lectures. A similar number of the students voiced their 'uncomfortable' feeling during the lectures, while 29.1 per cent of the participants partially disagreed with the premise of this item. Moreover, besides students feeling uncomfortable during EMI lectures, 21.5 per cent and 26.6 per cent of the respondents answered they strongly agreed and partially agreed, respectively, that EMI lectures make them more anxious. The responses to the statements in the questionnaire were supported and further explained by the interviewees. One student commented on their feelings in such a classroom environment by stating:

> To me, there is usually a feeling of a non-stop pressure [in EMI classes] not only to cope with understanding the language of the lecture but also to not to be able to answer questions if called by the lecturer. (Student 4)

Finally, regarding the learner's perspectives on the English-language competence in preparation for the EMI courses, Table 18.3 shows that the average mean is 3.53.

Table 18.3 Students' Perceptions of the Impact of EMI on Language Skills (Values in %)

Item	5=SA	4=A	3=Not Sure	2=D	1=SD	Mean (SD)
I do not have an adequate level of English to easily understand the course textbooks	32.1	24.1	13.1	27	3.8	3.26 (1.2)
The level of English used in the coursebook is higher than my English level	20.7	22.8	27.4	19.8	9.3	3.47 (1.2)
The level of English used in the coursebooks does not match the language level we learned in school	30.4	21.1	18.6	24.9	5.1	3.71 (1.2)
The school's English-language level is much lower than the required level at my university/college	37.1	22.4	19.4	16.9	4.2	3.71 (1.2)
Total average score						3.53

As shown in Table 18.3, the majority of the respondents to the first statements agreed that they 'do not have an adequate level of English to easily understand the textbooks' (56.2 per cent). Equally 30.4 per cent of the participants strongly agreed and 21.1 per cent partially agreed that the 'English level used in the coursebook does not match the language level they learned in high school'. Specifically, a total of 43.5 per cent of the participants agreed that the 'English used in the course book is higher than their English level'. Significantly, most of the respondents (59.5 per cent) believed that the 'high school's English language level is much lower than the required level for their colleges'.

When interviewees were asked how they deal with language challenges in EMI lectures, a few strategies were suggested.

> Having a bilingual teacher is helpful, so I prefer to be in a class of bilingual instructors if I have a choice, because there is a chance that the teacher can explain it in Arabic. (Student 1)

Another interviewee added that

> specialized dictionaries are helpful too, but time-consuming ... sometimes I just sit next to another classmate who is good in English. (Student 3)

Student 2 also discussed the issue of misunderstanding exam questions, which ultimately affects their grades:

> We face many problems when answering exam questions, as misunderstanding a small part of the question could mean we miss the whole question. This not only affects my current grades but also my overall average.

Discussion

The descriptive statistics, which included the means and standard deviations of the total responses in Table 18.1, reflect a negative effect of EMI on learners' comprehension of lectures. More than half of the responses indicated that they encountered difficulties in comprehending the contents of the lectures. Similarly, learners' responses and interview comments indicated a negative overall attitude towards the impact of EMI on their academic knowledge. The findings confirm those of Phuong and Nguyen's (2019) study where one-third of their students regarded comprehending lectures presented in English as difficult, particularly for academic concepts and terms. However, contrary to the overwhelmingly negative attitude in this respect, most of the respondents in the present study did not feel EMI was a hindrance to their academic achievement. At first, this might appear contradictory, but they did not agree that academic achievement depended solely on the medium of instruction but also on other factors. Interestingly, those who were hesitant to agree or disagree represented 27.4 per cent of the respondents. Learners distinguished between the challenges they face during EMI lessons and their academic achievement, which shows that they might see EMI as a challenge to be overcome but not a great obstacle to their academic development. Furthermore, EMI, as indicated by one of the interviewees, can play an encouraging role in motivating learners to improve their language skills, a view that casts a positive light on this method of instruction.

Table 18.2 clearly reveals the learners' experiences with EMI at the personal level. More than 50 per cent agreed that during EMI lessons they experienced anxiety, discomfort and inhibition to ask lecturers questions in English. Additionally, others explained that teachers' use of EMI was one of the reasons they were unwilling to communicate in English and demotivated them to participate in classroom discussions. This is consistent with Huanga's (2015) study, which found a significant negative correlation between anxiety and achievement during EMI courses. Furthermore, the same study concluded that the stress due to content comprehension and peer competition resulted from students' learning difficulties experienced through such a medium of instruction.

Concerning language skills, the results show a significant gap between the perception of the respondents' language skills and the language of the coursebooks. The participants believed the language level of the coursebooks was higher than their language proficiency. Such discrepancy in language skills, according to the respondents, is due to the lower language proficiency in their previous schooling, which students felt had been below the required level for college courses. The responses indicate gaps between their language skills and what is needed to understand EMI coursebooks and lectures. Based on the quantitative and qualitative data of the study, the participants showed that college students are in great need of successful preparation in an English programme that bridges the transitional stage from studying general English in high schools to learning English for academic purposes (EAP) and/or English for specific purposes (ESP) in preparation for college EMI courses. Such a need for language support was also reported in other studies (e.g. Galloway and Ruegg 2020; Yildiz et al. 2017; Karakaş 2017).

Another solution proposed by some of the interviewees was to have bilingual teachers. A proposal regarding respondents' preference for bilingual teachers who can code-switch between Arabic and English as a medium of instruction to overcome language barriers was iterated in a previous study in the Kuwaiti context (see Alenezi 2010). Many of the interviewees expressed that they would rather ask their classmates to explain difficult terminologies in their shared first language than asking the teachers in English, a practice also reported in Phuong and Nguyen's (2019) study. Additionally, Phuong and Nguyen (2019) reported that students allocate a long time to understanding the language first, then comprehending the content. Similar sentiments were expressed by one of the interviewees in the present study regarding wasting a lot of time understanding a basic idea, a challenge students face during lectures and while reading coursebooks. Nevertheless, few interviewees perceived these challenges in language abilities as a motivator to develop their language skills further.

Implications

The findings of this study present several pedagogical implications. Since lectures are the main source of information, students' incomprehension during lectures means their learning experience is affected and could interrupt their knowledge acquisition. Rather, in many cases, lectures have become a source of disruption and miscomprehension, which could lead to their being perceived as undesirable and boring (Alazemi 2020). It is recommended that more Arabic be used in lectures, especially in areas where students encounter difficulties. Furthermore, there seems to be a lack of rigorous practical steps followed to implement an effective learning programme properly. Thus, further analysis of EMI classrooms is needed to help identify problematic areas and find feasible solutions.

Another implication for educational practices is related to exams as a major source of evaluation material. It could be stressful and harmful to students' careers if they obtain low grades not because of academic incapability but rather due to language barriers. Therefore, teachers could add an Arabic translation to every question to provide students with a better opportunity to answer correctly; such a proposal has been explored in translanguaging literature (see Poza 2017; Kersten and Ludwig 2018).

A final implication is the use of imported English textbooks that are not written for Arab learners. These cause some complications because they are written at a higher English level, which does not suit Kuwaiti students. Therefore, KU and PAAET must encourage their teachers to write customized textbooks that serve the needs of their students, possibly done in collaboration with renowned international publishers. Teachers in both institutions have already taken similar steps as they have developed their own pamphlets and distributed them to their students according to their needs.

References

Alazemi, A. (2020), 'The effect of the policy of English as medium of instruction on Arabic in Kuwait', in S. Troudi (ed.), *Critical Issues in Teaching English and Language Education*, 41–66, Cham, Switzerland: Palgrave Macmillan. Available online: https://doi.org/10.1007/978-3-030-53297-0_3.

Al-Bustan, S. A., and Al-Bustan, L. (2009), 'Investigating students' attitudes and preferences towards learning English at Kuwait University', *College Student Journal*, 43 (2): 454–63.

Alenezi, A. A. (2010), 'Students' language attitude towards using code-switching as a medium of instruction in the college of health sciences: An exploratory study', *ARECLS*, 7: 1–22.

Canagarajah, S. (1999), *Resisting Linguistic Imperialism in English Teaching*, Oxford: Oxford University Press.

Canagarajah, S. (2006), 'Ethnographic methods in language policy', in T. Ricento (ed.), *An Introduction to Language Policy: Theory and Method*, 153–69, Oxford: Blackwell.

Galloway, N., and Ruegg, R. (2020), 'The provision of student support on English Medium Instruction programmes in Japan and China', *Journal of English for Academic Purposes*, 45. DOI:10.1016/j.jeap.2020.100846.

Galloway, N., Numajiri, T., and Rees, N. (2020), 'The "internationalization", or "Englishisation", of higher education in East Asia', *Higher Education*, 80: 396–414. doi.org/10.1007/s10734-019-00486-1.

Hajjaj, A. (1997), 'The communicative teaching of English in the public schools of Kuwait: Where the main problems lie', *Language Centre Journal*, 6 (2): 27–36.

Huanga, D. (2015), 'Exploring and assessing effectiveness of English medium instruction courses: The students' perspectives', *Procedia - Social and Behavioural Sciences*, 173: 71–78. DOI: 10.1016/j.sbspro.2015.02.033.

Karakaş, A. (2017), 'The forgotten voices in higher education: Students' satisfaction with English-medium instruction', *Journal of English as an International Language*, 12 (1): 1–14.

Kersten, S., and Ludwig, C. (2018), 'Translanguaging and multilingual picturebooks: Gloria Anzaldúa's friends from the other side/Amigos Del Otro Lado', *Children's Literature in English Language Education*, 6 (2): 7–27.

Kuwait University (2016), 'Kuwait University statistics', *The Office of the Vice President for Planning*, 1–7.

Pennycook, A. (2001), *Critical Applied Linguistics: A Critical Introduction*, Mahwah, NJ: Lawrence Erlbaum.

Phuong, H., and Nguyen, T. (2019), 'Students' perceptions towards the benefits and drawbacks of EMI classes', *English Language Teaching*, 12 (5): 88–100. DOI: 10.5539/elt.v12n5p88.

Poza, L. (2017), 'Translanguaging: Definitions, implications, and further needs in burgeoning inquiry', *Berkeley Review of Education*, 6 (2): 101–28. DOI: 10.5070/B86110060.

Ramanathan, V., and Morgan, B. (2007), 'TESOL and policy enactments: Perspectives from practice', *TESOL Quarterly*, 41 (3): 447–63.

Ricento, T. (2010), 'Language policy and globalization', in N. Coupland (ed.), *The Handbook of Language and Globalization*, 123–41, Oxford: Wiley-Blackwell.

Sawwan, K. (1987), 'Communicative language teaching in Kuwait', *Annual English Teaching Report*, 4 (2): 112–47.

Sewell, E. H. (2008), 'Language policy and globalization: Communication and public policy', Proceedings of the 2008 International Colloquium on Communication.

Shields, P. M., and Rangarajan, N. (2013), *A Playbook for Research Methods: Integrating Conceptual Frameworks and Project Management*, United States: New Forums.

Yıldız, M., Soruç, A., and Griffiths, C. (2017), 'Challenges and needs of students in the EMI (English as a medium of instruction) classroom', *KSJ* 5 (4): 387–402. DOI: 10.30438/ksj.2017.5.4.1.

19

English-Language Proficiency Pre- and Post-immersion Courses in Mexico for Pre-sessional Students at a Bilingual International and Sustainable University

Myrna Escalona Sibaja and Gabriela Zamarrón Pérez

Introduction

The implementation of English-medium instruction (EMI) programmes in higher education (HE) has been accompanied by empirical research conducted in Europe, Asia, Middle East and Latin America, in non-English-speaking countries. Nonetheless, as stated by researchers on the subject, there are important research gaps to be addressed, namely: the effects of EMI on learning, the kind of English used, academics' proficiency of language to teach through EMI, the effectiveness of EMI programmes in tertiary education, language assessment systems and so forth.

In addition to the aforementioned research gaps, researchers on the subject concur that there is an urge to conduct studies in countries where EMI has not been sufficiently investigated – although EMI programmes have been run for a considerable period. This is, as confirmed in a recent systematic review of EMI research (Macaro et al. 2017), the case of Argentina, Brazil, Colombia, Chile, Venezuela and Mexico (Escalona 2020) in Latin America.

In the case of Mexico (the country of the authors), for instance, Bilingual International and Sustainable (BIS) universities developed and implemented what they call an Immersion to English Language Course that aims to develop basic English-language skills in pre-sessional students who are willing to enter an EMI undergraduate programme at these HE institutions. Unfortunately, there is scarce information of the content, characteristics and, more importantly, effectiveness of the programme that was implemented in 2012.

The aims of this chapter, then, are to portray the full programme of the Immersion to English Language Course developed for pre-sessional students at forty-five BIS universities spread across Mexico, analyse potential students' English-language proficiency pre- and post-participation in an immersion course, appraise the effectiveness of the course and report on pre-sessional students' confidence to start an EMI programme after taking the Immersion to English Language Course.

Literature review

Whether for academic international opportunities or as a requirement to access bilingual tertiary education, HE institutions in non-Anglophone countries are providing their domestic students with pre-sessional or preparatory English-language support courses – the preparatory has been identified as being implemented, mainly, in Turkey and the Arab Gulf (Curle et al. 2020: 28). The approach of such courses may vary from institution to institution – it can be on English for specific purposes (ESP), English for academic purposes (EAP) or English as a foreign language (EFL) and focused on introducing discipline-specific language, developing academic communication and study skills (Schmidt-Unterberger 2018; Curle et al. 2020: 28) or flourishing all language skills or only one; nevertheless, stakeholders concur that the aim is to develop English-language skills in students that would allow them to attend lectures in English within their country or abroad.

The curriculum and duration of pre-sessional courses are based on institutional contexts and specific needs. Therefore, there is a vast array of programmes; for instance, the English Foundation Programme offered at the United Arab Emirates universities lasts one term and involves twenty hours of instruction per week for eight to ten weeks with focus on ESP (Rogier 2012); the Intensive English Learning Programme provided by the science college in a Saudi public university lasts one semester that entails four courses focused on reading, writing, listening and grammar (Alhamami 2019); and the Immersion to English Language Course offered at BIS institutions lasts four months and involves teaching-learning EFL.

To keep pre-sessional courses updated, relevant and effective, there should be a 'mode of inquiry in which stakeholders within language programmes collect, learn from, and use evidence' (Davis and Mackay 2018) to promote the improvement of a curriculum, and assess its effectiveness and efficiency, as well as participants' attitudes within the context of the particular institution involved (Griffee and Gorsuch 2016). Unfortunately, the evaluation of language programmes, which includes pre-sessional courses, is not always a priority for a number of reasons: there is not a budget assigned for such activities, there is no time, there is not a single person for that specific activity, it is not seen as a need and so forth. Whatever the reason, there are language programmes that have been run for a considerable time, and the assessment of them has been undervalued by stakeholders. This is the case of the Immersion to English Language Course implemented at the forty-five BIS universities spread across Mexico; since its implementation in 2012 at the Technological University of El Retoño, its relevance and effectiveness have neither been assessed nor improved. Thus, the authors considered that it was a timely topic for research.

The study

Context: BIS universities in Mexico

The implementation of the first BIS technological university, the Technological University of El Retoño (UTR), was followed by the first BIS polytechnic university in 2013, the Polytechnic University of Santa Rosa Jauregui. Currently, of the forty-five BIS universities in Mexico, twenty-nine[1] are technological and sixteen polytechnic (see Figure 19.1), and they have offered education to 26,711 students from rural and/or marginalized communities with no other options to access HE – this just in 2019 (CGUTyP 2017, 2018a, 2019b, 2020).

The academic modality at BIS universities

Programmes offered at BIS universities are based on training cycles that allow students to develop competences for their professional profiles. However, what distinguishes the BIS institutions is that they have added one term for a pre-sessional course to immerse students into the target language, English (see Figures 19.2 and 19.3).

Immersion to English language: Pre-sessional course at BIS universities

The first step towards taking classes in English at BIS universities is the pre-sessional course, Immersion to English Language. This course is mandatory

Figure 19.1 Map of the Mexican Republic that displays the location of the first technological BIS university in Mexico, established in the state of Aguascalientes, as well as the current forty-four BIS technological and polytechnic universities. Developed by the authors.

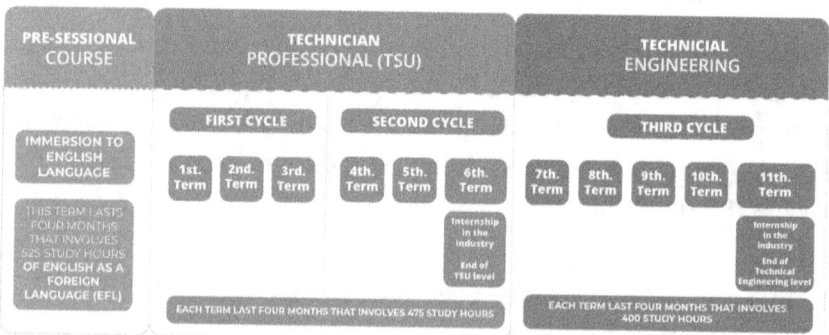

Figure 19.2 Pre-sessional course and training cycles implemented at technological BIS institutions. Developed by the authors.

English-Language Proficiency in Mexico   243

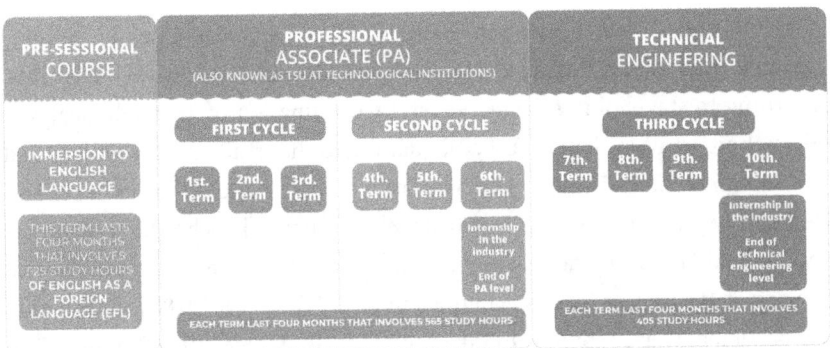

Figure 19.3 Pre-sessional course and training cycles implemented at polytechnic BIS institutions. Developed by the authors.

for all pre-sessional students holding confirmed offers to one of the academic options offered by the BIS institutions, and no previous knowledge of the target language is required. Nonetheless, prior to being enrolled, potential students should take a diagnostic evaluation, the iTEP BIS Universities Placement Test[2] – it evaluates grammar, listening, vocabulary, reading and writing, and the results are the basis on which participants are grouped by mastery level of the English language. Furthermore, if a pre-sessional student demonstrates a B2 English level, the university offers him/her an additional language linked to the needs of the productive sector of the region where the BIS institution is located. These languages could be French, Japanese and German, among others (UTR 2015, 2018b; UPMH 2018; CGUTyP 2018b, 2019a).

The pre-sessional course contemplates 525 hours of study in the target language – albeit changes were made in the UTR in September 2020, after the present research was finished. These hours are distributed in a fifteen-week term, 35 hours a week. During this period, the learners attend classes 7 hours a day, 5 hours with one English teacher and 2 hours with another (CGUTyP, 2018b, 2019a). Both English teachers focus their classes on the curriculum developed for the pre-sessional course, which comprises two main activities. First, to introduce learners into the English language through basic grammar, vocabulary and expressions that would allow them to communicate in working, social and personal contexts. Second, to provide workshops that aim to stretch participants' listening, speaking, reading and writing skills, as well as offer further practice of grammar and vocabulary. Figure 19.4 shows detailed information on the units and topics included in the curriculum of the pre-sessional course.

At the end of the Immersion to the English Language Course, the pre-sessional students are expected to demonstrate mastery of level A2. This, according to stakeholders at the General Coordination of Technological and Polytechnic Universities (CGUTyP), guarantees that students can understand and communicate in everyday situations and handle vocabulary and elementary grammatical structure from which they will anchor their technical and general language knowledge in parallel, which enables them to take two subjects in the foreign language in the first term (CGUTyP 2018b). To this end, the participants are required to take the iTEP BIS Universities Progress Test. Those pre-sessional learners who are not able to achieve the required A2 level are invited to enrol the next academic year. Nonetheless, the institution is open

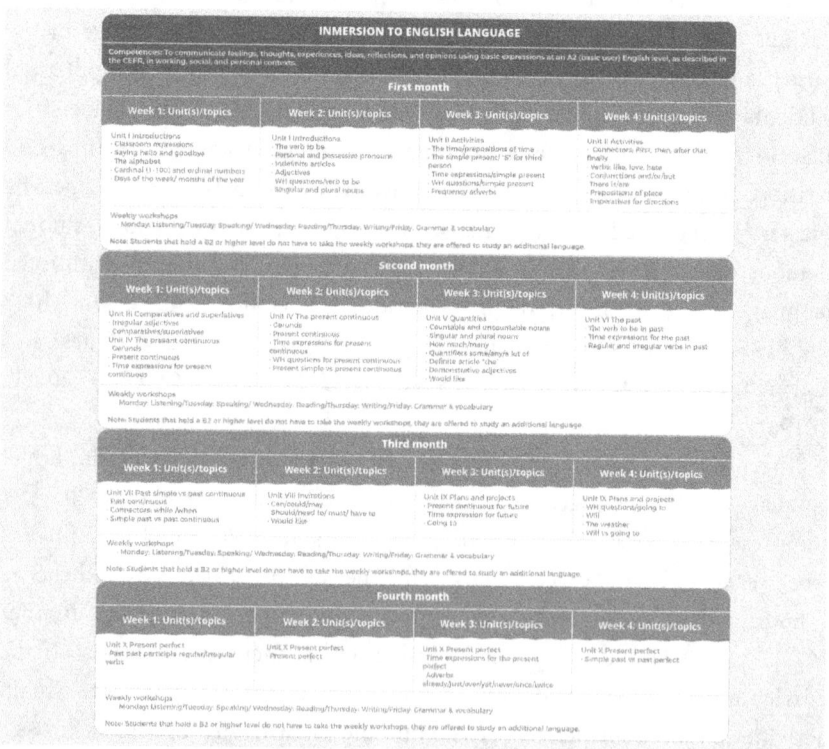

Figure 19.4 Overview of pre-sessional course for EMI in Mexico. Developed by the authors.

to accept those students whose results are close to A2 English proficiency, if the student signs a letter of commitment and compromises to attend additional and free-of-charge English classes on Saturdays for fourteen weeks. After the Immersion to English Language Course in 2019, sixty-eight students (almost 20 per cent of the participants) were accepted with this specific justification (UTR 2019a, 2020).

Research questions

Based on the dearth of information about the effectiveness of the Immersion to English Language Course implemented at BIS universities eight years ago, the researchers came up with the following research questions:

1. How effective is the pre-sessional course to develop participants' intended English proficiency required by the BIS university?
2. How confident are the pre-sessional students about starting an EMI programme after the immersion course?

Methodology

All data collected for this exploratory case study (Duff 2008; Yin 2003, 2009) were required, accessed and obtained via e-mail, Google drive and Google forms, respectively. Information was gathered between April and August 2020 from three main sources: documents that belong to the UTR, the CGUTyP and an online survey disseminated in July–August 2020 to students who participated in the Immersion to the English Language Course in September 2019.

Regarding the online survey, it entailed a mix of open-ended and closed-ended questions, and it was developed in two main sections. The first one focused on students' confidence to start an academic programme in English after their participation in the Immersion to English Language Course at the UTR, with a total of thirteen questions. Those thirteen questions contemplated students' confidence in general and in listening, speaking, reading, writing, grammar and vocabulary, after having taken the pre-sessional course. The last section was provided to obtain further information, to clarify or expand answers to the given questions or to provide other information that participants considered relevant for the improvement of the current pre-sessional course offered by the UTR.

Participants and their selection

A total of 350 students enrolled to the Immersion to English Language Course implemented in September 2019. Four groups were created based on the English proficiency they reported when they entered the pre-sessional course (see Table 19.1).

Data analysis and findings

Descriptive statistics (Cohen et al. 2011), document analysis and thematic analysis (Guest et al. 2012) were used to describe and summarize all data collected for this exploratory case study. The findings are presented in two tables. The first is pre-sessional students' English proficiency pre-post their participation in the immersion course. The second shows questionnaire response data reporting students' confidence in general in listening, speaking, reading, writing, grammar and vocabulary, after their participation in the pre-sessional course.

The results of pre-sessional students' English proficiency are shown in Table 19.1.

A total of 101 students, out of 350 that participated in the Immersion to English Language Course in 2019, completed the questionnaire. These included 63 out of 138 in the A1 group, 21 out of 134 in the A2 group, 16 out of 58 in the B1 group, and 1 out of 20 in the B2 group.

Results from the survey are not separated by groups. Rather, they are presented as a whole because it was found that the responses coincided. The outcomes, then, are presented in Tables 19.2.

Additionally, students stated that they felt confident in listening, speaking, writing, reading, grammar and vocabulary for three main reasons: activities done in class, teacher's support and intrinsic motivation; and not confident

Table 19.1 Participants' Proficiency Levels before and after the Pre-sessional Course

Before Pre-sessional: Proficiency Level	Number of Participants	After Pre-sessional Proficiency Level (%)				
		A1	A2	B1	B2	C1
A1	138	53.66	31.96	14.5		
A2	134	29.9	30.6	37.3	2.2	
B1	58	5.2	13.8	53.4	22.4	5
B2	20			5	40	55

Table 19.2 Respondents' Confidence Levels after Their Participation in the Immersion to English Language Course (Values in %)

	In general*	Listening	Speaking	Reading	Writing	Grammar and Vocab
Extremely confident	2.88	12.8	0	15.84	10.89	13.86
Slightly confident	36.64	19.80	24.75	43.56	32.67	32.67
Confident	45.55	46.53	48.51	37.62	42.57	43.56
Not confident	4.91	20.79	9.90	1.98	9.90	8.91
Not confident at all	0	0	6.93	0.99	3.96	0.99

*Students were grouped based on their self-reported proficiency levels before their participation in the Immersion to English Language Course.

because there was a need to use the language in real scenarios, and it was difficult to understand a variety of accents in English.

Discussion, recommendations and further research

To achieve the aims of our research was complex, mainly because the documents accessed had never been used or provided as a whole or even in parts. However, the hard work was worthwhile as we have been able to depict a full programme that has been implemented at the UTR for eight years, examine participants' language pre- and post-participation and pre-sessional students' confidence to start an EMI programme after taking the Immersion to English Language Course. Based on the results, we have shown that the pre-sessional course may not have been as effective as expected for those students holding the lowest English proficiency. However, the outcomes demonstrate that students holding a B2 English level benefitted more, with 55 per cent of the participants improving to a C1 English proficiency, whereas 53.66 per cent of those participants holding an A1 stayed at the same level.

In the light of the contradictory findings, then, there are some research questions to be addressed and recommendations to be considered.

Questions for further research

After attending the Immersion to English Language Course in 2019:

1. How did students feel attending the two subjects taught in English in the first term: confident and encouraged or demotivated and frustrated?
2. How many students actually passed the two subjects taught in English in the first term?

Regarding the pre-sessional courses taught from 2012 to 2018:

1. What were the results after the Immersion to English Language Course from 2012 to 2018?
2. Were the results in those years better than in 2019? If so, how? Why? What was different?

Recommendations

A whole-year programme

The current pre-sessional course has had a more positive impact on those students with an intermediate English proficiency. Based on this fact, the UTR may want to consider providing a whole-year programme that would be the basis for those potential students holding low English proficiency levels. In this way, the BIS institution would make sure that by the time students start their former classes in the career of their choice, they would hold a strong A2 level or above. It would also be better than accepting students with commitment letters – as done after the Immersion Course provided in 2019.

A six-month pre-sessional course

This would provide students at the UTR with more solid knowledge of basic English. After the six months, the students could attend the free-of-charge four-month English course (currently offered) while starting their formal career.

An online course

The possibility of an online English course, previous to the pre-sessional course, should be thoroughly analysed. This would provide pre-sessional students with an opportunity to practice the most basic English-language structures.

Monthly mock-tests

Applying monthly mock-evaluations – as part of the strategies in the pre-sessional course – of the official test applied at the BIS would be useful to indicate whether students are making progress, as well as help students become familiar with the structure of the test. Monthly evaluations would provide the teachers with evidence to offer further practice or one-to-one extra help to students left behind.

EAP and ESP

The BIS universities could implement EAP or ESP for students holding an intermediate English level, B1 and B2, respectively, to provide a more challenging pre-sessional course as well as develop other English-language skills in pre-sessional students.

Self-assessment promotion

Teachers could provide several opportunities for self-assessment of students' English proficiency, in order to develop self-learning strategies that would be helpful in determining the factors involved in their individual progress. For this purpose, the institution could provide students with an auto evaluation test and give them an opportunity to analyse their results as a group or individually.

Finally, the hope of the researchers is that this study will provide insight into and understanding of the implementation of a pre-sessional course that has been implemented for eight years in the BIS modality, specifically at the UTR, but more importantly, that the results will be used to make better decisions and improve future practices overall.

Notes

1. The Technological University Franco-Mexicana belongs to the BIS modality since 2019, although the medium of instruction in this institution is French. This HE institution is located in the state of Nuevo Leon, in north-eastern Mexico (Law of the state of Nuevo Leon 2019; Noticias 28 NL 2019).
2. BIS universities used to use the free downloadable For-Real Test as their placement test from 2012 to 2017. In 2018 the International Test of English Proficiency developed the iTEP BIS Universities Placement Test exclusively for these HE institutions (UTR 2018a,b).

References

Alhamami, M. (2019), 'Language of instruction policy in science programs: Science university student's voices', *Journal Pendidikan IAP Indonesia*. DOI: 10.15294//jpii.v8i1.17086.

CGUTyP (2013), 'Introduction to the English language curriculum, Asignatura de Introducción a la lengua inglesa', unpublished document developed by the General Coordination of Technological and Polytechnic universities, approved and released to BIS universities in 2013.

CGUTyP (2017), 'Tema 6. Modalidad Bilingüe, Internacional y Sustentable (BIS)', unpublished document developed by a group of stakeholders at the General Coordination of Technological and Polytechnic universities in 2017. (This document will be integrated into the Blue Book and was released in 2018 to technological and polytechnic universities.)

CGUTyP (2018a), 'Fundamentos de Gestión de la Modalidad BIS', PowerPoint presentation developed by a group of stakeholders at the General Coordination of Technological and Polytechnic universities in 2018 for promotional purposes of the BIS modality and presented in September 2018 to potential BIS institutions.

CGUTyP (2018b), 'BIS universities. Universidades Tecnológicas y Politécnicas Bilingues, Internacionales y Sustentables', unpublished document developed by a group of stakeholders at the General Coordination of Technological and Polytechnic universities in 2017–18 and released in 2019 to BIS universities.

CGUTyP (2019a), 'BIS universities. Universidades Tecnológicas y Politécnicas Bilingues, Internacionales y Sustentables. Manual de operación de la modalidad Bilingüe, Internacional y Sustentables (BIS)', unpublished document developed by the General Coordination of Technological and Polytechnic universities in 2019 and presented at a national meeting with the new Ministry of Education on 2 October 2019.

CGUTyP (2019b), 'Matrícula BIS en el Subsistema de Universidades Tecnológicas y Politécnicas. Ciclo escolar 2019–2020', unpublished internal document.

CGUTyP (2020), 'BIS universities spread in Mexico, power point', unpublished internal document.

Cohen, L., Manion, L., and Morrison, K. (2011), *Research Methods in Education*, USA: Routledge.

Curle, S., Jablonkai, R., and Mittelmejer, J. (2020), *English in Higher Education – English Medium. Part 1: Literature Review. Teaching English*, British Council. Available online: https://www.researchgate.net/publication/344352859_English_in_higher_education_-_English_medium_Part_1_Literature_review (accessed 24 December 2020).

Davis, J., and Mackay, T. (2018), *A Guide to Useful Evaluation of Language Programs*, Georgetown University Press.

Duff, P. (2008), *Case Study Research in Applied Linguistics*, Routledge.

Escalona Sibaja, M. (2020), 'Professional development for EMI faculty in Mexico: The case of bilingual, international, and sustainable universities', Routledge Focus on English Medium Instruction in Higher Education.

Griffee, D., and Gorsuch, G. (2016), *Evaluating Second Language Courses*, Information Age.

Guest, G., Macquuen, K., and Namey, E. (2012), *Applied Thematic Analysis*, SAGE.

Law of the State of Nuevo León (2019), 'Ley que crea la Universidad Tecnológica Bilingüe Franco-Mexicana de Nuevo León. (2019, June 03). Available online: http://www.hcnl.gob.mx/trabajo_legislativo/leyes/leyes/ley_que_crea_la_universidad_tecnologica_bilingue_franco_mexicana_de_nuevo_leon/ (accessed 25 June 2020).

Macaro, E., Curle, S., Pun, J., An, J., and Dearden, J. (2017), 'A systematic review of English medium instruction in higher education', State-of-the-Art Article, Cambridge University Press.

Noticias 28 NL (2019), '[TV local news] Entrega Estado Universidad Tecnológica Bilingüe Franco Mexicana. (2019, October 04)'. Available online: https://www.youtube.com/watch?v=XtS6hbVkgqs (accessed 25 June 2020).

Rogier, D. (2012), 'The effects of English-medium instruction on language proficiency of students enrolled in higher education in the UAE', a dissertation submitted to the University of Exeter for the degree of Doctor of Education in TESOL. Submission date June 2012.

Schmidt-Unterberger, B. (2018), 'The English-medium paradigm: A conceptualization of English-medium teaching in higher education', *International Journal of Bilingual Education and Bilingualism*, 21 (5): 527–39. DOI: 10.1080/13670050.2018.1491949.

UPMH (2018), 'Internal document, meeting minutes: Meeting at Universidad Politécnica Metropolitana de Hidalgo', Meeting to agree on improvements for BIS universities.

UTR (2015), 'Internal document, English department: Manual académico de buenas prácticas para las universidades tecnológicas en el sistema BIS', unpublished document developed by the English coordination at the Technological University of El Retoño in 2015 and released in 2015 to BIS universities.

UTR (2018a), 'Internal document: The benefits of iTEP placement', unpublished document developed by the Technological University of El Retoño on 25 January 2018, document released in 2018 to BIS universities.

UTR (2018b), 'Internal document: iTEP BIS Universities Placement Test', unpublished document developed by the Technological University of El Retoño on 12 March 2018, document released in 2018 to BIS universities.

UTR (2019a), 'Internal document: Letter of commitment', unpublished document developed by the Academic Department at the Technological University of El Retoño.

UTR (2019b), 'Internal document: Students grouped by English proficiency before the immersion to English language course', unpublished document developed by the Academic Department at the Technological University of El Retoño.

UTR (2020), 'Internal document: Students enrolled in January 2020 and signed a letter of commitment', unpublished document developed by the Academic Department at the Technological University of El Retoño.

Yin, R. (2003), *Case Study Research: Design and Methods*, 3rd edn, London: SAGE.

Yin, R. (2009), *Case Study Research: Design and Methods*, 4th edn, Thousand Oaks, CA: SAGE.

20

The Englishization of Higher Education in a Dutch University Context: The Glocalization of English-Medium Instruction

Robert Wilkinson and René Gabriëls

Introduction

The Netherlands has long been one of the countries at the forefront of the now global trend towards English-medium instruction (EMI). It was one of the first countries to initiate EMI in a full undergraduate programme, as opposed to incidental EMI courses within a programme largely in the local first language (L1), that is, in Dutch (Jochems 1991). The early implementation of EMI programmes predates European harmonization under the Bologna Declaration of the common first phase (bachelor's) and second phase (master's) levels. EMI programmes began in the late 1980s at Maastricht University and spread rapidly to the technical universities of Delft, Eindhoven, Twente and Wageningen, as well as to the University of Groningen by the early 1990s (van der Wende 1996).

In 2002, Dutch government policy mandated the rapid introduction of the two-phase Bologna structure (Litjens 2005), which, coupled with the widespread participation of universities in the Erasmus exchange system (Luijten-Lub et al. 2005), underpinned a stellar growth in EMI programmes at all Dutch universities. By 2019, almost a third of all bachelor's programmes and over three-quarters of all master's programmes had become fully EMI, with at least a further 10 per cent of programmes offering the choice between a Dutch-medium and an English-medium variant (VSNU 2020). It is not surprising that this extraordinary switch away from the L1 to English has generated considerable controversy and resistance (Breetvelt 2018; Gabriëls and Wilkinson 2020) leading to a landmark court case in 2018. A campaign group, Beter Onderwijs Nederland (BON, Better Education Netherlands), took two Dutch universities, Maastricht and Twente, to court accusing them of breaking the Dutch law on higher education for their failure to offer Dutch students programmes in Dutch, arguing that the quality of EMI programmes was inadequate.

This chapter reports research into EMI in the Netherlands. Although the focus of the empirical research is on the micro level (in particular students' perceptions of EMI), we explicitly place it in the context of both the university's language policy (the meso level) and the national and transnational developments related to higher education (macro level). First, this chapter considers the global-local nexus of EMI, before outlining the case of EMI at a Dutch university. The dilemmas identified by the case offer an interpretation of EMI implementation in higher education. Finally, we draw conclusions with regard to further research into EMI in practice.

The global-local nexus of EMI

The tremendous growth of EMI programmes is usually described in terms of the internationalization of higher education (Bowles and Murphy 2020; Malfatti 2020). For example, de Wit et al. (2015: 29) in a report for the European Parliament defined the internationalization of higher education as

> the intentional process of integrating an international, intercultural, or global dimension into the purpose, functions or delivery of post-secondary education, in order to enhance the quality of education and research for all students and staff, and to make a meaningful contribution to society.

Over time, the concept of internationalization has been used not only to refer to the cross-border mobility of students and staff but also to the increase in cross-cultural disciplinary content and EMI programmes. Most often university administrators and politicians use the concept of internationalization to justify their policy and usually provide it with a positive connotation (cf. Bowles and Murphy 2020).

De Wit et al.'s definition of 'internationalization' is anything but clear. The use of the expression 'international dimension' to define the concept of internationalization makes the definition somehow circular. The definition relates the international, intercultural and global dimensions, without clarifying the differences, let alone the mutual relationships. Moreover, it is wrongly suggested that the phenomena described by the concept of internationalization are only the outcomes of intentional acts. This overlooks the fact that the intentional actions of individuals are often determined covertly by social structures. Therefore, the way in which de Wit interprets the concept of internationalization cannot do justice to the issue of agency and structure, which is important for a better understanding of the global advance of EMI programmes.

The exponential growth in EMI provision in higher education is incorrectly interpreted in terms of internationalization because the advance of EMI programmes is a transnational rather than an international phenomenon. Internationalization literally refers to processes that take place between nation states, whether or not the result of intent. EMI expansion is only partly the outcome of developments between nation states (consider e.g. the impact of the Erasmus Programme and Bologna Declaration). In part, the expansion can be attributed to intentional partnerships between universities that are locally active and that build transnational networks. For example, universities from one and the same nation state can be part of very different transnational networks and have different (language) policies. Predominantly, the growth of EMI programmes (we will return to this later) can be attributed to economic globalization, which has not only led to a general denationalization of policy (Zürn 1998) but also to the emergence of a global market of education and research (Cantwell and Kauppinen 2014).

Instead of internationalization, it is better to talk about the growth of EMI provision in higher education in terms of glocalization. The concept of glocalization indicates that the intensification of dependencies beyond national borders in very different domains inherent in globalization attunes with the articulation of local particularities. The latter is often referred to by the term 'localization'. Robertson (1998) stresses that globalization and localization are not mutually exclusive because the global and the local are different sides of the same coin. He argues that

> capitalism has to accommodate itself both to the materiality of the heliocentric global world, with its inherent space-time contingencies, and to the culturality of human life, including the 'making sense' – indeed the 'construction' – of the geosocial contingencies of in-group/out-group relations. (Robertson 1992: 173)

Language is an important phenomenon of the culturality of human life that cannot be seen in isolation from localization. Arguably, the development of EMI programmes is subject to both global localization and local globalization. The latter points to the phenomenon that universities at various locations comply with the increasingly global rules of the academic game. But simultaneously, on the basis of contingent factors, universities give their own shape to it, which indicates the former. For example, the embedding of EMI programmes at Dutch universities is often very different, a phenomenon that cannot be explained in terms of *inter*nationalization. Understanding EMI necessitates seeing seemingly contradictory developments – globalization and localization – in their relationship. We will illustrate this with a case.

Case: Maastricht University

The site of this study is Maastricht University in the southernmost part of the Netherlands. The university was founded in 1976 on the principles of problem-based learning (Barrows and Tamblyn 1980). The key approaches entailed small-group learning centred around a problem usually extracted from practice. Until the mid-1980s, all programmes were in Dutch, though the fundamental literature, especially in medicine, was in English. Higher education in the Netherlands has long required the ability to read original texts in other languages, particularly German, French and English. In the mid-1980s the first 'international' programme started at Maastricht University in international management, with the aim to take advantage of the proximity of the nearby universities in Aachen (Germany) and Liège (French-speaking Belgium). The goal was evidently local, but the problems addressed in international management were multidisciplinary and global. The programme allowed students and staff to experience learning not only in a second language (German or French) but also in a different national culture as well as a different institutional culture (for a history, see Wilkinson 2013). At Maastricht, the courses started in Dutch and gradually shifted to English. The programme was successful in terms of popularity, with student numbers doubling every year at first, and, without overt publicity, it began to attract students from abroad, especially Germany. The objective of this pioneering programme required students to acquire disciplinary competences in their first language (L1), a foreign language (German or French) and English. This, however, proved untenable. The three institutional cultures did not prove a good mix and local student competence in the foreign language was inadequate to take disciplinary courses. Moreover, international students often did not possess competence in Dutch, French or German. Hence, within a few years the programme became fully English-medium.

The recruitment success of the first programme did not go unnoticed. New programmes began in the economics faculty and others (health sciences, law, arts), as well as at other Dutch universities, stimulated perhaps by favourable

Dutch government policy. During this time, the late 1990s and 2000s, the focus at Maastricht shifted to the global level. Not until the early 2010s did the university strengthen its original emphasis as a regional international university rooted in its trilingual context, notwithstanding the attraction of its English-medium programmes and student-centred learning to students from all over the world.

On a meso level the university underscores its objective to retain graduates in the local trilingual region through the provision of advanced language courses that would allow them to seek jobs in Germany and French-speaking Belgium and France, as well as Dutch-speaking Flanders and the Netherlands. In essence this underpins the university's glocalized character. However, the dominance of international students – more than 55 per cent of full-time students (VSNU 2020) – has augmented controversy about EMI. The controversy concerns the perceived lack of opportunity for Dutch students to study their preferred courses in Dutch and the potential risk this poses for the harmony of Dutch society if knowledge is no longer being generated and disseminated in Dutch.

In a study of Maastricht University, Wilkinson (2013) found that the drivers for EMI changed over time, but initially (late 1980s) practical reasons of local geography prevailed, characterized as the cross-border phase. At that time, cooperation with universities immediately over the German and Belgian borders was paramount, which entailed multilingualism (Dutch, French and German). Only during the 1990s, and more so in the 2000s, did motivations extend beyond the region to Europe and to the world. This tendency should be set against the mission of Maastricht University today, which profiles the institution on local cooperation, including across local borders, as well as more globally in Europe and elsewhere. The university's latest annual report (Maastricht University 2020) emphasizes the close regional collaboration with the Euregion Maas-Rhine as one of its points of departure over thirty years ago. In other words, localization has played a critical role in the university's identity.

The Dutch law on higher education and scientific research (Wet op hoger onderwijs en wetenschappelijk onderzoek, WHW), dating from 1992, is currently being revised in the light of the public controversy spearheaded by the campaign group BON and highlighted by the court case mentioned earlier that BON brought against Twente and Maastricht in 2018. BON charged the universities with failing to fulfil their obligations to Dutch students by not offering teaching in Dutch, as required under Dutch law, and thereby undermining the quality of higher education. BON argued that it was not against English but against English-only. BON may have lost the case, but the court required the minister of education to re-examine Art. 7.2 of the higher education law which specifies which language may be used for instruction. The policy can be interpreted as 'Dutch, unless' (Edwards 2020), since a sub-clause allows institutions to use a language other than Dutch if the specific nature, the organization or the quality of the education, or the origins of the students makes it necessary. In the eyes of BON, universities have been very free in their interpretation of this clause. The minister's proposed amendment to the law entails little change.

According to BON, a massive increase in EMI programmes would harm the quality of education and the Dutch-language proficiency of graduates. In addition, in a letter to a national newspaper, 194 eminent representatives from academia and the cultural sector expressed the concern that 'by not appreciating Dutch, they [the universities that embrace Englishization] are ignoring its important role in shaping our national identity and traditions' (BON 2019). The signatories also fear that Dutch will disappear as an academic language and that the budget spent on international students as a result of Englishization in higher education could reduce students' access to Dutch programmes. The challenge for the minister of education is how to square the conflicting interests of the different stakeholders. A Dutch Ministry of Finance report has underscored the dilemma of balancing the economic and cultural goals both of individuals and of Dutch society (Ministerie van Financiën 2019). For almost twenty years, economic reasoning prevailed as a response to globalization with only sporadic attention to what was happening to society. Universities began competing to promote their international credentials. The critics of educational policy and practice at Maastricht and other Dutch universities held that through their actions the institutions had become agents in the *verengelsing* (Englishization) of Dutch higher education. In brief, we may define 'Englishization' as the process of the English language increasingly gaining ground in social practices (in this case in higher education) where previously a different language was used.

As in many countries, Dutch universities as public institutions are subject to a neoliberal management policy, whereby they are obliged to function like private firms in a competitive educational market as demonstrated, for example, by university rankings. This policy has resulted in them using internationalization as a mechanism to engender a rapid rise in such rankings, as internationalization is the most easily manipulable component in ranking systems given the emphasis on numbers of international students and staff and publications in prestigious international journals which are English-medium (Piller and Cho 2013). Over a very short time, the education market in the Netherlands has changed radically, and one of the main drivers has been the growth of EMI.

At the micro level, we have looked at EMI practices in the Faculty of Arts and Social Sciences (FASoS) at Maastricht. The faculty follows the principles of small-group, student-centred learning. Generally, the learning principles underlying the EMI programmes do not differ from those underlying programmes in Dutch. But distinctions are evident in the nature of the topics (and problems) analysed as well as the literature the students consult. At FASoS, the topics tend to be transnational and the literature is almost totally in English. The reason may be because students come from more than seventy countries, with a considerable number claiming a bilingual background and many having experienced living for extended periods in several different countries. In a study of the perceptions of 237 students relative to the Englishization controversy in the Netherlands, Gabriëls and Wilkinson (2020) found that students who generally have consciously opted for an EMI programme, report doing so for job or career reasons (personal economic perspectives). The students quite strongly disagreed with the claims in the Dutch debate that EMI leads to lower quality, but they agreed with the claims regarding cultural identity, in particular that EMI leads to a dominance of knowledge in the English language. Significantly, Dutch students (n=42) tended to hold slightly stronger opinions than their international colleagues (n=195), aligning more strongly with the critics of Englishization. These findings may be interpreted in the light of glocalization. The more strongly one is tied to the local area (i.e. the Netherlands), the more strongly one feels the need for the education to reflect the local cultural identity.

The political economy of EMI practices

The glocalization of EMI as shown above underlines the nature of the global language system which is a subsystem of the world system. It is noteworthy that on a macro level the global language system is characterized by diversity and connectedness. De Swaan (2002) points out that not only do multilingual people, such as students and staff in higher education, keep the different language groups together but the global language system is not separate from another subsystem of the world system, namely the economy. That is why it is important to study the political economy of EMI practices, which will differ according to national context.

According to de Swaan, the communication value of a language must be determined by figuring out its position within the language system. Two indicators are important for this: the prevalence and the centrality of a language.

The prevalence of a language is the percentage of speakers of a specific language within a language system and indicates how many people can be addressed in that language. The centrality of a language is the percentage of multilingual speakers among all multilingual persons who speak that language within a language system. English is the pivot of the global language system: 'People who want to learn a foreign language expect others to choose English, and that is why they decide to learn it themselves. Moreover, the introduction of available and feasible alternatives to English is blocked by rivalry between the other language groups' (De Swaan 2002: 229).

The political economy of EMI practices is mainly determined by the fact that capitalism is forced to accommodate itself to the culturality of human life (Robertson 1998), which is partly constituted by language and entails in-group/out-group relations. The case showed that the accommodation of the neoliberal form of capitalism to the culturality of human life in the Netherlands has led to a public controversy. Certain stakeholders, under the banner of internationalization, support the increase of EMI programmes. For example, university administrators manage Dutch universities according to a revenue model, whereby attracting foreign students and staff serves the economic interests of the university. In contrast, other stakeholders emphasize that the Englishization of higher education is detrimental to Dutch culture. For instance, BON and several academics argue that not only will Dutch disappear as an academic language (which would be bad for the cultural identity of the country), but Englishization will also widen the gap between the English-speaking academic world and the everyday world in which Dutch is spoken, which perpetuates the existing in-group/out-group relationships.

The fact that university administrators, supported by various ministers of education, use the earnings model to underpin their language policy reflects the neoliberal New Public Management (NPM) that they have embraced. As a result, in no way do they serve the interests of stakeholders who have publicly criticized Englishization. According to NPM, government institutions must be run in the same way as companies. By modelling themselves as companies, universities would not only be better armed against the ever-increasing competition in higher education but also be able to excel (Münch 2007).

Due to the enormous influence of NPM, higher education has become a global market where universities compete to get the best possible return from education and research. Rankings are judged as an indicator of the market position of a university, and the ranking system itself has partly led to the Englishization of higher education. The number of EMI programmes, for example, serves to indicate how high a university should be ranked. The number of publications in so-called 'high-impact' international journals that are mostly Anglophone also determines the ranking. Scholars who publish in English are attracted and the incidence of publishing in a language other than English is low (Boussebaa and Brown 2017).

The foregoing highlights two dilemmas associated with the Englishization of higher education in the Netherlands and elsewhere, related to conflicting interests of different stakeholders. The first dilemma concerns the incompatibility of an economic and cultural value. While the proponents of more EMI programmes in the wake of the earnings model maintain an economic value (return), the opponents of Englishization defend a cultural value (the preservation of the language-bound cultural identity of a country). The second dilemma is that, given the legislation, the voice of some stakeholders is better heard by politicians than that of other stakeholders. The public controversy about Englishization is a power struggle in which the interests of stakeholders who are concerned about the future of Dutch as an academic language and the growing gap between science and society are hardly addressed. The case showed that although the lawsuit led to an amendment to the law, the revised law can be interpreted such that universities can continue their language policy and do not have to worry about the consequences of the Englishization for Dutch culture.

Conclusion

We have argued that the growth of EMI provisions is better characterized in terms of glocalization than internationalization. The concept of glocalization offers the possibility to simultaneously emphasize the intensification of dependencies beyond national borders in higher education and to underscore its localized articulation by universities. We have illustrated this through the case of Maastricht University. Although universities in the Netherlands are subject to the same global neoliberal NPM regime, there are local differences in its translation. For example, while Maastricht University, focused on a transnational Euregion, promotes a multilingual language policy, the University of Twente has opted for a monolingual English approach. Maastricht University grounds its language policy in its own initiatives aimed at the local Euregion and is therefore transnational and not international in character. In contrast, from 1 January 2020, the universities of both Twente and Eindhoven have made English the official language in education, research management and administration.

However, in common with other universities, these three universities grapple with the two dilemmas we have outlined. The first dilemma (the tension between the economic and the cultural value of higher education) raises the question to what extent higher education should be a private or a common good. This question concerns the issue of linguistic justice. The second dilemma (that regarding Englishization politicians are more attuned to the voice of some stakeholders than of others) raises the question of fairness to all those affected by the growth of EMI. This concerns power relations and is an issue of educational democracy. Researchers and practitioners would be wise to reflect on these dilemmas. If the two dilemmas are not resolved, EMI will be politicized.

References

Barrows, H. S. and Tamblyn, R. (1980), *Problem-Based Learning: An Approach to Medical Education*, New York: Springer.

BON (2019), *Oproep aan de Tweede Kamer van 194 prominenten: volledige tekst* (Appeal to the Second Chamber by 194 eminent scholars: full text). Available online: https://www.beteronderwijsnederland.nl/nieuws/2019/03/oproep-tk-nederlands-volledig/ (accessed 2 August 2019).

Boussebaa, M., and Brown, A. D. (2017), 'Englishization, identity, regulation and imperialism', *Organization Studies*, 38 (1): 7–29.

Bowles, H., and Murphy, A. C. (2020), 'EMI and the internationalization of universities: An overview', in H. Bowles and A. C. Murphy (eds), *English-Medium Instruction and the Internationalization of Universities*, 1–26, London: Palgrave Macmillan.

Breetvelt, I. (2018), 'English-medium instruction in Dutch higher education: A policy reconstruction and impact study', *L1-Educational Studies Language and Literature*, 18: 1–24. Available online: https://doi.org/10.17239/L1ESLL-2018.18.03.10 (accessed 30 June 2019).

Cantwell, B., and Kauppinen, I., eds (2014), *Academic Capitalism in the Age of Globalization*, Baltimore: John Hopkins University Press.

De Swaan, A. (2002), *Woorden van de Wereld. Het Mondiale Talenstelsel* [Words of the world: The world language system], Amsterdam: Bert Bakker.

De Wit, H., Hunter, F.,Howard, L., and Egron-Polak, E. (2015), *Internationalisation of Higher Education*, European Parliament. Available online: http://www.europarl.europa.eu/studies (accessed 4 December 2020).

Edwards, A. (2020), 'Language policy and the law: How Dutch universities legally justify English-medium instruction', *Dutch Journal of Applied Linguistics*, 9 (1–2): 38–59. Available online: https://doi.org/10.1075/dujal.19028.edw (accessed 16 November 2020).

Gabriëls, R., and Wilkinson, R. (2020), 'Resistance to EMI in the Netherlands', in H. Bowles and A. C. Murphy (eds), *English-Medium Instruction and the Internationalization of Universities*, 49–75, London: Palgrave Macmillan.

Jochems, W. (1991), 'The effects of learning and teaching in a foreign language', *European Journal of Engineering Education*, 16 (4): 309–16.

Litjens, J. (2005), 'The Europeanisation of higher education in the Netherlands', *European Educational Research Journal*, 4: 208–18.

Luijten-Lub, A., van der Wende, M., and Huisman, J. (2005), 'On competition and cooperation: A comparative analysis of national policies for internationalization of higher education in seven Western European countries', *Journal of Studies in International Education*, 9: 147–63.

Maastricht University (2020), *Jaarverslag 2019* (Annual report), Maastricht: Universiteit Maastricht.

Malfatti, G. (2020), *People-Centered Approaches toward the Internationalization of Higher Education*, Hershey: IGI Global.

Ministerie van Financiën (2019), *IBO Internationalisering van het (hoger) onderwijs* (Internationalization of (higher) education), Inspectie der Rijksfinanciën/Bureau Strategische Analyse.

Münch, R. (2007), *Die akademische Elite. Zur sozialen Konstruktion wissenschaftlicher Exzellenz* [The academic elite: On the social construction of academic excellence], Frankfurt-am-Main: Suhrkamp.

Piller, I., and Cho, J. (2013), 'Neoliberalism as language policy: Language', *Society*, 42: 23–44.

Robertson, R. (1992), *Globalization: Social Theory and Global Culture*, London: Sage.

Robertson, R. (1998), 'Glokalisierung: Homogenität und Heterogenität in Raum und Zeit' [Glocalization: Homogeneity and heterogeneity in space and time], in U. Beck (ed.), *Perspektiven der Weltgesellschaft* [Perspectives of world society], 192–220, Frankfurt-am-Main: Suhrkamp.

Van der Wende, M. (1996), 'Mobility reviewed: Trends and themes in the Netherlands', *European Journal of Education*, 31: 223–42.

VSNU (2020), *Opleidingstaal universiteiten* [Instructional language in universities]. Available online: https://vsnu.nl/taal-en-opleiding.html (accessed 13 November 2020).

Wilkinson, R. (2013), 'English-medium instruction at a Dutch university: Challenges and pitfalls', in A. Doíz, D. Lasagabaster and J. M. Sierra (eds), *English-Medium Instruction at Universities: Global Challenges*, 3–24, Bristol: Multilingual Matters.

Zürn, M. (1998), *Regieren jenseits des Nationalstaates. Globalisierung und Denationalisierung als Chance* [Rule beyond the nation state: Globalization and denationalization as an opportunity], Frankfurt-am-Main: Suhrkamp.

21

English-Medium Instruction in Tunisian Higher Education: A Desired Target but with Uncertain Consequences

Khawla Badwan

Introduction

The global spread of English-medium instruction (EMI) in higher education (HE) has attracted a lot of research attention in the past few years. Most of this research directs attention to the role of neoliberal ideologies in education that seek to justify the increasing dominance of English as the medium of instruction at the tertiary level. Neoliberal buzzwords such as knowledge-based economy, human capital, linguistic capital, social mobility, competition, innovation, internationalization and job market (Holborrow 2013; Hultgren 2019) are often invoked to rationalize decisions for educational language policies supportive of English. These neoliberal discourses are inextricably linked with globalization, which has driven the internationalization of HE as a sector. Internationalization means different things in different places and to different stakeholders. For example, Coleman (2013) explains that internationalization entails some sort of competition such as world university rankings, international exchanges and opportunities, attracting fee-paying international students and recruiting better-qualified international staff and gifted research students. For this competition to be logistically operationalized, a key linguistic tax needs to be paid. That is, the need to adopt one global language to facilitate global movement, exchanges and comparisons.

This language is English, with its colonial history, ideological hegemony, economic power, political authority and social dominance. Li (2013) argues that this spread of English has significantly contributed to the disruption of local language ecologies in multilingual societies around the world, producing ideological preferences for English as the language of instruction particularly at higher levels of study. Commenting on this situation, Phillipson (2009) describes the increasing offerings of university degrees through the medium of English as a pandemic that gives English an unprecedented global status and privileges its native speakers. In addition, it creates a system of linguistic stratification (Piller 2016), whereby English dominates the market and hence 'becomes the norm against which the prices of the other modes of expression, and with them the values of the various competences, are defined' (Bourdieu 1977: 652). Consequently, the ideological apparatus associated with English in HE produces dreams and aspirations in the minds of university students who might be (mis)led to believe that English is the answer to their social mobility challenges. Responding to this, Liyanage and Canagarajah (2019: 432) maintain that there is 'no guarantee that English proficiency will improve or change people's life conditions'.

This chapter discusses university lecturers' views towards the status of English-medium instruction in Tunisian HE. It starts by presenting a brief contextual background about Tunisia and its educational language policies before it problematizes EMI as a label. After that, the chapter presents three key challenges associated with EMI, namely: access issues, inequality and epistemic injustice. The sections that follow introduce the study's research questions which are followed by the study's methodological design and research findings. Finally, the chapter concludes with some recommendations for policymakers and HE practitioners relevant in Tunisia and beyond.

Contextual background

Tunisia is a North African country with a population of 1,18,82,127, according to the latest United Nations estimates (Worldometers 2020). It gained its independence from France in 1956. The country's income level as classified by the World Bank (2019) is lower middle income. Sociolinguistically, Tunisia is a highly multilingual country. Its residents speak different varieties of Arabic, including Darjah Arabic and Standard Arabic, in addition to French, Berber and some Italian and English repertoires.

Regarding the official language policies in Tunisia, the Tunisian constitution specifies Arabic as the official, national language of the country. It does not specify the country's first and second foreign languages, and therefore, there is no official policy that regulates the status of French, which is a dominant colonial language in the country. Primary education is through the medium of Arabic. French and English are introduced as foreign language subjects in grades 3 and 6, respectively. Moving to secondary education, Tunisian students are faced with a major linguistic challenge since the medium of instruction of some school subjects such as maths and science changes from Arabic to French, while the rest of the school subjects, such as history, religion, literature, geography and civic education, are taught in Arabic. English continues to be taught as a foreign language in secondary education.

As for HE, the majority of university programmes are taught through the medium of French, with the exception of disciplines such as history, philosophy, journalism, Islamic studies and Arabic literature, which are taught in Standard Arabic. However, some universities in the capital city of Tunis have gradually started to shift from French as a medium of instruction to English-medium instruction in academic programmes related to disciplines such as business, engineering and law. This is mainly to access recent research and publications, to encourage international investments, to attract talents and to create new job opportunities for the Tunisian youth. The chapter comments on this shift in the medium of instruction and on how university lecturers respond to it.

Problematizing EMI as a label

There are two key inherent problems with the term 'English as a medium of instruction', both highly relevant to the Tunisian context. First, a medium of instruction, argues Kyeyune (2003), should be an enabling tool – a tool through which learning, teaching, sharing, discussing and debating occurs. However, by describing English-medium instruction, the term misleadingly suggests that the linguistic ability to perform these educational tasks is already established. In many EMI contexts, English cannot be described as a tool or a medium that enables teaching and learning. Rather, it is a *barrier* that prevents teachers from further elaborating the content of their sessions and inhibits learners from critically engaging with the content of their lessons.

The second problem with the term is in relation to the E. With reference to the role of English in EMI settings, Pecorari and Malmström (2018: 499) explain that 'it is the language used for instructional purposes'. Yet, there is no consensus on the type of English used in these contexts because each has its own characteristics (Doiz et al., 2013: 219), its language ideologies and its scope for accessing and assessing linguistic resources (Busch 2012: 520). That said, the exclusive reference to English in the term hides and undermines the translingual practices that occur in multilingual classrooms, giving the impression that learning in EMI contexts occurs exclusively through English monolingual norms. As such, the term is ideologically loaded with connotations that reinforce the supremacy of English which leaves other languages and repertoires unrecognized and undermined.

Having problematized the label which I continue to use here bearing in mind its caveats, I now move to problematizing EMI as an educational quest.

EMI as an educational quest: Issues of access, inequality and epistemic injustice

In this section, I discuss some of the challenges caused by the use of English-medium instruction in contexts, such as those in Tunisia, where English is not a main language for the majority of the population. Namely, I discuss issues of access, inequality and epistemic injustice.

Issues of access refer to the linguistic disparity between individuals that is mainly attributed to unequal access to economic and technological resources. While state education in Tunisia offers the teaching of English as a foreign language from grade 6, there is a difference between English as a subject and English-medium instruction. The former is mainly taught in Tunisia through grammar rules and thematic vocabulary lists, whereas the latter requires advanced linguistic proficiency that enables not only the expression and understanding of academic content but also communicative skills to discuss, negotiate, analyse and debate. This means that while state education offers English as a subject to all students, not all students are equally equipped with the advanced linguistic repertoires required for EMI. This lack of linguistic resources requires individual investment in developing additional repertoires. Access to these repertoires requires economic resources (e.g. private tutoring), as well as technological resources (e.g. online tutoring, online educational resources). This access is not equally distributed across the society and is mainly mediated through social class. As a result, those with access to advanced English repertoires are granted privilege in an educational arrangement thought to be just. Such an arrangement does not take into consideration regional, socio-economic and infrastructural disparities and their impact on the quality of education that individuals receive.

Inequality is another challenge relevant to the Tunisian context which is directly linked to the first. The unequal distribution of linguistic resources creates unequal distribution of social capital. In her study on how university students conceptualize English in EMI, Kuteeva (2020) discusses two types of inequality in EMI settings. First, she explains that native varieties of English are valued by the students who tend to assign low status to postcolonial and English as a lingua franca (ELF) varieties of English. This creates a situation of linguistic privilege (Piller 2016), favouring English native speakers. Second, she argues that English creates a mechanism of elite formation among university students, disadvantaging those who resort to trans-lingual practices. Commenting on this, she maintains that 'translanguaging can … function as a mechanism of exclusion and reinforcement of language standards by a group of "elite" translinguals'.

In addition to issues of access and inequality, EMI programmes can be complicit in producing epistemic injustice. This challenge is concerned with the role of language in decolonial deconstruction and knowledge production. Stroud and Kerfoot (2020: 3) explain that knowledge production through European languages leads to insidious consequences such as exclusionary language policies and oppressive language ideologies. By insisting on the supremacy of English in EMI programmes, multilingual and multimodal semiotic resources become invisible, leading to the misrecognition of multilingual identities and the downgrading of knowledge produced in languages other than English.

The discussion of these challenges highlights the need to carefully consider the consequences of developing educational policies based on the exclusive use of English. In the following sections, I explore how university lecturers in a Tunisian institution view the shift to English and highlight some wider social implications of this educational policy.

The study

Utilizing qualitative content analysis of interview data with four university lecturers, this chapter addresses the following research question:

How do Tunisian university lecturers talk about the suitability of embracing English as a medium of instruction in higher education?

The case reported herein is part of a larger British Council project that explored readiness for EMI in Tunisia in different HE institutions (Badwan 2019a). This case was chosen because it comes from a public institution that has already

Table 21.1 Participant Details for EMI in Tunisia Study

Interview no.	Duration	Gender	Discipline
Interview 1	40:44	Male	Mathematics
Interview 2	13:50	Female	Mathematics
Interview 3	38:28	Female	Marketing
Interview 4	38:40	Male	International politics

embraced EMI. Students admitted to this institution need to meet a high entry requirement based on their baccalaureate exam. They also need to pass a locally designed English test.

After obtaining permission to access the institution, I introduced myself to many lecturers and described the project and what participation entails. Four participants volunteered to take part in the study. Interviews took place in a quiet classroom. Table 21.1 provides details about the participants and the duration of the semi-structured interviews.

Findings: Lecturers' professional anxieties

While discussing EMI and its value to their students, the lecturers in this case study reported sentiments of professional anxieties for three reasons. I present the reasons in relation to interview data below.

Uncertainty about the suitability of EMI

Lecturers' interviews indicate that while they are convinced that English enables their students to study and work abroad, they maintain the view that French is a de facto prerequisite for employment in Tunisia. The lecturer in interview (1), while highlighting that the decision to use EMI in his institution was made based on using language as a differentiation marker and as a strategy for brand-building and attracting students, explains that

> most enterprises, most businesses in Tunisia require French so students need to make sure that their French is good enough to communicate. (Interview 1)

This tension between the prestigious global status of English and the dominant status of French in the country was featured in the feedback the institution received from parents and employers as the lecturer in interview (4) demonstrates:

> The only serious criticism we've received is that 80% of our students remain in Tunisia. 15% leave, go. It is an issue with brain drain but it is a relatively small percentage and I am for an open door policy. The ones who stay in Tunisia are then asked to switch from commercial English to commercial French. That's why we started to teach two business courses in French to respond to the Tunisian market.

In addition, the above quotation shows how English is ideologically perceived as a tool that facilitates brain drain, which is a common view that was echoed by several educators in the wider study. It is worth highlighting that French was not linked to brain drain even though many educators explained that many of their graduates work in France after completing their academic qualifications. Concerns about brain drain and retaining graduates were raised by the lecturer in interview (3):

> We're preparing students to what? Are you preparing them for the Tunisian market? Maybe then there is no need for English. But if you are preparing them to leave the country, this is happening now and we don't have to hide this. We are preparing them to go to Germany, Canada. Again, we are preparing them for what? We should provide positions and an environment that welcomes them. Otherwise, they'll be depressed, anxious and will create problems. Some are going abroad and this is a short term solution as they are not asking the government to employ them but we are preparing them for others who did not invest in them or spend money to educate them. So we are losing. We are avoiding problems but we are losing but providing people to work for other countries.

This lecturer expresses a sense of professional anxiety, as she is not sure about the purpose of the education she delivers. She is also concerned about the social consequences of the mismatch between educational language polices and employment requirements, and how this could cause unemployment and mental health problems among the Tunisian youth. Later in the interview, she admits that it is hard to be certain about what her students need:

> Sometimes English is a barrier. If they learn everything in English and are employed in a company where everything is required in French, it is difficult for them to shift to French again. At the same time, they will have access to new opportunities. It is hard to tell.

On the other hand, the lecturer in interview (2) seems more confident that EMI is part of a wider social change that aims to challenge the status of French:

> The mentality in Tunisia is changing. Parents are pushing their kids to study in English from a young age. English definitely has future here. The Tunisians are trying to detach themselves from the French influence. There is a mind-set change in the country.

Lecturers' responses above reflect some wider debates in Tunisia regarding the language of instruction in HE and its alignment with local and global demands. EMI, in this complex socio-political context, offers both an opportunity and a barrier in a chicken-and-egg situation. Should change start with the language of instruction in HE or should it start with employers changing the linguistic expectations they place on university graduates? Due to the lack of coordination between policy influencers, the lecturers expressed a sense of professional anxiety regarding the shift to English (see also Badwan 2019b).

Concerns about students' readiness for EMI

Two of the participants in this study raised concerns about students' readiness for EMI. The lecturer in interview (3) argues that

> I do not think that all students are prepared for such an experience. They need to be prepared earlier to make them ready for HE in English

Moreover, she highlights that readiness for EMI across the country is not consistent. In the following quotation, she draws attention to regional disparities and how they influence educational language policies:

> I worked in another part of Tunisia and even if I teach in French they don't understand it. There are differences between regions. English worked in pioneering schools but when we consider other schools, other regions they are very different.

Similarly, the lecturer in interview (2) explains the types of language skills that her students need to develop further in order to improve readiness for EMI:

> They don't have a problem understanding me but they have a problem with practising it because they don't use it outside university ... Students are capable of expressing themselves in writing but they are not very comfortable speaking in English.

Both lecturers explain that they resort to trans-lingual practices to engage students and to offer them the chance to discuss and comment on academic content. Without these practices, the students could feel alienated and silenced. In addition, the lecturer in interview (3) explains that the use of Arabic Darjah changes the feel in the room especially when she notices that her students are tired.

Nonetheless, the other two lecturers who did not raise concerns about EMI readiness did not make a distinction between general English skills and the academic repertoires required for EMI. For example, the lecturer in interview (1) reports that they recruit the most competitive students with the highest baccalaureate English results and hence he does not see issues concerning readiness for EMI. In a similar vein, the lecturer in interview (4) argues that younger generations are more proficient in English:

> The new generation have smart phones to listen to things all the time. The difference between this generation and the one before is massive. Current 18 years are relatively comfortable with English

These views suggest the complexity of discussing readiness for EMI. Without an awareness about the range of repertoires and skills required for successful engagement with EMI programmes, the common perception that younger generations are attached to their devices and hence are more proficient in English could significantly cover the linguistic challenges caused by EMI policies.

Questions about the identity of the country and its education system

Commenting on language educational policies in Tunisian education, two lecturers mention concerns about the identity of the country and its education system. For instance, the lecturer in interview (3) speaks about the need for a national policy and explains that the majority of the students require advanced French repertoires:

> I don't know what they [the government] will be doing with French but if the government will have relations with English-speaking countries English will be mandatory. Otherwise, English might work for the short term ... We have a lot of funding and projects that require French in Tunisia. Students want to study abroad but UK's costs of education is very high and it will not work for the majority.

In addition, the lecturer in interview (4) shares the concern that the spread of EMI raises questions about the identity of Tunisia:

> We expect that many other public universities will start giving courses or even full programmes in English. I would expect other types of arguments regarding the identity of the country ... I am not for a full replacement ... Tunisian university education gives little importance to Arabic unless you are going to study Islamic studies.

In other words, the lecturers in this theme call for a wider discussion about language in education and the implications of existing policies and practices on the national identity of the country and its education system.

Discussion and conclusions

The findings of this case study indicate that while EMI remains a desired outcome in response to neoliberal pressures that seek to homogenize the global HE sector, the spread of EMI in Tunisia continues to raise questions about its suitability for local demands and concerns about language access and social inequalities. For many university lecturers, English is not seen as an enabling tool that facilitates learning and becoming. Rather, it is a linguistic barrier with uncertain consequences. So what needs to be done to address this educational challenge?

Kyeyune (2003: 179) explains that 'many educators believe in the logic of suggesting that if children are failing to learn through English, the obvious alternative is the mother tongue'. However, this suggestion is without challenges. One of the key challenges is domain loss and lack of academic resources in Arabic. One possible middle grounds solution is to consider multilingual education and training in trans-languaging as the medium of instruction. This is an equitable solution in a highly multilingual country. University lecturers and students have access to a range of shared multilingual resources that they can draw on and utilize. In doing so, education can contribute to addressing issues of epistemic injustices by validating the multilingual identities of individuals and recognizing alternative ways of knowledge production that are not mainly governed by Anglo-centric norms.

To address the concerns of uncertainty raised by the lecturers in this study, it is important for policymakers at different levels, be it national or local, to engage with a range of language policy influencers such as teachers, students, parents, employers and educational funding agencies in order to develop a coherent policy that aligns the education system with local and global demands (Badwan 2019b). As part of these wider national consultations, it is crucial to draw attention to issues of language access, inequality and epistemic injustice and to consider policies that address these challenges in order to produce just arrangements. As such, this study agrees with Kirkpatrick's (2019) recommendation that the implementation of EMI cannot be successful without engaging with all stakeholders. It is possible that these consultations could push language policies in different directions as tensions between the local and the global emerge. However, I would argue that the surfacing of these tensions is beneficial to developing national and local decisions about educational priorities. Coordinating these efforts and consultations means offering the Tunisian youth more certainty about the language(s) of instructions and the value of their university degrees.

References

Badwan, K. (2019a), 'Exploring the potential of English as a medium of instruction in higher education in Tunisia', *British Council Report*. Available online: https://e-space.mmu.ac.uk/623468/1/Final%20KB%20REport%20%20Teaching%20for%20Success%20HE%20Tunisia%20Report%20FINAL_Web.pdf.

Badwan, K. (2019b), 'Agency in educational language planning: Perspectives from higher education in Tunisia', *Current Issues in Language Planning*, 22 (1–2): 99–116. DOI:10.1080/14664208.2019.1700056.

Bourdieu, P. (1977), 'The economics of linguistic exchanges', *Social Science Information*, 16 (6): 645–68.

Busch, B. (2012), 'The linguistic repertoire revisited', *Applied Linguistics*, 33 (5): 503–23. DOI:10.1093/applin/ams056.

Coleman, J. (2013), 'Forward', in A. Doiz, D. Lasagabaster and J. Sierra (eds), *English-Medium Instruction at Universities: Global Challenges*, xiii–xv, Bristol: Multilingual Matters.

Doiz, A., Lasagabaster, D., and Sierra, J. M. (2013), *English-Medium Instruction at Universities: Global Challenges*, Bristol: Multilingual Matters.

Holborrow, M. (2013), 'Applied linguistics in the neoliberal university: Ideological keywords and social agency', *Applied Linguistics Review*, 4 (2): 229–57.

Hultgren, A. (2019), 'The drive towards EMI in non-English-dominant European HE: The role of university rankings', *Language Teaching*, 52 (2): 233–6. DOI:10.1017/S0261444816000380.

Kirkpatrick, A. (2019), 'The rise of EMI: Challenges for Asia', *Language Teaching*, 52(2): 237-40. DOI:10.1017/S0261444816000380.

Kuteeva, M. (2020), 'Revisiting the "E" in EMI: Students' perceptions of standard English, lingua franca and translingual practices', *International Journal of Bilingual Education and Bilingualism*, 23 (3): 287–300. DOI: 10.1080/13670050.2019.1637395.

Kyeyune, R. (2003), 'Challenges of using English as a medium of instruction in multilingual contexts: A view from Ugandan classrooms', *Language Culture and Curriculum*, 16 (2): 173–84. DOI: 10.1080/07908310308666666.

Li, D. (2013), 'Linguistic hegemony or linguistic capital? Internationalisation and English-medium instruction at the Chinese University of Hong Kong', in A. Doiz, D. Lasagabaster and J. Sierra (eds), *English-Medium Instruction at Universities: Global Challenges*, 65–83, Bristol: Multilingual Matters.

Liyanage, I., and Canagarajah, S. (2019), 'Shame in English language teaching: Desirable pedagogical possibilities for Kiribati in neoliberal times', *TESOL Quarterly*, 53: 430–55. Available online: https://doi.org/10.1002/tesq.494.

Pecorari, D., and Malmström, H. (2018), 'At the crossroads of TESOL and English medium instruction', *TESOL Quarterly*, 52 (3): 497–515. DOI:10.1002/tesq.470.

Phillipson, R. (2009), 'English in higher education: Panacea or pandemic?', *Angles on the English-Speaking World*, 9: 29–57.

Piller, I. (2016), *Linguistic Diversity and Social Justice*, Oxford: Oxford University Press.

Stroud, C., and Kerfoot, C. (2020), 'Decolonising higher education: Multilingualism, linguistic citizenship & epistemic justice', *Working Papers in Urban Language & Literacies*, paper 265.

World Bank (2019), 'World Bank country and lending groups'. Available online: https://datahelpdesk.worldbank.org/knowledgebase/articles/906519-world-bank-country-and-lending-groups.

Worldometers (2020). 'Tunisian population'. Available online: http://www.worldometers.info/worldpopulation/tunisia-population/.

Index

academic development 230, 234
academic disciplines 63, 113, 117, 119, 213
academic lingua franca 14
academic issues 225, 227
accreditation 26, 103, 105, 120
applied linguists xiii, 47, 81, 125
applied linguistics 2, 9, 49, 177
   critical 225, 227
   mainstream 225
Amharic 59, 61, 66–67
Arabic 226, 228–9, 233, 235, 266–7, 273–4
Armenia – *see* South Caucasus
Austria 99–107, 151
Azerbaijan – *see* South Caucasus

Bangladesh 13–22
Brazil 25–32, 239
bilingual
   instruction 36, 40–2, 73–5, 90–4, 131, 166, 177, 239–40
   teachers 73, 166, 233–4
bilingualism, elite 80
Bologna Declaration 25, 52, 253, 255
Bologna structure 253

capital
   human 14, 64–5, 80, 173, 265
   linguistic 75, 78, 265
   symbolic 75, 80
China 35–43, 92, 201, 214
Ciência sem Fronteiras – *see* "Science without Borders"
classroom environment 231–2
Colombia 111–21, 239
colonial rule 13–17, 20–1
commodified courses 77–8
communicative competence 111, 116, 118
conflicting interests 259, 261
content and language integrated learning (CLIL) 13, 49, 54, 112, 199, 201

competition 18, 37, 48, 52–3, 62, 64, 76, 80, 105, 107, 112, 126, 128, 132, 152, 173, 234, 258, 265
comprehension issues 66, 225–36
creativity 30, 178, 200–8
critical applied linguistics – *see* applied linguistics, critical
critical approach 55, 227
critical awareness 103–4
culturality 255, 260
culturalist discourse 128, 130–2

decolonial perspective 112, 120, 269
Denmark 47–55, 103,
   higher education in 49–52
discourse 40, 71–2, 75–7, 80, 167
double first-class initiative 35, 39
Dutch higher education – *see* Netherlands, higher education in

ecological perspectives and approaches 32, 80, 117, 120–121
educational practices 235,
educational democracy 262
educational reforms 36, 54, 227
elitism 74–75
Englishisation/Englishization 35, 131–2, 253–62
employability 61, 100, 103, 107, 178, 190
English as a medium of instruction
   actors 16–17, 49, 125,
   bottom–up implementation of 2, 28, 37, 117
   content–language collaboration 41, 112, 120
   definition of 153–4, 199
English-only 30, 36, 62–3, 79–80, 85, 92, 199, 200, 257
English-medium education (EME) 50, 73–4, 78, 99, 192

English-medium programmes
(EMPs) 99, 133, 257 – *see also*
Vietnamese EMI programmes
incentives for/drivers of 26–8, 35–8,
48–9, 52–5, 153, 195, 257–8
institutional support for 92, 114,
118–9, 134
debates around 21, 49, 60, 120, 125–34,
161–2, 164, 168–9
policy 42, 53–4, 60, 62–7, 72–78, 86–8,
93, 150, 152, 157, 174–177, 225, 227
English as a global lingua franca 2–3,
13–14
English for academic purposes (EAP) 3,
13, 42, 88, 138, 180, 202, 234,
240, 249
English proficiency tests 41, 78,
103, 178–9
English proficiency 3, 19, 38–41, 62,
88–91, 115, 117, 120, 173–4, 178–80,
213, 227–8
English textbooks – *see* textbooks
epistemic injustice 266, 268–9, 274–5
Erasmus Programme 253, 255
Estonia 125–34
Ethiopia 59–67, 73
exclusion 120, 269

free-market economy 75
foreign language competence 114

gatekeeping 103, 107
Georgia – *see* South Caucasus
German as the medium of instruction
102–104
Globalisation/globalization 37, 60–2, 78,
116–17, 199, 255–6, 265–6
global-local nexus 254–6
glocalization 259–61
graduation requirement 116, 119

higher education-policy 49–50, 54,
63–5, 75–8
Hong Kong 42, 199–211

identity
• cultural 193, 259–61
• national 258, 274
institutional cultures 28, 167

intercultural perspective 112
intercultural competence 116, 191
international
staff 51, 131–2, 265
students 14, 36–9, 77–8, 92–3, 102–7,
126–28, 130–4, 150–3, 188–94, 221,
256–8, 265
tests – *see* 'English proficiency tests'
internationalists 126–33
internationalisation/internationalization
at home 28, 31, 76, 93, 111
of curricula (IoC) 112, 179
of extracurricular activities 27, 120
of experience 27, 30, 145
of higher education 14, 16, 26, 35–8,
41–42, 62, 75–81, 85, 100–4, 106–7,
115–17, 120–1, 125–34, 151–3,
178–80, 189–92, 199, 214, 254–62,
265–6
Italy 102, 137–46, 151

Japan 9, 37, 78, 92, 113, 213–22

knowledge acquisition and
dissemination 53, 66–7, 78, 86,
100, 120, 154–155, 163–4,
213–22, 235
Kuwait 225–36

language
access 274–5
hierarchies 17, 80, 269
minoritized 120, 164
support 19, 21, 27, 41, 63–6, 86–9, 103,
214, 222, 234, 240
system 259–60
Languages without Borders 27
lingua academica – *see* academic
lingua franca
linguistic privilege 269

mainstream applied linguistics – *see*
applied linguistics, mainstream
medium of instruction roadmap 75, 77
Mercosul 26
Mexico 111, 239–49
mixed method research 66
multimodalities 199–209

Multimodalities-Entextualisation Cycle
    (MEC) – *see* multimodalities

nationalism 14–15, 73–5
Nepal 71–81
neoliberal ideologies 48, 72, 265
neoliberal management policy 258
neoliberalism 14–16, 72, 75–8
neoliberalism, hidden agenda of 78, 80
new public management 260–1
Netherlands 25, 50, 51, 176, 253–62
    higher education in 25, 50, 253–62

placement tests 226, 243
Poland 149–59
PRINT Programa Institucional de
    Internacionalização
Programa Institucional de
    Internacionalização 27
professional development xii, 41, 89,
    139, 189
policy
    language (LP) 17, 49, 53, 60, 67, 80–1,
        92, 100–1, 112, 115–17, 127,
        161–9, 171, 254, 260–1, 274,
    macro-level 15, 42, 86–90, 92,
        195–6, 227
    makers 37, 54–5, 59, 67, 76, 93, 163,
        195, 225, 227–8, 274–5, 274
political economy 49–50, 179, 259–61
power relations 262

quality management 102
quasi-colonialism 72–3, 75

research universities 100–7
road mapping framework 113–14

science subjects 226
science without Borders 26
social consequences 20, 271
social stratification 80
South Africa 161–9
South Caucasus 187–96
student mobility 26, 106, 116

tensions with English and
    multilingualism 115–6
territorial approach 116–7, 120
textbooks 39, 74–5, 168, 174, 214, 227,
    232–3, 235–6
translanguaging 162, 164, 167, 199–209,
    235, 269
transnational education 38–9, 175
transnational networks 255
trans-semiotizing 199–209
trans-semiotic agency 200, 203–4, 208
Tunisia 265–275
Turkey 85–94, 188, 189, 240

Universities of Applied Sciences
    (UAS) 100–1
university rankings 103, 258, 265,
University of Tartu 126–32

Vietnam 173–180
Vietnamese EMI programmes
    advanced 175–176
    high quality 175–175
    joint 175–176
    Professional Oriented Higher
        Education (POHE) 175–176

www.ingramcontent.com/pod-product-compliance
Lightning Source LLC
Chambersburg PA
CBHW052154300426
44115CB00011B/1666